BETWEEN SHADOW
and SUN

BETWEEN SHADOW and SUN

A Husband's Journey Through Gender – A Wife's Labor of Love

Revised & Expanded Edition

Tina Madison White

Kumquat Publishing • USA

BETWEEN SHADOW and SUN

A Husband's Journey Through Gender –
A Wife's Labor of Love

1. White, Tina Madison—Biography. 2. Transsexuals—United States—Biography. 3. Family relationships—United States. 4. Gender Identity—United States—Psychological Aspects. 5. Transsexuals—United States—Psychology. 6. Families—United States. 7. Gender Identity—United States—Religious Aspects I. Title

Cover Design: Cover Design: Rob Allen @n23art
Author's Photo: Cassandra Storm

Kumquat Publishing
Hoboken, NJ

First Edition – Revised and Expanded with Appendix
Note: Revisions are minor and largely stylistic. A few passages were expanded to add clarity. Appendices that were held back from the first printing have been added back in.

DEDICATION

To the wonderful people who have helped me on my journey. You offered me your love, support, and confidence. You saw the person inside and gentled me into my future. Your friendships are my greatest treasure.

I dedicate this book to each and every one of you.

... But pride of place goes to Mary.

CONTENTS

FOREWORD

I MET MY KNIGHT in shining armor in 1997, on a flight from Columbus to Chicago. Who would have thought that I would meet my soulmate on an airplane?

We married a year later and enjoyed a wonderful life. Tom made me laugh every day. He was manly and muscular. When he held me in his arms, I felt safe and secure. He was smart and thoughtful. I loved to introduce him to others as my husband.

My friends loved Tom, too. If they expressed any concern, it was that he sometimes seemed too good to be true. How could a man be that kind, loving, and empathetic? Tom would later joke that women liked him because he was a man as a woman would design him. How true that proved to be!

I cannot lie. I was crushed when I lost my Tommy. I cried for years. My knight in shining armor was transforming right in front of me. He was turning himself from my handsome warrior into a hulking beast of a woman. The sight of him made me cringe.

Yet, the person inside him never left. I have never known someone to wrestle so valiantly with his demons. He thought about his family constantly. He failed, over and over, to redeem himself. But he never stopped trying. How could I not love such a person?

In the course of Tom's search for identity, I met many more transgender women. I met crossdressers, transsexuals, and genderqueers. At first, they horrified me. Why would men (or women) do this to themselves?

But as I came to know them, I realized: these are just people. They are deeply caring and vulnerable, each one beautiful in her own way. Gradually, my attitude shifted. It was now society that horrified me.

Why do we treat these men and women with such contempt? What are we afraid of?

BUT SYMPATHY is not the same as blind loyalty. While I was determined that I would stick around to see Tom through his transition, I wasn't sure that I would stay.

In the end, I decided to remain. Tina is now my best friend. Even today, I mourn the loss of my husband. But I cannot imagine life without Tina. She is my soulmate. When I look at her, I see a beautiful, happy woman. My friends miss Tom, too. But they continue to admire our loving companionship. And they have come to love Tina just as much as they did Tom.

THIS BOOK is Tina's story. What I like most about it is her willingness to share her most private thoughts and her effort to incorporate the words and feelings of those around her.

Read her story and let me know … was I right to stick around?

Mary White

August 2015

PREFACE

WHEN I TRANSITIONED, my fondest hope was that I would finally put my gender behind me. All I wanted was to love my family, live a meaningful life, and to pursue my career transforming companies. Why would I choose to publish a book about the very thing I want most to forget?

I am encouraged by the growing attention paid to transgender men, women, and children. But I am concerned by its focus. It continues to set us apart: it highlights our physical differences and wardrobe choices. Too often, it dwells on our failed family relationships.

YES, WE ARE DIFFERENT. Being transgender involves different notions about sex, clothing, and genitalia. But, in most other respects, we are much like anyone else. Being transgender involves a struggle with two questions that challenge everyone at some point in their life: *Who the hell am I? Where do I fit in?*

Some people struggle with their religion, their sexual orientation, their social class, their family role, their purpose in life. We struggle with our gender. It is painful in a way that others cannot imagine.

If you want to understand us, look past our exteriors. Get to know the person inside us. Unfortunately, many of us hide that person from you (and from ourselves) for most of our lives. When we finally bring the person we hide inside out into the open, we are anxious to silence any discussion about our identity. We want to put a painful past behind us and to move on.

In these pages, I have tried to share the person inside me as honestly as I know how. You will learn, for example, that for most of my life, I was deeply transphobic. I wanted nothing more than to be the man that everyone around me so loved and depended on. I wanted to be a good husband, a loving father, and a gentle friend.

But, all the while, I was haunted by the nagging suspicion that I was, in fact, a woman. It followed me everywhere. "Anything but this," I prayed, "God, help me, anything but this."

For forty years, I tried every imaginable cure for what I took to be a broken sense of manhood. Today, I am proud to be the woman that I am. But I openly confess that I tried my damndest not to take this path.

One of the reasons I wrote this book was to invite you into the mind of a transgender person. What did I think about all those years? Why did it take me so long to transition? What led me to my eventual decision?

Follow my struggles, experiments, and failures. At the end, I leave it to you to decide: *Who do you think I am? Do I offer more to the world as the person I tried to be for fifty years or as the person that I am today?*

I ALSO WROTE this book in order to share my family's experience of my transition—especially my wife, Mary. Sadly, many transgender people experience the loss and breakup of their families when they finally reveal the person inside. But that is by no means a universal outcome. Mary and I know of many couples and families that have remained together after a parent or child transitioned. We need to hear more of their stories.

My family is still working out their feelings about the new me—our journey isn't over. But, based on our progress so far, I would describe our transition together as a success. We remain loving. We continue to communicate. I enjoy greater intimacy with most members of my family than I ever did before. They report that I am more joyful and more giving of myself.

Mary and I have learned a lot during the past few years. The second reason I wrote this book was in order to share our experiences and some of what we have learned.

One thing I learned is that, when families do break apart, it isn't fair to assume—as people often do—that the family is transphobic or that the person transitioning is self-absorbed. It is a lot more complicated than that. Family members have to reinterpret and reconsider a lot of things. There is grief and anger to work through. The learning curves are steep for everyone involved.

Mary and I don't consider ourselves a success because we are still married. We feel successful because we worked together to help the other to find their best possible future. Mary didn't run for the hills; I didn't disappear into my new wardrobe. We took the time to work things out. We listened. We problem-solved. We grew as individuals.

MY PARENTS, siblings, children, and grandchildren struggled mightily with my change. They were variously confused, hurt, and angry. Some worried about my soul. Everyone worried about Mary and everyone missed Tom. No one was particularly tickled to meet Tina. But, like Mary, they stuck around.

I have tried, without violating their privacy, to share my family's reactions to my transition and our efforts to work through all of the change. How would we redefine our past? How would we work out our future? While this book is autobiographical, I have shared—with my family's permission—many of their letters to me in which they vented their deepest hurts and anxieties.

I have tried not to sugarcoat my impact on my family. I have even shared some pictures that —to be honest—I would rather consign to the trash heap. I want you to see all of the person that I was asking my family to love.

I MUST MAKE an immediate qualification: Transgender people are as diverse as the rest of the world. When we gather in groups of any size, we resemble a human version of Noah's Ark. We embody every race, religion, creed, and social class.

There are transgender truckers, waiters, executives, farmers, soldiers, students, accountants, musicians, sex workers, programmers, doctors, teachers, and lawyers—all in the same room. It's pretty damn cool!

You are reading the story of one transgender person. I am certain that many share my feelings and struggles. I am equally certain that others will bridle at being likened to me.

With apologies to the latter, here is my story ...

INTRODUCTION

AT PRINCETON, LOCKER ROOMS were a special trial for me. Usually, I dried and dressed myself in an inconspicuous corner, listening over my shoulder to the conversations around me. Jocks and athletes alternately pushed their way into and out of the gray, swinging doors in the men's locker room at Dillon Gymnasium. Some were headed into the sweat-filled fog of the shower room, others to the fresh air and combat outside.

One afternoon, I listened to a pair from the school's tennis team as they compared notes from the night before. They sprawled languidly on their towels, their sweaty backs pasted against marble tiles that had long since yellowed with age. As they dressed to return to their classes, they kept up a constant chatter. "You went down on her without making her douche first? Dude, that's crude! What did that skank smell like?"

Their banter ricocheted among the lockers. Everyone within earshot laughed. Soon, other men erupted with vulgar quips of their own. The air filled with echoes of innuendo, each one vying with the others for masculine approval.

In my corner, I felt my anxiety mount. How could they talk about women that way? It was disgusting. I felt violated. Was this a sign of maturity on my part or another example of my lack of manliness?

FALSE START

What are little boys made of, made of?
What are little boys made of?
 Snips and snails, and puppy dog's tails,
 That's what little boys are made of.

What are little girls made of, made of?
What are little girls made of?
 Sugar and spice and everything nice,
 That's what little girls are made of.

— 19ᵗʰ Century Nursery Rhyme

As BEST AS I CAN REMEMBER, I was six when I wondered for the first time if there might be something different about me. One cold February night, my family and I gathered around our black-and-white television to watch the TV debut of Rodgers & Hammerstein's *Cinderella*.

I was spellbound by Ginger Rogers as the queen and Celeste Holm as the fairy godmother. But I dreamed of being Cinderella! I wanted to have Lesley Ann Warren's doe eyes and radiant cheeks. Even though her face had been artfully rouged with coal dust, she positively sparkled. I longed to have her voice. For weeks after the show, I fell asleep repeating her lines: *In my own little corner, in my own little chair, I can be whatever I want to be!*

I found nothing interesting about the prince or king. The prince seemed a bit of a prig, prancing about in his tights, and the king struck me as an elderly boor. They were stage props who were there to propel the action, all of which centered on the women.

Though I wanted most to be Cinderella, I would gladly have traded places with any of the women who sang and danced across the screen that night—even Cinderella's evil stepsister, Prunella. Each time Prunella curtsied gracelessly to the prince, her kneecaps rent the air with an audible crack. Even so, I found her a more compelling character than were any of the men. But I never shared these feelings with my family; somehow, I knew that this was something to keep private.

MY UPBRINGING was fairly conventional and middle class. I was born in the Hell's Kitchen neighborhood of New York City. But at the time of the *Cinderella* debut, my family lived on the campus of a Presbyterian seminary on Chicago's north side. My father was pursuing a doctoral degree in theology and managing an outreach program for inner city teens. My mother spent most of her time caring for their five children, two girls, two boys—and me.

We lived in an old brownstone that backed onto the seminary campus. It was a wonderful place for a child. We were protected from the dangers of the world by a tall, wrought-iron fence that marked the border between our Middle Earth and the great urban wilderness beyond. Within our realm, we were safe, so we spent our time inventing dangers of our own. We reenacted World War II with GI Joes, reclaimed the West from the Indians, and hunted one another down, killing each other with our finger guns, "Kapow, Kapow!" … "Bedoo, Bedoo!" We scaled trees that, compared to our small frames, stretched into another world. To climb them was to own all that I could survey. It was an idyllic life.

THERE WAS, OF COURSE, the ordinary mischief that occurred between boys and girls. Our neighbor, Stephen, loved to chase my twin sister, Anne Louise, around the house. He threatened to strip naked as soon as he cornered her. But Anne Louise was fleet of foot, and Stephen, to my knowledge, never got further than exposing his underwear. As soon as he tried to remove his pants, Anne Louise sprinted past him into another part of the house. I ran after them both, laughing and egging them on as they zigzagged from one room to the next.

Stephen liked to play at my house, where he could antagonize my sister. I preferred to play at his, where I could surround myself with nudes. Stephen's father, a noted painter of the '60s, often made a study of the female figure. To my memory, the walls of their house were festooned with the images of half-naked women, distorted into shapes and colors that excited the imagination. Whenever I could, I found an excuse to set up our board games where I could sneak a peek at the canvases on the walls around us. They were more exotic than erotic. The muscular sinews and deep-set eyes of the models communicated a raw, womanly power.

I ENGAGED IN INNOCENT ESCAPADES of my own. Once, I was caught in bed with another six-year-old, George Anne. We had dared each other into a showdown: "You show me yours, and I'll show you mine."

We hid ourselves beneath the covers at opposite ends of her bed and removed our clothes. We were just about to pull away the covers on the count of three when the bedroom door opened. Her mother popped her head through the door, "What are you two up ..." She never finished her sentence; we never finished our game.

These acts of curiosity aside, I spent most of my early youth digging holes, lighting fires, climbing trees, and riding bikes.

WHEN I WAS NINE, my parents moved our family to Washington D.C. My father took on an administrative role supporting all of the Presbyterian churches in the D.C. metropolitan area. My mother pursued a doctorate of her own, then went on to teach political science at the American University.

With our parents so busy, we, the kids, ruled the house. This was an era in which children still walked themselves to school and managed their own extracurricular lives. Our parents periodically emerged from the woodwork to cook dinner, arrange vacations, and attend school plays and concerts.

Anne Louise and my older sister, Mary Fran, shared the second floor with Mom and Dad. My two younger brothers, David and Graham, ruled the kingdom that was the third floor. It did not take them long to pockmark the walls of their bedroom with blows from their broomstick spears and Tinker Toy arrows. Ever jealous of their little kingdom, I let it be known that they had drawn their bull's eyes around the holes after the fact. I rationalized my invented truth: their aim could not possibly be that good.

As the oldest boy, I was given dominion over the basement. My headquarters, my bedroom, was a converted garage. My parents had redecorated it with the dark brown paneling and linoleum tile so characteristic of the 1970s. My mother fretted constantly about my physical remoteness, but I reveled in my private world.

I played pick-up basketball after school and peewee football on weekends. I mowed yards and delivered the city's afternoon newspaper for spending money. I learned how to whittle and etch wood with the Cub Scouts and to read a compass and navigate the wilderness with the Boy Scouts. My friends and I filled our bookshelves with model airplanes and cars. When I outgrew the plastic models, I started to sketch intricate blueprints of underwater cities. I looked forward to a future as a world-famous SCUBA diver, architect, and oceanographer.

WHILE I BUSIED MYSELF with all these dirt-digging, wood-carving, and city-planning activities, I began to struggle with thoughts and feelings I did not understand.

At first, it was subtle. Like other boys of my generation, I watched adventure shows, such as *Batman*, *I Spy*, and *Mission Impossible*. But each TV season, I found myself gravitating increasingly toward shows that featured female characters.

I loved to watch Marlo Thomas on *That Girl* and longed to know what it would be like to be her. Whenever she pouted, "Oh, Donald," I pouted with her. When I watched the *Dick Van Dyke Show* with my family, I laughed at Dick but identified with his wife, Laura. I followed her manic ups and downs as though they were my own.

But it wasn't just the glamorous stars who drew me into their orbits. On the *Dick Van Dyke Show*, I was as interested in Dick's co-writer,

Sally Rogers, as I was in Laura Petrie. On *I Love Lucy*, I felt a special bond with Ethyl Mertz. I envied Sally Field's girlish exuberance in *Gidget* and *The Flying Nun*.

I READ FICTION with a similar, divided response to male and female characters. On rainy afternoons, I often took refuge in my basement stronghold. I sprawled on the floor amid a litter of books and went adventuring. I solved crimes with Frank and Joe Hardy; I dirtied my feet in the Mississippi with Huck Finn and Tom Sawyer. Adventure novels were the moral compass of my youth. Good triumphed over evil. Bravery, pluck, and youth won out. Frank and Joe got their man. What could be more hopeful?

But as much as I envied my heroes their adventures, I rarely identified with their interiors. I connected more deeply with female protagonists like Nancy Drew and Pippi Longstocking.

Pippi was imaginative, brave, and unconventional. Where Frank and Joe Hardy were often more grown up than the grownups, Pippi was proud to be a child! I longed to be her. I wanted her pigtails and her long, gangly legs. I wanted to talk with her careless bravado.

While I enjoyed following Frank and Joe's adventures, I rarely found myself wondering what they were feeling inside. In contrast, I connected emotionally with Nancy and her best friends, Bess and George. I was particularly intrigued by George for, like me, she had a boy's name. I imagined myself in the back of Nancy's blue convertible, laughing and sleuthing with the other girls.

At the time, I didn't worry about this duality. If I thought about it at all, I supposed that it had more to do with how men and women were portrayed in fiction. I assumed that I was simply expansive enough to enjoy both worlds. But as I grew older, my acts of imagination began to evolve into flights of fantasy.

WHEN ALONE IN THE HOUSE, I began to explore the second floor with a new curiosity, especially my mother's closet and my sisters' dressers. I tried on their dresses, blouses, and swimsuits. I did it with a mixture of fascination, perplexity, and horror. I didn't know what to make of my feelings.

I wasn't old enough to think of this as something erotic. I only knew that I felt a sense of calm and peace when dressed as a girl. But I as often felt unsettled. Somewhere in the deep recesses of my mind, I sensed that something was horribly wrong.

Whenever I could, I slipped into my mother's closet. I sat, enveloped by a dark void. After making certain that the rest of the house was empty, I crept upstairs to my parents' bedroom. I paused at the closet door. Listen. Wait. Listen again. All I could hear was the silence of an empty house—silent but for the rhythmic pounding of my heart: *Thump-thump … thump-thump … thump-thump.*

I looked around my parents' bedroom one last time, took a deep breath, and opened the closet door. I leaned in, pulled the knob behind me, and fell into the inky blackness. For a moment, I hunkered by the door, checking one more time for sounds from outside. When I was finally convinced that all was safe, I sank into the darkness of the furthest corner. Relief.

I didn't do anything. I just sat in the dark, surrounded by an invisible forest of dresses, blouses, and slacks. They hung about me like vines in the Garden of Eden. My body relaxed into a Zen-like calm. I felt as though I were a pool of water collapsing into its center.

I would sit like this for an hour and imagine myself as … what … a woman? Was I imagining another life for myself? Was I retreating into the comfort of my mother's womb? I was never quite certain. I just imagined myself alive and without form in a different world. I drifted into a timeless peace.

AT OTHER TIMES, I felt compelled to try things on. It wasn't the clothes that interested me as much as the sense of becoming encased in a cocoon of femininity. I fantasized that, if I wore the clothes long enough, they would turn me into a girl.

I tried on as many different items as I could, one ear cocked for the sound of someone returning home. Once dressed, I applied face creams, sampled perfumes, and crimsoned my lips. The sweet smells, gentle lotions, and smooth fabrics lulled me into a dreamy serenity.

Sometimes, I took it further. Perhaps it was quantity that mattered. If I wore enough clothes all at once, would that turn me into a girl? I added layer after layer of everything I could lay my hands on. Soon, I was wrapped in a thick shell of cotton, Lycra, nylon, and wool. I looked nothing like a girl; but I imagined that I had now been compressed inside one. Perhaps if I did it often enough, my wish would come true. Perhaps all those layers would reshape my being.

WHEN DRESSING WASN'T AN OPTION, I studied our family's Sears catalog. If I was going to be a girl, I had to learn about sizes and colors. I had to understand the difference between nylon, spandex, and rayon. What was so special about Lycra and Antron III? I had to understand the pros, cons, and care instructions for linen, cotton, and wool. I studied the reference section in the middle of the catalog as though it were the *Encyclopedia Britannica*. I imagined a staff of feminine fashion experts patiently educating me about textiles, collar types, and sizing.

One of the first things I learned from Sears is that everything has a season. If it was spring, I didn't waste time on the winter catalog. Those clothes were already out of date. I shopped the spring catalog for dresses and the summer catalog for swimwear and casual clothes. In the winter, I looked at nightgowns, scarves, and gloves.

My favorite catalog arrived in the fall, just as the leaves were starting to yellow. This one was twice as thick as the other catalogs. Most of the added pages were devoted to women's fashion. Here, I would find the greatest variety of fabrics, patterns, and colors. There was an especially large assortment of outfits made from linen and wool. I had been given to believe that these two fabrics marked the woman of distinction.

Men loved the revealing nature of women's spring and summer fashions. But women, it seemed, lived for the fall. In spring and summer, I was told, women dressed to impress the men. But in the fall, they dressed to impress each other. If I wanted to belong to the sisterhood, I told myself, I had to master the fall.

During these moments of seclusion and fantasy, I felt a tremendous sense of peace. But immediately thereafter, I would become consumed by feelings of guilt and disgust. What was the matter with me? This was OK for girls, but I was a boy!

As IF TO COMPENSATE, I busied myself with boyish activities and surrounded myself with male friends. I built model airplanes with my neighbor, Chris. I chopped down trees and went fishing with Jimmy. I rode bikes through Rock Creek Park with my school chum,

With Twin Sister, Anne Louise

Charlie. I camped the C&O Canal with a trio of friends: Albert, Gerald, and Kirby. At Albert's house, we bet donuts on games of chess. At my house, we came to blows bidding for New York Avenue in Monopoly.

I played pick-up basketball. No one picked me first, but they usually picked me third or fourth. That counted for something, didn't it?

I spent hours practicing on my own. I practiced my release at the free-throw line and my turnaround jumper from the corners. I dribbled and snaked my way past imaginary opponents.

At night, I fell asleep listening to my grandfather's A.M. clock radio. If I balanced my hand in just the right way on the right, rear corner of the radio, I could pull in the voice of the excitable Johnny Most, play-by-play announcer for the invincible Boston Celtics. I imagined myself on the court, running the ball with all-stars, John Havlicek and Jo Jo White. One day, I would play for Boston.

I ALSO COMFORTED MYSELF with the thought that I was developing a healthy attraction for girls. More importantly, girls were developing an attraction for me. One of my friends informed me that Chris Holland, a really cute girl in my church group, had blushingly described me as a hunk. Martha Marvin, a popular cheerleader two grades ahead of me, started an imaginary Tom White fan club. One day, she gave me a copy of the group's invented minutes.

Tom White Fan Club—Meeting Minutes   *April 1975*

Chairman: Ann Leffingwell   *Secretary: Martha Marvin*

Motion was made by Angela Abruzzo to write a letter to Tom. The group took a vote—affirmative (21–6). The letter was composed by the group and taken down by Alice Marvin, the scribe. The letter included sweet nothings and compliments. It also asked Tom to send an 8"x10" autographed glossy photograph for each member of the group. Then the group read a collection of Tom's latest poems, some of which brought Chris Holland to tears. Miss Kitty Nesbitt asked each member to contribute 50 cents to buy Tom a floral arrangement. The motion was passed, and Miss Kitty collected $31.00 and ordered a large arrangement from an FTD florist. Brenda Baker moved for adjournment, and Chris Chadsey seconded.

THINGS SEEMED TO BE GOING WELL. Most of the time, I managed to shove my dressing episodes out of my mind. But, once in a while, the world seemed to laugh at my predicament. One such occasion was the celebration of my sixteenth birthday.

My family had gathered, as usual, around the dining room table. Anne Louise and I had blown out the candles on our separate cakes and had served everyone their double portion of confection and ice cream. Now it was time for the presents.

When her turn came, my mother handed me something heavy that was wrapped in fancy paper. She had always considered gift wrap a wasteful expense. Why had she taken such pains to adorn this particular gift? Why was she grinning so? She was usually so reserved.

Whatever it was, it was heavy, flexible, and rectangular—like a Sears catalog. Oh my God! Was she on to me? Was she about to give me my own Sears catalog? To this day, I don't know if that was a terrifying thought or a hopeful wish.

I gently teased back the paper wrapping, revealing the contents an inch at a time ... What the hell? Was this a joke? There I was, staring at the cover of the 1973 bestseller, *Our Bodies, Ourselves*, the feminist atlas of modern womanhood.

"Now that you're sixteen," my mother explained, "I thought it important for you to understand women better."

Such was the feminist perspective at the time: men needed to be educated. They needed to understand the world as experienced by women. Oh, if my mother only knew!

In the months that followed, I studied *Our Bodies* as though preparing for a final exam. My favorite page was the one that diagrammed the fallopian tubes. Wouldn't it be marvelous if I could have those, too? Perhaps I would develop some if I stared long enough. At the time, we were studying the theory of spontaneous generation in science. Maybe I would be the first to prove it possible.

From the netherworld of my subconscious, I could faintly hear the echoes of Cinderella: *I can be whatever I want to be ...*

AT ABOUT THIS TIME, I started my first serious relationship. Peggy, a girl at our church, had deputized her friend Angela to persuade me to invite Peggy to the upcoming church social. Ange had agreed to do it, but at the last second, changed her mind. Instead, she asked, would I be interested in taking her?

Of course!

Our relationship developed as did many high school romances. We went on dates and day trips. We held hands. Ange taught me how to kiss a girl ("Stop pressing so hard! ... Don't slobber. I'm not a postage stamp, for God's sake!"). She tutored me in slow dancing ("You're supposed to be leading. ... Oh, forget it! Just watch my feet."). I motored her to restaurants and shopping malls in my parents' lime-green Vega. We chose Barry Manilow's "Mandy" as our song.

Ange's household was awash in estrogen. When we weren't out on dates, we hung out in her kitchen with her mother, Betsy, or downstairs with her sisters, Gina and Vicki. Ange's father, Tommy, had long since resigned himself to a home that spun on a feminine axis. In fact, he seemed to spin on one as well. By day, he worked for the Department of Energy. At night, he disappeared into his art studio where he chain-smoked Marlboro cigarettes and painted Cubist mosaics of female nudes. I often joined him there after bidding Angela goodnight.

The only other masculine presence in the Abruzzo household was the family's German Shepard, Max. One day, I was loitering in the kitchen, watching Betsy at work on one of her recipes. I loved to watch her cook. Tommy wandered through. "Here Max! Come boy, come."

Max trotted in. Ange turned to her father, "Where are you going, Daddy?"

"I'm taking Max to the vet. It's time to have him neutered." He looked at me and grinned, "Want to come along, Tom?"

Ange scowled, "Dad! That's disgusting!"

"Maybe another time," I responded.

I WAS LIVING IN MY FANTASY UNIVERSE, a household that revolved around the women and that welcomed me into their world. Ange, Gina, and Vicki fought over clothes, prattled on about boys, and practiced gymnastics together. I watched them with fascination. When they invited me into their melees, I felt a warm sense of belonging. Maybe this guy thing would work out after all. I liked being around girls. They seemed to like having me around.

THE CAPSTONE OF OUR ROMANCE was Ange's high school prom. I wanted to make it a fairy-tale evening. I dressed myself in a tuxedo of pastel green—ghastly to think of now, but fashionable in the disco '70s. I wrapped a corsage around Ange's wrist; she pinned a rose boutonniere to my lapel. I wooed her with a romantic dinner at a suburban steak house.

We hung out at the prom with our best friends, Alice and David. We spent most of the night on the dance floor until the school principal called it an evening. I escorted Ange to my lime-green chariot and whisked her off to the Jefferson Memorial, our favorite spot for midnight romance. She was radiant; I was in love. We were prince and princess.

Except for one thing: Ange had no idea that, all night long, I had been wishing that it was I wearing the dress and the corsage. I wanted to be the one to be wooed. I wanted to be bubbly, giggly, and cute. I wanted Alice to be my best friend—not David.

The best I could hope for was to experience these things through Ange. I focused instead on being the perfect gentleman. This wasn't difficult to do. I simply did everything I wished that a gentleman would do for me.

IN THE TENTH GRADE, I decided to switch from public to private school. At the time, public schools in D.C. were in a state of chaos. I had been mugged, held at knife-point, and repeatedly harassed.

I had several options to choose from, most of them coeducational. But I chose The Heights, an all-boys school run by the conservative Catholic order, Opus Dei. Publicly, I reasoned that The Heights was my best option. It had academic rigor; the class sizes were small; the teachers were strict. The boys attended school wearing oxford shirts, jackets, and ties. After three years of public school chaos, I explained, I wanted order and discipline.

Privately, I hoped that adolescing in a community of boys and male teachers would do something to fix my growing discomfort with all things masculine. I also hoped that the school's religious fervor might rekindle my waning faith. For reasons I couldn't understand, my confidence in God, church, and doctrine had begun to weaken. I was as troubled by this as I was by my confusion with gender. Might they be connected?

I joined the school's basketball and soccer teams. I tried out for baseball. I went on religious retreats and enrolled in theology classes. I became friends with my high school teachers, adopting them as big brothers. Meanwhile, I became a deacon at my neighborhood Presbyterian church. I became more involved in our youth groups and spent more time with our pastors.

I NEVER SHARED my troubled feelings about gender and faith with anyone. I was too ashamed. I hoped that I could fix these lapses on my own. I captured my carefully concealed feelings in my journal:

Dear Tom,

I hate your guts! Why must you be so miserably pathetic? Why don't you just crawl into a hole and die?

I don't hate you. I pity and despise you. Goddamn you.

Why can't you be happy? Why are you so restrained? What are you hiding?

Damn it! Oh, you ass. You are just a mask. A miserable, putty mask. A brainless, stupid mask.

This was my teenage universe: Priests, acolytes, and teenage boys occupied my weekdays; Ange, her sisters, and my youth group filled my weekends. At night, I found refuge in my basement stronghold. There, I fed my imagination with books, blueprints, catalogs, and old-time radio shows.

Superficially, I excelled. I got good grades and made modest contributions to my sports teams. My friends looked up to me. They admired my intellect and trusted my sincerity. If someone felt troubled, they often came to me for advice.

Inside, I felt confused and disheartened. Though I got along with other guys, I never felt close to them. Though I was attracted to women, I spent most of my time wondering what it would be like to be them. Though I attempted to order my life with religious discipline, my faith was in continual retreat.

Everyone thought of me as a gentle leader; I considered myself a fraud. Part of my problem was that my outward success worked against me. To let anyone know of my doubts and anxieties would be to risk losing their admiration. At the time, others' respect was the only thing sustaining me. I had to fix this on my own.

The only time I seemed to feel a measure of peace was in the company of girls.

∾

AT EIGHTEEN, I enrolled at Princeton University. I shared a suite in Lockhart Hall with two other freshmen, John and Jed. John would later captain Princeton's varsity basketball team and found a successful investment management company. Jed would graduate *summa cum laude*, study acting at the Julliard School, and settle down as the well-published law school professor he is today.

To be sure, they had their quirks. John kept a poster of Tweety Bird in his bedroom. Jed loved to pace our living room late at night, discoursing to John and me on his two favorite topics: women and philosophy.

I was fascinated by their ease and confidence. They knew what they wanted and went for it, never seeming to struggle. I, on the other hand, was uncertain of even my identity. Who was I? What did I want to achieve? What did I want to be known for?

For the time being, I settled on serving as an amusement to my roommates. I learned to hide my anxiety behind the mask of a gentle, irrepressible clown. I did it well. One day, I entered our suite to find John lying on his belly, pounding his fists and feet on the floor. He was laughing uncontrollably. From the corner, Jed watched both of us, amused.

"What's so funny, John? What are you laughing at?"

"I don't know," he gasped. "I just saw you and couldn't help myself. You are so damn funny."

From the corner, Jed chuckled, "you two are something else."

At least I had a character to play.

I assured myself that I could match Jed and John measure for measure. I was at least as intelligent and well-read as they were. But, in truth, I couldn't come close to their achievements. Yes, I had the brains. But something was missing. I didn't bubble with their self-assurance. I felt empty and without direction.

LIKE MANY OF MY GENERATION, I began to explore sexual intimacy while in college. The other men in my class seemed to take unbridled joy in their potency. In the locker room, they crowed about their exploits. They bragged about their conquests over hands of poker. They compared notes on their girlfriends' anatomy and willingness to put out. Such talk both mortified and intimidated me.

My body was bursting with the same testosterone that coursed through my classmates' bodies. My masculine groin responded to a pretty face or a rounded curve with as much ardor as did that of any other teenage boy. Unfortunately, my mind did not cooperate. I battled between the urge to bed a woman and the desire to be her.

When I was younger, I had found my confusion about gender vaguely troubling. But as I matured, my body developed into a potent hormone factory. I became confused.

Sometimes, the only way I got through an evening of sexual intimacy with a woman was to imagine myself in a female role. I tried to orchestrate our tumble so that I ended up the one beneath. I imagined that it was I being caressed and penetrated. I still thought of my partner as a woman, but I reveled in her strength and ardor. I imagined myself enveloped and consumed by her feminine energy.

At other times, I found distraction by throwing myself into my partner's pleasure. Thanks to *Our Bodies, Ourselves*, I knew the details of female anatomy in a way that few men did. I used my knowledge of the clitoris and the G-spot to my partner's delight and to my personal advantage. Fortunately for me, there were women who enjoyed a change from the more typical masculine come-ons. I didn't captain a sports team; I didn't lead a band. But I was a gentle and considerate lover. I had to be.

IT WASN'T THAT I HAD a lot of sexual encounters. I was too timid. My body confused me.

In our teen years, we start to explore our bodies. Men stare at their developing muscles and note each new appearance of hair. They detect new smells and wonder at unfamiliar discharges. Touch takes on new meaning: we touch ourselves; we touch each other. Many teenagers explore this new physical world with rapt fascination.

But for the transgender teen, this stage of life can be terrifying. When I touched myself, I was touching something foreign. When I touched a woman, I was touching the possibilities within me. What did it all mean?

IN MY SOPHOMORE YEAR, I visited Ange at Sarah Lawrence College. There I met a classmate of hers, Joel. He was a gangly, awkward freshman. To Ange and the largely female student body, Joel was an amusing distraction. He described himself as a male lesbian: he loved women but felt that he was a woman, too. He imagined himself one of the girls. I joined Ange and her friends in laughing at poor Joel. What a silly idea! It made no sense. Right?

For years after, I privately teased myself that I, too, might be a male lesbian. With my limited sexual vocabulary, this was about as close as I could come in the 1980s to describing what I felt inside. As always, I never shared these sentiments with anyone. I didn't want to become the object of open ridicule—like Joel.

As I HAD DONE at The Heights, I tried to solve my problem by spending more time in the company of men. In my junior year, I joined the Ivy Club, a selective, all-male eating establishment. One of the things that I liked most about Ivy was that it was generally regarded as the more genteel and intellectual of the men's eating clubs. I hoped that I might find it easier to bond there.

On autumn Sundays, many of the men of Ivy gathered in our upstairs living room for an afternoon of televised football. They sprawled across the furniture, swigged their beers, and exchanged sports commentary and campus gossip. It was our barbershop.

How I longed to feel a part of the comradery! I rose extra early on such days and studied the sports page over coffee. Maybe if I memorized enough information, I could contribute to the armchair deliberations. But such ambitions always eluded me: by game time, I had forgotten every piece of sports trivia and insight. I sat quietly in the corner, marveling at everyone else's command of the game and witty repartee. Why couldn't I be like them?

On the outside, I remained a model of congeniality. I had many casual friends. On the inside, I slipped deeper into isolation and shame. I continued to struggle with the urge to cross-dress. Once in a while, I purchased an article of clothing to wear in the privacy of my room. But after a few weeks, I guiltily disposed of it in the trash.

IN 1983, a year after graduating from Princeton, I married Sally, a fellow student. I had developed a crush on Sally two years before. But it wasn't until the end of her junior year that she took any notice of me. Much like my freshman roommates, Jed and John, Sally was a driven, focused achiever. She knew what she wanted and went after it.

We had strikingly different personalities. At the time, I thought of our differences as yin and yang: her hard-edged intensity complemented my postured, easy-going congeniality. I liked her sense of direction and desire for structure. She was also very beautiful.

Shortly after our wedding, we moved to Chicago. There we threw ourselves into our new life together. Sally went to work for a consulting firm. I became a commercial loan officer, then an investment-banking officer. After a couple of years, I returned to business school and earned an MBA. Upon graduating, I became a management consultant. Meanwhile, Sally returned to academia and pursued a PhD.

For fifteen years, I crisscrossed North America, working for banks, airlines, steel companies, chemical plants, and transportation giants. I threw myself into pricing strategies, reorganizations, downsizings, mergers, and process reengineering initiatives.

At home, Sally and I began to design our future together. We filled our apartment with furniture and artwork. We escaped on weekends to nearby scenic towns, state parks, and bed and breakfasts. I built bookshelves and window seats. When I had time, I played tennis and basketball.

I THREW MYSELF into all these activities with a ferocious intensity. I often worked at the bank late into the night, only returning home in time for breakfast and a shower. I did this partly for love of the work. Someone in our bank had purchased a new machine called a "desktop computer". I was fascinated by its possibilities. I taught myself spreadsheet programming and began to think of ways to transform our commercial lending operations.

I teased Sally that this was all her fault. A year before we moved to Chicago, I had been working for a small consulting firm in Princeton, New Jersey. My boss, Dr. Kapoor, and I were constantly dreaming up new business ventures that involved portable computers. They were nicknamed *luggables* then, because they were the size, shape, and weight of a sewing machine.

One day, in a fit of scorn, Sally laid into me: "You two don't know the first thing about computers. It's embarrassing!" That week, I bought a book on BASIC programming. When the office closed on Friday, I stayed behind and opened the book to page one. I didn't leave until Sunday afternoon. I only left then because I had a date with Sally that evening. I wanted to tell her all that I had learned.

BUT I WAS ALSO DRAWN to my work at the bank because it brought me welcome distraction. Idle moments offered an opportunity for my gender anxieties to resurface. I was happiest when busy.

I hated that I had these feminine feelings inside me and searched constantly for ways to get rid of them. All I want, I thought, is to be a good man and a caring husband.

Over the next fifteen years, a predictable pattern emerged. Though the timing varied, it approximated a two-year cycle: for a year or two, my efforts to keep myself preoccupied worked. I distracted myself with new duties at home, a new service line at work, a new sport. I always had something to work toward.

But, eventually I would start to think about my womanhood. Why couldn't I be a woman? Why couldn't I dress like one? I tried desperately to repress these thoughts. My efforts worked for a while, but only built up the pressure. It was just a matter of time before the dam would burst. When it finally did, it was terrible. I became consumed by thoughts of womanhood and the need to cross-dress.

It was terrible for me; it was terrible for Sally. She was the only other person who knew of my struggles—although I tried hard to keep them from her. But keeping such secrets is almost impossible in a relationship as intimate as marriage. Sally tried to tolerate my episodes. But we agreed that this wasn't something that belonged in a marriage. Most of the time, I held it at bay. But not all of the time.

EVERY COUPLE OF YEARS, the ache for this other side of me grew to unbearable proportions. At first, it took over my nights. I lay awake, imagining what it would be like if only I could be a woman. I dreamed about it: I dreamed about being pregnant, pushing a stroller, and caring for my baby. I dreamed about sitting on the beach with girlfriends, chatting away idly. Sally had a few girlfriends who went canoeing each year in Minnesota. Oh, how I longed to go with them and to share their adventures—but as a woman.

Eventually, my thoughts invaded my days. I wondered how to get closer to the women I knew and further away from the men. Since most of my life outside the family involved work, I focused my efforts there.

In their spare time, the guys on my consulting team tended to talk about things like automotive engineering, home construction projects, and strippers. I tried to connect with them. I even joined them at a couple of strip clubs. But I found these too depressing. The last time I went, I excused myself a few minutes into the evening and spent the rest of the night waiting in the parking lot. I sat in the back of our car, quietly reading the Bible while my colleagues emptied their wallets on twenty-dollar lap dances.

Figuring out how to connect to the women I worked with was complicated. I was committed to my marriage and had no interest in anything more than friendship. But personal conversations between a man and a woman on a business trip are easily misunderstood. I worried that my womanly feelings would betray me. It would be too easy to fall into awkward topics: "That dress is so flattering on you, where did you get it?" "Do you ever think about having children?" These were the sorts of questions that sprang casually to my mind.

Once my thoughts had invaded my nights and filled my days, they began to annex my body. I lost weight. I shaved my arms, my chest, and my legs. I stopped doing anything that might build muscle.

I purchased women's clothes and wore them when I could find time alone. I didn't buy fantasy wear—at least not as the term is generally understood. My fantasy was to be real. Except for a few items of risqué lingerie, I shopped for attire at the business and casual end of the spectrum: a gray pencil skirt, a pair of women's khakis, an oxford blouse.

At the height of these cycles, I ventured outdoors. I wanted to feel real. How could I do that hiding in a basement or bathroom? I set the alarm for 4 a.m. Upon waking, I dressed in a layer of women's athletic wear, then a layer of men's. I eased the door open and sprinted toward the nearest unlit street. Once I was cloaked in the safety of darkness, I removed my men's sweatshirt. But I always jogged at the ready: I ran holding the waist of the sweatshirt in both hands so that I could throw it on should anyone appear on the sidewalk ahead of me.

On other occasions, I drove to an isolated park. I drove until I found a place where there were no other cars. One day, I found an empty parking lot. At the far end, a picnic bench lay within ten feet of the curb. I reasoned that, if anyone entered the park, I could quickly return to the car. I got a book and a Diet Coke and sat down to read. I was out in the world as a woman. I even took my first Polaroid to commemorate the occasion.

EACH TIME the cycle repeated itself, it persisted for a couple of months. I quietly disappeared from all sports activities—from basketball, tennis, and gym. I had to wait for my body hair to grow back. Until then, I could only appear in public in long pants and long sleeves. I didn't dare to venture into a locker room.

Eventually, the shame and isolation grew unbearable. I purged my stash of clothing, regrew my hair, and vowed never to do it again. This cycle repeated itself over and over.

PURGING CLOTHING was especially painful. It brought so many different forces into play. Each item of clothing was invested with a special meaning to me. It had taken me two hours to buy a simple, brown woolen skirt because I had been so frightened of detection. But it had been worth it. That skirt had, if only for a few weeks, invested me with a feeling that my womanhood was real. Throwing it away was like tossing aside my hope.

I was torn, too, by the matter of waste. I had spent family money on these items. I knew from history that this cycle would almost certainly repeat itself. Why not save the clothes for then? But purging is an act of faith: if I had any hope of escaping these feelings, everything had to go.

Finally, there was the question of security. What if someone caught me disposing of these things? I went through my discards two or three times to make certain that nothing was there that could be connected to me. To this day, I mourn the destruction of my first Polaroid. At the time, it was a source of shame and potential exposure. Today, I remember it for the smile that was on my face. It is my first memory of the woman I am today.

FALSE CURES

Myself when young did eagerly frequent
Doctor and saint, and heard great argument
About it and about: but evermore
Came out by the same door as in I went.

— *Rubaiyat of Omar Khayyam, First Edition, 1859,*
Quatrain 27

MANY SEEM TO THINK that crossdressing is something that people like me do for fun. No doubt, there are crossdressers who enjoy the practice. I did not. It was horrible. It degraded me. I worried that it degraded women. But I couldn't help it.

Today, I understand that this was simply the real person inside me, screaming to be let out. I was following my true north. But back then, I thought that there was something terribly wrong with me. As I cycled through each crossdressing episode, I worked frantically to understand and to fix my problem.

With Twin, Anne Louise, in Hansel & Gretel

Over the course of thirty years, I developed a number of theories to explain my self-loathing and gender confusion. I researched them. I read books. I poured through scientific studies, religious tracts, and spiritual memoirs. I consulted specialists, therapists, and ministers. I conducted experiments, using myself as the human guinea pig.

Did any theory fit my facts and feelings? Did the interventions I tried make them go away? Each exploration consumed months or years of effort.

People often ask me why it took me so long to figure out that I am a transsexual woman. The reason is simple: I consumed thirty years desperately pursuing every other possibility. Three in particular interested me: Was it something in my family upbringing? Did I just need to get right with God? Had something in my past shattered my sense of manhood?

THE FIRST AREA I explored was my family history.

With Family

I had been raised in a pretty normal and healthy middle-class home. So far as my brothers, sisters, and I knew, we got along with each other as well as did any other siblings. My parents weren't exactly Italian with their love, but they took good care of us. With their careers and so many children to manage, Mom and Dad functioned more like camp counselors than family intimates.

But I was looking back on my childhood from the vantage point of the 1980s. This was the heyday of family systems therapy. Magazines were full of new buzzwords, such as the birth order effect, attachment theory, and genograms. The notion underlying these frameworks was that you couldn't understand and diagnose an individual without understanding the social system that they had grown up in.

Alice Miller's *Prisoners of Childhood* particularly impressed me. Miller explored the distinction between healthy and unhealthy narcissism. Healthy narcissism equated to strong self-esteem. Miller defined it as a state of feeling genuinely alive. It resulted from having access to one's true self and authentic feelings. Unhealthy narcissism came about when the true self faced solitary confinement within a false self.

I didn't consider myself a narcissist. But the notion of a false self had a ring of truth to it. Something about me felt very false. According to Miller, the key to finding our true selves lay in examining our unresolved childhood conflicts, which so many of us lock away and hide. What, I wondered, might I be hiding? Was there something in my family history that could explain my low self-esteem and gender anxiety?

I BEGAN MY EXPLORATIONS with my mother. Between her career and children, she had stretched herself pretty thin. In the mornings and afternoons, we children fended for ourselves. At night, the family gathered over Crock-Pot casseroles and other recipes for the time-constrained career woman. We were on our own when it came to homework.

I wondered: Might I be trying to fill an emptiness that stemmed from a lack of bonding and connection with my mother? Was I creating a more reliable woman to fill that void?

From birth, I had had to compete with two sisters for my mother's scarce time. My chief competitor was my twin sister, Anne Louise. In therapy sessions, I wondered aloud: Had Anne been breastfed first? Had she gotten more time and attention from my mother because she was a girl? Had I been treated differently because I was a boy?

I found several published studies suggesting that baby boys were held and cuddled less frequently than were girls. They were spoken to differently. They were treated more independently. Some feminists took this data to suggest that boys were encouraged to be more independent. I took it in the opposite direction: Had I learned that girls were loved more than boys were? Did I want to be a girl so that I, too, would feel loved?

I spent several years in therapy exploring questions like these. My mother must have known which days my appointments fell on. Immediately after each session, I telephoned her and subjected her to a grueling cross-examination: "What did you do for Anne Louise that you didn't do for me?" "Why did you put me in the basement?" "Did you prefer Mary Fran and Anne Louise to me?" "Do you think that you breastfed us enough?"

MY FATHER WAS THE NEXT to fall under my microscope. I was his firstborn son. As a result, I had grown up with the understanding that the two of us were supposed to have a special connection. Isn't that why I had followed him around everywhere? Hadn't I made him the center of my universe?

Dad was deeply invested in his work as a minister. At church, he was a charismatic and expressive leader. But he rarely expressed himself so openly at home. He conveyed more love and compassion while leading a weekend retreat than he might share at home in a year. At our summer home, he often took me on daylong fishing trips. He lit his cigars, baited my hooks, and hauled my catches into the boat. But he said hardly a word the entire time.

I wondered why he hadn't been closer to me, his firstborn son. Weren't we supposed to have that special bond thing going? He preached his religious convictions to perfect strangers, but never shared them with me. Was I that unimportant? Shouldn't he care for my soul?

In *Finding Our Fathers,* Samuel Osherson suggested that the nine-to-five office workday had robbed modern households of a masculine presence and little boys of a critical emotional bond. Picking up on this, I began to study the writings of a school of philosophers and poets who were part of the then-fashionable movement to rediscover masculine spirituality. These included Robert Bly, Robert Moore, and Joseph Campbell.

I wondered: was I imagining myself as a woman because I had lacked a personal connection to a masculine role model? Is that why my masculine identity was so underdeveloped?

I CONSIDERED MY SISTERS NEXT. Could my gender issues be explained by my dynamic with them? I had spent a lot of my early youth in the company of my twin, Anne Louise, and my older sister, Mary Fran. Perhaps I had just wanted to belong to their circle. Had I felt left out of their games? Had I subconsciously modeled myself after them? Is this why I had so thoroughly enjoyed being around Ange and her sisters later on?

When I reviewed this theory with my mother, she brought up another possibility. Had I felt the need to overcompensate for the lack of conventional femininity in our household? My mother and sisters were all pretty, but they weren't particularly feminine—at least, not as defined at the time by the media. "Were you trying to fill a feminine void in the family?" my mother later wondered.

Finally, I considered my younger brothers, and with them, the entire family. Once David and Graham arrived on the scene, I found myself the odd man out among three natural pairings: my two parents, my two sisters, and my two brothers. While I never felt excluded, I always felt that I orbited on the periphery of these duos. Did it make me feel lonely? Did I try to compensate in some way? Had living alone in the basement driven me to create a family within me?

As I CYCLED into and out of my crossdressing episodes, I examined these possibilities over and over. I was certain that the key to my issues lay buried somewhere in my family history. But I could never make the accusation stick.

Yes, my mother and father were busy and distracted. But they were always there. Dinner may have been a quickly prepared casserole, but we dined every night as a family. My father may not have said much on our fishing trips, but he always invited me.

When I finally asked him why he had never shared his religion with me, he explained that he had been so worried about foisting his views on us that he worked hard not to. He had known many ministers to destroy their children by imposing their dogma on them. I considered: he *had* taken me on many of his church retreats. He left it to me to make of them what I wanted to.

My mother would not or could not recall the details of my breastfeeding schedule. But I couldn't recall feeling lonely or anxious when I was young. If anything, having a twin sister gave me a ready playmate. Anne Louise and I shared a fairly fluid set of friends—boys and girls. Children moved to and fro between the households in our neighborhood. I had lots of friends, male and female, while growing up.

As for wanting to imitate my mother and sisters, there is this: I was a child of the '60s, living in a liberated household. Neither my sisters nor my mother were into more than the most basic makeup, perfume, and jewelry. We had few, if any, Barbie dolls in our home. From the beginning, I had expressed my womanhood differently than did anyone else in my family. My sisters were the first to point out that I clearly hadn't learned to dress and act like a woman from them.

BUT MOST IMPORTANT, I realized, was the fact that it was I who had isolated myself from the family, not the other way around. During my teen years in particular, I often refused family invitations to go on field trips. "I'm too busy," I explained. "I want to be on my own."

The second statement was closer to the truth. At our summer home, for example, the family often went on boating excursions to a beach on the other side of Narragansett Bay. Everyone packed themselves into my father's eighteen-foot aluminum outboard. We were alternately soaked and sunned as my father skippered the craft across the water. Once at the beach, we tumbled out of the boat and onto the shore. We snorkeled, bodysurfed, sunbathed, and picnicked until the tides turned sufficiently to allow the boat back into the channel. Then we returned home.

In truth, I loved these beach outings. I often didn't go on them though, because, packed as we were in my parents' summerhouse, these trips were my only opportunity during summer vacation to explore my secret life. Our summer home was a reconstructed Montgomery Ward kit house—a relic of the 1930s. It was not designed to hold a family of seven, let alone all of the guests and relatives who regularly descended on our summer Eden.

So, instead of joining my family, I stood on the shore, waving goodbye to them as they puttered around the bend. As soon as the sound of the outboard motor had died away, I sprinted back to the house. I sorted through my sisters' and mother's clothing and laid out my options. There weren't too many choices, mostly sundresses, shorts, blouses, and swimsuits.

At times like this, I resented my mother and sisters for their basic tastes in clothing. My mother, for example, favored polyester pants with an elastic lining. She said that they were economical and comfortable. I would not, for the life of me, put them on. My sisters favored blue jeans. I already had plenty of those.

With the house to myself, I could sunbathe, swim, cook, garden—anything. My favorite escape was to swim and kayak in our cove. I worried about getting caught: our shoreline was dotted with so many summerhouses. Anyone sitting on a sundeck with a pair of field glasses might spot me from afar. But I was giddy with the idea that I was claiming new territory for the new me. The further I ventured from our shore, the larger my secret universe became.

These flights to freedom were always short-lived. An hour or so before my family was destined to return, I cleaned everything off and put it back where I had found it. If I had worn makeup, I scrubbed my face to remove any evidence. When I finished, I pulled out my drafting paper and began to sketch plans for another underwater city.

My family felt hurt by my refusals to join them on these outings. Meanwhile, I resented them for ... well, for what? I wasn't sure at the time. I only knew that I felt angry and annoyed.

In retrospect, I realize that I desperately wanted to fit in and to have fun with everyone. Far from being an occasion for joy, my dressing episodes were a source of guilt and isolation.

I SPENT TWENTY YEARS exploring these family systems explanations before I finally let them go. They did nothing to explain my misplaced sense of gender. They did nothing to reduce my sense of isolation. In fact, they left me feeling as lonely and as desperate as ever. And, in attempting to blame my family, I had only extended my years of isolation from them.

৵

EVEN AS I WAS DISSECTING each member of my family, I explored a second line of questioning: Did my problems stem from a loss of faith and my separation from the Church? Had Modernism corrupted my soul? Did I need Jesus to fix me?

I had grown up surrounded by the Church. Before our family moved to Chicago, we had lived in New York City. There, my father had served as the pastor to a Black and Hispanic congregation in the Hell's Kitchen neighborhood of Manhattan. I was so proud of him.

Every Sunday morning, my mother dressed us for church and corralled us into a pew near the front of the sanctuary. I rarely sat still. One day, I grew especially restless. Before my mother knew what was happening, I had slid to the floor and darted into the aisle. Dressed in black corduroys and a white oxford shirt, I paraded toward where my father stood. Even as he addressed the congregation, I raised my voice in chant: "I want my Daddy! ... I want my Daddy!"

My father continued his homily; I continued my steady advance. Nobody dared to interrupt our strange duet. When I reached his side, I clamped my fist about his index finger, turned to face the parishioners, and beamed. I don't know why, but my father's index finger was a magical thing to me. I was clutching the center of my universe. So long as I held onto it, I was invincible.

Somehow, my father managed to finish his sermon and restore me to my mother. For the rest of his tenure in New York, she never allowed me to sit nearest the aisle again. She always made sure that an adult sentry guarded either end of the pew.

Sometime later, my twin sister, Anne Louise, and I were invited to a meeting of the church elders. This was big stuff! There we were, sitting amongst the leaders of our church as our father led them in an Easter Sunday prayer. We were barely big enough to stretch our legs the length of the seats.

When the prayer was over, the room remained quiet. Anne Louise and I looked up to see all of the elders smiling at us. A door swung open; a woman entered the room bearing a birthday cake. Everyone started to sing "Happy Birthday" as she placed the cake before us. Even at that young age, I knew that this gesture had little to do with Anne Louise and me. It was a sign of respect for my father. How cool was that! And on that year, my birthday happened to coincide with the second birth of Jesus. Even cooler.

I LOVED TO WATCH my father in action. He was a natural leader with a gift of unassuming authority. With each word he spoke, he drew people out of themselves.

One time, he fashioned a sermon after an UltraBrite toothpaste commercial. The premise of the commercial was that UltraBrite made your teeth so bright that, if you blew someone a kiss, they would physically feel it. As soon as the loyal UltraBrite consumer blew their kiss, a lipstick imprint would appear on the smiling recipient's cheek.

My father faced his parishioners. "Love doesn't just come along like …" Here, he imitated the happy recipient of the air kiss, touching his cheek where the kiss had landed. He went on to explain the hard work of love and the importance of Christ and compassion. I marveled. Where did he come up with this stuff?

After an hour with my father, people felt loved and connected. His presence made the room feel bigger; he made each person feel bigger, and I, his son, felt bigger by association.

WHEN I ENTERED JUNIOR HIGH SCHOOL, my parents started to send me to a Presbyterian summer camp in Virginia. Early on, I earned the nickname, Motor Mouth. My counselors were constantly after me to "tone it down." The one exception was morning wakeup call. Then, they were only too willing to let me loose on my fellow campers. I raced from campsite to campsite, shouting, "Rise and shine! Wake up! Wake up!"

By high school, my nickname had sweetened to Reverend Tom. I had advanced from inflicting others with my voice to infecting them with my ideas. I had inherited my father's gift.

One summer afternoon, I was sitting at a picnic bench, talking to two especially pretty campers in our group, Darla and Jenny. They had earned nicknames of their own: Sugar Lips and Swivel Hips. Denny, my chief rival for their affection, came running out of the woods, shouting with excitement.

"Tom! Tom! You'll never guess what I just did!"

"What is it, Denny?"

"I found a black widow spider. I was just about to kill it. Then I remembered what you said earlier about life being sacred and all. I walked it a mile into the woods and set it free."

"You are an idiot!" I teased. I didn't recall saying anything of the kind. But it didn't matter. I felt my father's power within me. Cool.

AT THE TIME, I didn't have conscious designs to become a minister, and my father never pressured me to become one. But it was often at the back of my mind. I had inherited from him the ability to inspire others to reach beyond themselves. I was a thoughtful listener and a persuasive speaker. Maybe I had his gift.

By this time, my father had risen to a privileged rank in the Presbyterian Church. He was now an Executive Presbyter, the leader of over 100 churches in the D.C. area. Instead of guiding a flock of parishioners, he now guided their spiritual leaders. Instead of leading church services, he led retreats.

I often went along on his retreats. I loved to watch my dad in action. He really knew how to draw people into thoughtful discussion. One weekend, he opened a gathering of church elders by addressing them as follows: "I want all of you to arrange yourselves in a single line. Position yourselves along that wall to reflect your level of influence in this group. If you think that you are the most influential, stand to the far left. If you think you are the least influential, stand to the far right. No talking."

The elders exchanged embarrassed blushes as they shuffled into position. Some who started at the left found themselves pushed to the right as others stepped in. For a few minutes, people stepped into and out of line as they pushed their way into a new position. The silence was broken only by nervous chuckles and the shuffle of feet. At last, my father called time. "Very well," he said. "One of the things we are going to explore this weekend is how you all function as a group. Remember your positions. Let us pray."

With that, he led them through a series of exercises and discussions. I watched in fascination as he layered one exercise upon another to draw everyone out of themselves. Through a mixture of scripture, group facilitation and personal alchemy, he softened the egos in the room and drew the elders into two days of heartfelt discussion. Was their mission to grow membership or to live God's word? What did God's word mean to their mission? I was amazed to see how much spiritual growth my father could create in a weekend. I wanted to be just like him.

BUT IN MY MID-TEENS, my spiritual world began to fall apart. No one else was aware of it, but I could feel my faith slipping away. I still mouthed all the right words, but I no longer believed them. Although I tried, I found that I could not will myself into belief.

I had grown up confident in the love of Christ and secure in his message of salvation. The church hadn't been forced upon me. In fact, far from it: I had willingly adopted "Reverend Tom" as a vital part of my identity. My spiritual strength had moved me up the social pyramid from likeable clown to influential leader. I had counted on it to be there for the rest of my life.

So when it left me, I began to panic. What had I done to deserve this?

This was the 1970s. The liberal church was under attack. Attendance had begun to fall. Newspapers were trumpeting the rise of the secular society. Was I losing my soul to science?

On the far right, religious conservatives argued that the church had become too humanistic. The only solution, they insisted, was for people to confess their sins and to give themselves over to God. Had I followed my father down the wrong spiritual path? Had my faith weakened because I had rooted it in spirituality and acts rather than in doctrine and prayer?

To make matters worse, even as my faith was slipping away, my confusion over my gender was steadily mounting. I worried that the two were related.

These two worries are what drove me to attend The Heights. Opus Dei was known for being one of the strictest, most disciplined religious orders in the world. I admired their sense of conviction and their focus on order. I hoped that, if I spent enough time with them, their sensibilities would rub off on me.

I remained connected with the Heights for five years. In fact, when I took a year off from Princeton, I spent half of it teaching science in their after-school program and counseling at their summer camp. But for all my efforts, things never came together. I wanted to share Opus Dei's beliefs. I wanted to feel the strength of their convictions. But I could not.

AS I BECAME AN ADULT, I started to flail around for answers. This was no small matter. There were days when I didn't even want to get out of bed. If God was no longer speaking to me, what was the point? I felt abandoned and betrayed. I prayed for signs. I tried bargaining: "God, if you speak to me again, I will be extra good. I will do whatever you say." I never received a reply.

At several points during my twenties and thirties, I explored other religious ideas and organizations. I was especially attracted to those that leaned toward evangelism and strict biblical interpretation. If I truly believed in something, wouldn't I want to evangelize? If I was feeling lost and rudderless, didn't I need the discipline of specific commandments? Perhaps Opus Dei had provided me with the wrong sort of discipline and the wrong set of laws. What else was out there?

If nothing else, the United States is rich with religious variety. You can spend decades shopping the pews and prayer rooms for something that suits your taste. At various points, I entertained affiliations with Unitarians, Episcopalians, Catholics, Buddhists, Methodists, and Presbyterians. I explored the basic tenets of Islam, Judaism, and Hinduism.

WHILE ON A BUSINESS TRIP—before I married Sally—I even spent several days on a farm in Boonville, California, a guest of Sun Myung Moon's Unification Church. There, I braided garlic stalks with other lost souls and listened as our hosts educated us about their worldview. It was enticing. Their explanation of the spiritual universe was simple and vivid. I wanted to believe it.

More important, every one of our hosts seemed to be lit from within by the power of love and the spirit of peace. I could feel their light wash over me.

Throughout the weekend, I watched my fellow pilgrims with fascination. Most of them had come from broken homes. They were society's outcasts, gathered up, like me, in the streets of San Francisco. This was probably the first time that some of them had experienced what it was like to have another human look them in the eyes and say, "I love you." Our hosts said this often. Each time, they delivered the words with a loving gaze that lingered like a caress. Who could blame my fellow guests if they cast their lot with this group of tender-hearted souls? What, after all, were they giving up?

But I wasn't a social outcast. My family wasn't broken. I was just lost. As much as I enjoyed learning about the Unification belief system, it struck me as an artfully constructed mythology. It was a tale too neatly told. I returned to San Francisco and the business world on Monday.

WHENEVER I VISITED my parents, I borrowed from my father's library of religious philosophers. I examined the works of luminaries, such as Reinhold Niebuhr, Karl Barth, and Dietrich Bonhoeffer. Surely, one of them could help me. They offered more than a disembodied theology. They offered spiritually grounded commentary on some of the most vexing problems facing modern man.

I often wondered if it was simply that I lacked discipline. I tried to be more ascetic. I tried to be obedient to a creed that had yet to reveal itself to me.

I searched for a religious guide who might ignite in me a spark of hope and spirituality. The closest I came was a chance meeting with a British missionary in Hong Kong. He didn't try to get me to believe or do anything. He simply talked about his profound love affair with Jesus Christ. Like any lover, he couldn't stop talking about the object of his affection. I was captivated by his passion and jealous of his certainty.

But, try as I might, I could not kindle such a spark within me.

Something always seemed to be missing. With each failed effort, I only felt more ashamed and despondent. I was probably more ashamed by my lack of faith than I was by my gender confusion. Wasn't the former more important? If only I could reach God, I thought, I might beg his forgiveness and guidance. I prayed for help. None came.

All the while, I told no one.

෴

WHAT DID ALL OF THIS have to do with my confusion about gender? How might religion save me? I considered several possibilities. Perhaps I was just a lowly sinner. According to this line of reasoning, my problems had nothing to do with me. Everyone since the fall of Adam and Eve had wrestled with one demon or another. Gender was mine.

Man's greatest sin, I reasoned, lay in trying to fix our problems on our own. This was the sin of pride. My only hope was to give myself over to God and to pray for salvation. Each time I tried a new church on for size, I was essentially hoping that I would connect with God and free myself from my horrid desires. When it didn't happen, I moved on to another church, another creed, another theologian.

A VARIATION on this theme was the notion that I was uniquely perverted. Perhaps there was something distinctively shameful about me. I had often heard religious leaders lump people with feelings like mine together with the dregs of society—with pedophiles and sexual predators. Was it possible that I was something that vile and despicable?

If so, I imagined that my only solution was to separate myself from society and to pursue a life of chastity. I would become a monk or join a holy order. I would protect the world from people like me and spend a lifetime alone seeking penance. I was not fit to be part of the world. I considered this possibility at several points in my life. The first time was while attending the Heights; the last came shortly after the end of my marriage to Sally. But I could not follow this path unless I was called to it. To do so would be to commit an even greater hypocrisy.

I was never called.

THE LAST of the religiously rooted theories I entertained was that my gender troubles were born of shame and despair. Perhaps my sense of shame and degradation had left me feeling so completely alone that I needed to create a soulmate to comfort me. Like Adam, I needed an Eve. Perhaps my desire to experience womanhood was born of the need to have someone in my life who wasn't ashamed of me. Alone in the world, I needed to create someone who would willingly complete me.

Journal Entry   *February 1995*

Dear God,

I am a sinner. A lowly, lowly sinner. I am writing to you asking for strength and absolution. I have never felt this low in my life. ... I know I am a man, and a good one at that. ... But I feel so alone in the world.

Loneliness worries me. I have done few things that I regret. But those regrets that I have were all conceived in loneliness. I have felt alone and unloved for so many years. Bunyan was right: The greatest sin of all is despair. Help me not to despair, God.

If despair was the issue, the solution wasn't to address my gender confusion but rather to address my isolation. This is where my efforts to belong to social groups and sports teams had come into play. It is partly why marriage was so important to me: I wasn't just looking for a friend and a lover; I was looking for someone to redeem my soul.

I DIDN'T EXPLORE these causes and cures in sequence. They were different expressions of the same desperate trope. I bounced back and forth between them in confused desperation. But all involved the same cycle of activities: Pray. Study. Consult. Affiliate. Commit. Pray some more.

Nothing worked. The more people and texts I consulted, the more confused I became. I knew that I was a good and decent person at heart. I simply didn't understand why I couldn't take joy in myself and feel the love of others.

ॐ

MY THIRD LINE OF INQUIRY was my manliness. Proving my manliness had been a preoccupation for most of my life. Although I found many masculine feelings and behaviors distasteful, I envied the men who experienced and practiced them. They seemed so powerful, so at ease.

To all outward appearances, I was reasonably virile. Lots of pretty girls thought I was cute. My male friends would have described me as having a pleasant, easygoing masculinity. Why didn't I feel that way inside?

I was often preoccupied with the notion that I simply wasn't man enough. Perhaps, I thought, I am just inferior to other men. We can't all be good at everything. I was given a great mind and a gentle heart. Maybe my guy genes weren't as potent as everyone else's. If so, I just needed to accept it.

I certainly felt intimidated around men. Whether they were jocks or nerds, I felt exposed in their presence. They boiled with something inside them that I lacked. The remedy was simple: Man up! Play harder. If necessary, find a way to become comfortable objectifying women. That's what real men do, isn't it? Sally put it quite succinctly one day, "I just need a real man, damn it!"

MANNING UP is an all-too-common phenomenon with transsexuals. Ask former Navy Seal, Kristin Beck, or former Navy pilot and NASA flight surgeon, Dr. Christine McGinn. Ask the 150,000 other transgender military personnel who have served in the armed forces or who are currently on active duty. Talk to Olympian Caitlin Jenner or to Kimberly Reed, once the golden-boy quarterback of her Helena, Montana high school football team. Mortgage banker Gina Duncan pursued manliness as an all-star linebacker for her high school's undefeated football team and as its homecoming king.

So many of the transsexuals I know have the same story. Hoping for a cure, they gravitate to particularly manly careers and pastimes: military service, construction work, weightlifting, football, martial arts.

Although I wasn't blessed with the athletic talents of Caitlin Jenner or Kimberly Reed, I tried my hand at just about every sport I could: basketball, tennis, football, baseball, soccer, street hockey, rugby, crew, golf, cross-country running, kayaking, hiking—even ultimate Frisbee. I was a middling athlete, but I was propelled by a desperate anxiety. I played hard.

In my early teens, for example, I decided to train as a long-distance runner. On my first day out, I set a goal of eight miles. After covering two miles, I developed a severe cramp. "Real men don't stop," I told myself. I ran the remaining six miles, ignoring the excruciating pain. For the next three weeks, I could barely walk.

A few years later, I was playing midfield for my high school soccer team. We were losing, two to one. It was the second-to-last game of the year and we needed the victory. I was far from the most talented player on the team, but I ran like the devil. I chased down one ball after another, trying to get it to our forwards.

At one point, an opponent and I rushed a loose ball at top speed. Our legs locked together in full kick. We circled each other in midair like a pair of conjoined helicopter blades. I fell to the ground with a thud that shook me to my core. Though groggy, I refused to leave the game.

Shortly after the final whistle blew, I collapsed on the sidelines and began to hyperventilate. The next thing I knew, my teammates had hoisted me in their arms and were carrying me to our van. Our coach ran through several red lights on the way to the emergency room. In between my labored breaths, I could hear my teammates worrying about me. I was a warrior now! I had finally entered the brotherhood.

When we got to the emergency room, we didn't even have to leave the waiting area. There, the doctor lay me on a stretcher. He calmly placed a brown paper bag over my mouth. With my team looking on, he explained, "Don't worry. He's just hyperventilating. He was probably shocked and upset by all the exertion. It will pass."

It did. But my shame and embarrassment did not.

For all my effort, it never felt like me on the playing field. Where other men seemed to be fueled by a fire in their belly, I was driven by high anxiety. Making a great play didn't give me a boyish sense of joy. It only made me feel less suspect. My worst fear was that the other men would pick up the scent of my anxiety and come in for the kill. Never let them know your fear. I never did.

WHILE I DIDN'T FEEL MANLY on the football field, my testosterone-infused body had no trouble feeling manly toward women. When I responded to the sight of a pretty face, a part of me hated the swelling sensation that bridled inside my zippered jeans. But another part of me loved it. Maybe, I thought, my problem is that I am too manly. Perhaps I am too attracted to women—so attracted that I seek their constant presence and approval.

Like many other men in the pre-Internet era, I purchased my share of *Playboy* and *Penthouse* magazines. But unlike other men, I stared at each picture, wondering why the woman on display couldn't be me. In 1981, when *Playboy* featured Tula, the transsexual Bond girl, my mind fairly exploded. Was that really possible? I had never heard of such a thing. Still, she seemed to be such an outlier; it never occurred to me that we might have something in common. I was just a broken man. She was in a league all her own.

By this logic, my problem was that I was too attracted to women. The solution was a familiar one: get back out there on the field and play your heart out. Dig into your career. Women will be your undoing. Be chaste. Whatever you do, don't think about sex. Tame the beast within.

SO WHAT WAS IT? Was I undermanned or oversexed? It didn't make any sense. I considered a third possibility: perhaps I was the model man for the future.

This was a time when traditional models of masculinity were under attack. Several popular movements encouraged men to consider new approaches. Some writers encouraged men to get in touch with their feminine side. Others, like Robert Moore, and Joseph Campbell went in the opposite direction: they advised their brethren to tap into the spiritual roots of their masculinity. Meanwhile, the hosts of *Queer Eye for the Straight Guy* taught American men how to become thoroughly modern metrosexuals.

Maybe, I thought, I have had it backwards. Maybe I have been misled by an outdated model of masculinity. Perhaps all the other men should be learning from me! My desire to imitate women might simply reflect the fact that I had more depth and breadth of soul than could be expressed through the masculine stereotype. Maybe I just needed to love the man I was.

By this logic, I should stop trying to imitate other men. I should stop borrowing from feminine ideals. I should define my own manhood. Be a leader.

One of the things I had liked about women's clothing was the opportunity it afforded to express an exacting sense of style. I tried to think of ways to express myself more richly as a man. I bought colorful shirts and ties. I picked out suits with European tailoring. I kitted myself with fancy colognes and badger-hair shaving brushes.

But this never worked either. I simply moved on to the next cycle of emotional ups and downs.

So I wandered through my twenties, thirties, and early forties. I journeyed through a seemingly endless cycle of peaks and valleys. With each cycle, I explored a new theory for my misplaced sense of gender. I tried new solutions. All of them failed. With each repetition, my sense of despair only deepened.

With Haley

One thing in my life felt uncomplicatedly wonderful: being a father. Several years after we married, Sally and I bore two children into the world. Haley joined us in 1989 and Cameron in 1991. I was head over heels in love with them.

I had conceived another daughter, Evelyne, while still an undergraduate at Princeton. Evelyne would later become a major part of my life and will figure prominently in these pages later on. But during the period covered in this chapter, she was growing up in New Jersey with her mother, Christine, and her stepfather, Mikel. At the moment, my family life centered on Sally, Haley, and Cam.

My consulting job involved a lot of time on the road. Most weeks, I was gone for four or five days. When I returned home, all I wanted was to hear Haley's and Cam's gleeful, "Daddy's home!" I dropped my briefcase and hauled them into my arms. We danced, we wrestled, we played hide-and-seek and tickle-monster. The house was our playground.

Even when I was exhausted from travel, I found ways for us to have fun. I stacked ten layers of blankets on top of Haley's bed. Then, while they hid their eyes, I slipped between two layers. "I'm ready!"

I closed my eyes and listened as the two of them bounced on top of me. Layer by layer, they giggled their way through the blankets. "Where are you, Daddy? Where are you?"

At last, a ray of light broke through the darkness. Two joyous faces peered in. "Oh, there you are, Daddy!"

I HATED BEING AWAY from Haley and Cam. When I was home, I recorded them on audiotape. I captured Haley growling like a tiger, talking with her make-believe friend, singing her ABCs. I preserved Cameron sputtering, burbling, and endlessly laughing. He always infected the room with his glee. I filled twenty cassettes with my children's echoes. Whenever I left home, I packed a couple of tapes in my briefcase. Each night, I fell asleep in my hotel room listening to the children's gurgles, stories, and songs and to Sally's nighttime lullabies.

When Haley and Cam were older, I took their favorite books with me on the road. On nights when they were interested, I read to them over the phone. One night, while on business in Cleveland, I had to attend a Cavaliers basketball game with my colleagues. One of them eyed the copy of *The Hardy Boys* in my hand. "Why did you bring that to the game? Aren't you a little old?"

Another colleague teased, "Maybe he's going to read to us."

During the second quarter, I quietly excused myself. I searched the stadium for a payphone as far from the noise as possible. I read a couple of chapters to Cam until he finally nodded off. I always knew when he was falling asleep because I randomly inserted nonsense into my narration. Usually I added, "… and then a naked boy ran across the lawn!" If Cam didn't respond with his reproachful "Oh, Dad", I knew he was asleep. I marked my place for the next reading.

SADLY, Sally and I divorced while Haley and Cam were still young. We had entered our marriage with such high hopes. We both tried hard to make it work. But our ten years together were burdened by too many episodes of pain and grief.

When we had married, I had thought of our differences as yin and yang—natural complements. As it turned out, our souls were 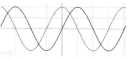 more like sine and cosine: two waves undulating about a shared axis, but forever out of cycle and often moving in opposite directions. We shared common values, but approached every situation with different instincts. All too often, we misunderstood each other. Over time, our misunderstandings evolved into a deepening sense of hurt and mistrust. In 1994, our marriage reached its breaking point.

Our divorce aggravated an anxiety that I had managed to suppress while we had been married. As much as I loved being a father, I never felt certain that I was qualified to be one. If my manhood was broken, what could I possibly pass along to Cameron and Haley? If I was constantly compelled to bury my feelings and to distract myself, how could I share myself with them? I marveled at my children. But I worried constantly that I would cripple them just by being around.

I LIVED FOR THE TIMES when my thoughts of womanhood went into remission. Only then did I feel like something approaching a real dad. I especially loved to take the kids for hikes, field trips, and campouts. Whenever we ventured outside, I tried to view the world through their eyes. What did infant Haley see when I lowered her nose to the first flower of spring? What did Cam experience when I carried him, swaddled and bundled, into his first Chicago blizzard?

When I was young, I had tutored myself about nature with books, encyclopedias, and magazines. I learned how cells work, how the moon was formed, and how fireflies fire. Now I longed to unlearn all of this. I wanted to enjoy life for the mystery that it was.

Rather than pass my knowledge along to Haley and Cam, I sought to absorb their childish innocence and wisdom. Never mind how the weather man reported today's snow ("this will add an hour to your commute"), I wanted to know how Haley and Cam saw it ("Look, Daddy, it's white outside!"). Unconsciously, I think that I was seeking a return to my days of youthful innocence. Knowledge and prayer had done little to help me; maybe my children could.

This was all well and good for me. But what of Haley and Cam? Didn't they deserve a real man for a father? I had often rationalized my business travel as a buffer device in an unhappy marriage. I began to wonder if it had also been a way of insulating myself from my sense of failure as a father.

A COUPLE OF YEARS after our divorce, Sally remarried. Her husband, Bob, struck me as sweet and likable. He had a wonderful manner with the kids. Now, I thought, my children will have a real father in their lives.

Sally and Bob tied the knot one sunny afternoon in a beautiful ceremony on the shores of Lake Michigan. I could tell that some of those attending the ceremony were worried about me: was it hard to watch Sally move on? Not at all. I was probably one of the happiest celebrants that day. In spite of our failure as a couple, I still loved Sally. Now she had her man; my kids had their father.

I reconciled myself to living on the periphery of my children's lives. I would stay far enough away to allow Sally and Bob to create an intact world for Haley and Cam. But I would stay close enough to watch their marvelous lives unfold. I also wanted to be on hand should they or their mother ever need me. Once in a while, they did.

Meanwhile, I took my own run at a couple of relationships. But they never developed: I wasn't ready. I needed some time to reflect. I moved to a Chicago neighborhood that I nicknamed Purgatory. No one—at least no single man in my income bracket—would think of impressing a date by bringing her there. Purgatory was my no-man's land. It was my retreat for introspection. What the hell was I?

I WAS on my own now. As Christmas approached that year, I worried about the children. They were so loving and sensitive, I was certain that they would notice that there were no presents for me under the tree. I didn't want them to be concerned.

So I took various things from around the apartment and wrapped them up in fancy paper. I attached a card to each and invented fictitious friends to send them to me. One of these friends, Ebenezer Kumquat, gave me a wonderful set of books, Winston Churchill's four-volume series, *A History of the English Speaking Peoples.*

When Christmas Day arrived, I proudly opened my presents. "Look! Here's another gift for me. Who is this one from? ... Oh my gosh! I haven't heard from Ebenezer in ages. I wonder what it could be."

Haley and Cam started to quiz me. "Who is Ebenezer?" "Why haven't we heard you or Mom talk about him before?" "Where is he now?"

On the spur of the moment, I manufactured a life almost as fantastic as my own. I had known Ebenezer in high school. He had grown up a wealthy, but lonely boy. He was now an eccentric who traveled the world, searching tropical forests for rare dyes with which to manufacture ink for calligraphy, his favorite hobby.

Over the next ten years, Ebenezer took on a life of his own. Although Haley and Cam have long since filed Ebenezer away with Santa Claus, Ebenezer and I have kept up our friendship. As I write this book, he is enjoying the life of a retired gentleman of leisure. He lives on the island of Majorca where he raises olive trees and sheep. In his spare time, he runs my publishing company.

NEW IDENTITIES

There will be time, there will be time
To prepare a face to meet the faces that you meet;
There will be time to murder and create …
And time yet for a hundred indecisions
And for a hundred visions and revisions,
Before the taking of a toast and tea.

— From The Love Song of J. Alfred Prufrock, T.S.
Elliot.

IT WAS DURING my sojourn in Purgatory that I met Mary.

I met her on an America West flight bound from Columbus, Ohio to Chicago. We were both returning home from our respective consulting assignments. She was a project manager at Unisys; I was an associate partner at Accenture.

I noticed Mary even as I wheeled my suitcase down the aisle. I was in a foul mood. I had been given a middle seat on a fully booked flight. Apparently, my stressful day

Skiing with Mary

wasn't over. But then I saw her. Her eyes and smile lit up my afternoon. She was cute! Was she in my row? Maybe this flight wouldn't be so bad.

"Hello!" she sparkled as I sat down.

"Hi."

Once the wheels were up, I dropped the seat tray in front of me and started to review the day's interview notes. I wasn't very good at talking to someone as pretty as she was. In fact, in all my years, I had never been the one to initiate conversation with a pretty stranger.

"Would you like some gum?" she asked.

"Yes. ... Thank you."

Mary later revealed that she had offered it because she thought that I had smoker's breath. As it turned out, it was the woman in the seat behind us. But the ice had been broken.

When I opened my notebook to work on my notes, Mary noticed a collection of pictures drawn by Haley and Cam. As with their voice recordings, I carried their artwork wherever I went.

"Oh, dear! You have baggage."

Baggage? I didn't know what she meant. Pointing to the pictures, she clarified, "Children. I have two myself. But mine are already grown. I make it a policy never to date people with baggage."

She said this with such friendly warmth, that I found it impossible to take offense. "Oh, you would have to meet my children before saying that. They are actually my greatest asset. They are amazing. How old are yours?"

"Twenty-six and twenty-four. I also have three grandchildren. Want to see?"

"You have grandchildren?" She looked so young. I found it difficult to picture her with grown-up children let alone grandchildren. I put my work away and we spent the rest of our flight talking about our families, friends, and careers.

AFTER THE FLIGHT, I did something I had never done before. I offered to give Mary a ride home. In the car, I asked her for her number. Two days later, I called her. The following week, I asked her out on a date. Up until now, I had never taken so much initiative to start a relationship. I was terrified. Would she call me back? Would she like me?

She did. For the next six months, Mary and I were practically inseparable. On Monday mornings, we commuted together to Columbus. On Thursday afternoons, we returned as a pair to Chicago. We ate together every night and typically talked late into the evening. We only parted company to sleep.

Romancing Mary brought with it the return of a familiar pattern: one of the few times I was able to completely forget my feminine side was when I lost myself in another woman. The more completely I immersed myself in her, the more completely I forgot about the woman inside me.

This led to an understandable if faulty bit of logic: my problem was that I was incomplete. Aren't we all? Isn't that why marriage is such a sacred bond? Man and woman complete each other. My feelings of womanhood were simply my subconscious telling me to find a mate.

Mary certainly enjoyed my thoughtful attentions. After our very first date, we stopped at a convenience store to pick up some beer. As I pulled into the parking lot, she muttered, "Oh, dear."

"What's the matter?"

"Never mind. I'll just come into the store with you."

"No, what do you need?"

"Well … I … I need to buy some tampons."

"Oh, I'd be happy to get them! What kind do you need?"

Mary was so impressed to be out with a man who wasn't threatened by the thought of picking up beer and tampons.

FOR MY PART, I was impressed by Mary's ability to be direct without creating distance or offence. Though she always spoke her mind, she did it in a way that conveyed warmth and intimacy. Several weeks into our relationship, I wrote a poem for her. It expressed a feeling that I hoped we shared.

Yesterday, you asked me how I slept with someone:
Alone on my side of the bed or nestled against them?
I returned home that night to a bed—and a life—that could not reply.

And yet, in the hollow of the night,
I awoke in darkness.
I found the warmth of my pillow lodged against me.

I imagined the smooth bend in your spine
Neatly contouring the curve of my chest.
The heat from your back soothed my belly.

And though I could not see it,
I imagined the smile of contentment on your face
As you lay, enveloped in the clutch of my arms.

I lightly squeezed the pillow and drifted back into the peace of my reply.

As Mary read the poem, I sat before her, a proud puppy presenting its precious bone. Mary's brows furrowed into a frown. "Hmmmm. It's nice. It's ... er ... very sweet. But ... where are the rhymes?"

God, how I loved that woman!

A FEW WEEKS LATER, Mary pushed the pause button on one of our evening conversations. "I really like you, Tom. But if we are going to date seriously, you are going to have to meet my friends. I need them to look you over. I have to warn you, though, if they don't approve of you, we can only be friends."

That was Mary: simple and direct.

Mary, a social being at heart, was concerned by my seeming solitude outside our relationship. Why wasn't someone as handsome and friendly as I surrounded by friends? Why hadn't I had to break off a relationship, as she had had to do? She needed to know what I would be like in the company of others. So she decided to arrange a night out with her buddies.

On the appointed night, I met about twenty of them at a bar near Wrigley Field. For three hours, I walked their gauntlet of gentle inquisition over beers and shots. "What do you do for a living?" "How old are your kids?" "You aren't a White Sox fan, are you?"

Apparently, my game was on. By the end of the night, everyone had signaled Mary with an enthusiastic thumbs-up.

OUR SECOND HURDLE was for Mary to meet my children. She still liked to tease me about my "baggage". This was one thing I had never worried about. Evelyne, Haley, and Cam were amazing. When Mary finally met them, she agreed. She met Haley and Cam first, and bonded quickly with them. In the months that followed, Mary and I spent half of our free time together at bars, beaches, and baseball games. We spent the other half with Haley and Cam in parks, museums, and on the sidelines of their soccer games.

BUT WHAT OF MY HIDDEN SELF? Wasn't that another obstacle to be crossed? Part of me clung to the hope that Mary would finally complete and cure me. We were so happy together. For a time, I felt that she might be the answer to my prayers.

But, inevitably, I began to feel the return of a feminine presence within. I didn't feel the need to express it outwardly yet, but I knew that it was only a matter of time. I decided that I owed it to Mary to tell her.

I guided us over this speed bump one sunny afternoon. We were crossing Michigan to visit Mary's daughter, Lindy, and her family. Midway through our journey, Mary turned to me. "What are your intentions for us? Before I introduce you to Lindy, I need to know where you see our relationship going."

"I am very in love with you," I said. "I think we still need a little more time to get to know one another, but my intention, as you put it, is that we get married one day."

I paused to let this sink in. "Speaking of which, I think that there is one thing you need to know about me before we get more serious … I have this … this occasional need to dress as a woman."

"What?!"

"It's called crossdressing. I hate it. I don't understand it. But every once in a while, feelings well up inside me that I can't control. I have to dress up."

"What do you mean, 'dress up'? What do you wear?"

"I don't know. Not fishnets and that kind of stuff. I wear pretty ordinary clothing. I just need to feel like a woman. But we don't need to go into those details. This isn't something you need to participate in. In fact, I don't want you to. I just need you know that it will happen at times."

"What do you mean, 'at times'? How often do you do this? How long have you been doing it?"

"I try not to do it. It varies, but it seems to return every year or two. It sticks around for a couple of months and then disappears. It's really weird. I don't understand it. I've been to therapy about it, but it's never helped."

"I've been to a therapist, too. It was useless."

"Like I said, you don't need to participate. I just need some space to do it in when it happens. When it does, I need you to be willing to look the other way."

Mary plied me with more questions. "Where do you dress?" "Do you go out?" "Do you do it with other people?"

When she had completed her interrogation, she lapsed into silence. After a few minutes, her face brightened. "Well, as long as I don't have to be part of it, why should I care?"

As Mary reports it today, she was so in love with me and so loved my gentle side that she thought it a worthwhile trade-off. Yes, it was weird. But she wrote it off as a harmless eccentricity.

Meanwhile, back in the car, I was stunned. Wow! That went over well. As we continued our eastward journey, I mused. Perhaps, I have been too hard on myself. Why couldn't I think as Mary did? When you got down to it, what was the harm in my occasionally dressing up? I was respectful of women. I was successful, loving, and considerate. What was the big deal?

This was the first time since my divorce that I had shared this part of me with anyone. I had half-expected Mary to shame and dismiss me. But, even though she now knew who and what I was, Mary still found me attractive.

"Just one more thing," she said. "Before we get to Lindy's, is there anything else about you that I need to know?"

Finally! I had found someone who might love the real me. True, I had volunteered that she need not participate in this part of my life. But I had someone I could talk to about it. And she didn't find me loathsome. The first chink in my armor had been penetrated.

A few months later, I revealed my secret to a second person—to my oldest daughter, Evelyne. Evelyne had gradually reentered my life a few years before. Her mother, Christine, and I had conceived her out of wedlock. I fully acknowledged my responsibility for Christine's pregnancy. I went to weekly Lamaze classes with Christine and attended Evelyne's birth.

With Evelyne

But throughout her pregnancy, I made it clear that I drew a line at birth. I felt certain that Evelyne would be better off if adopted into an intact family. I had no confidence in my ability to father someone—I was barely hanging on to my manhood! Nor did I feel that Christine and I could create a stable home together.

But Christine insisted on raising Evelyne. Other than support payments, I absented myself from their lives. At the time, I rationalized that a clean break was the only way to ensure that Christine moved on to find a suitable partner.

Two years later, Christine met and married a wonderful man, Mikel. Mikel was a talented chef who had trained at the Culinary Institute of America. Together, they bore a second daughter, Angela. Evelyne, I thought, has her family now.

But Christine felt differently. She wanted Evelyne to know her birth father. When Evelyne was halfway through elementary school, Christine and Mikel decided that she and I ought to meet. We began to see each other a couple of times a year and to exchange occasional letters.

When Evelyne entered high school, our relationship deepened. She had enrolled at Interlochen, an arts-focused boarding school in northern Michigan. Since the school was so much closer to Chicago than to New Jersey, Evelyne adopted my home as her base of operations.

This was our chance to finally get to know one another. Over the next couple of years, Evelyne and I spent a lot of time together driving between New Jersey, Illinois, and Michigan. We went on daddy-daughter vacations to Florida, Wisconsin, California, and Mexico. We memorized *The Love Song of J. Alfred Prufrock* together—or tried to. Evelyne introduced me to her talents with the harp, to her musical tastes, and to her many friends. I was always fascinated by and jealous of her easy intimacy with people.

Our time together afforded Evelyne the chance to ask me a lot of questions. When her mother had been pregnant with her, I had attended the Lamaze classes and had been there for her birth. Why hadn't I stayed around?

I couldn't give an honest answer without sharing something of my struggles with gender. I told her about my crossdressing and about my masculine insecurities. I explained that I was grateful today that her mother had held on to her and that she was now a part of my life. I had been wrong before. But at the time she was born, I had honestly thought that she would be better off in a well-formed home. I had stayed out of the picture until her mother and stepfather invited me to visit. I had wanted her to feel that she had a full-time mother and father.

As with Haley and Cam, I was thrilled to have the chance just to know Evelyne. She was happy to finally know me. She accepted my explanation without further discussion. We focused on growing closer.

THERE WERE NOW TWO WOMEN in my life who knew my secret. But after sharing it with them, I tried not to discuss it further. I didn't want it to be their burden. Nor did they. Like me, they counted on my ability to manage it.

I continued to think of myself as essentially masculine. My feminine side was a defect to be cured. Until I could correct it, my duty as husband and father was to protect my family by keeping this side of my life in quarantine. Still, I had made progress. I had moved from a life of utter shame and secrecy to a measure of self-acceptance and a whispered disclosure.

ONE AFTERNOON, six months after Mary and I met, I telephoned her mother from the Columbus airport. "Eleanor, how are you? ... No, everything's fine. ... Look, I'm calling to ask you a question. Can I have your permission to propose marriage to your daughter?"

"What?! ... Oh, for Pete's sake, Tom! You're crazy! ... Why are you asking me?"

"Because you're her mother."

"Well, aren't you sweet? Crazy, but sweet. ... Yes, of course you can!"

Mary and I were about to board the same flight that we had met on six months before. I approached two of the flight attendants as they prepared to board the plane. "Excuse me. I was wondering if you could do me a favor. Could you talk to the pilot and ask him to read a little announcement for me?"

I handed them a business card on the back of which I had scrawled my message. They read it and looked at each other, perplexed. "I didn't even know she was dating!"

They had misunderstood. They thought that I was planning to propose to an off-duty flight attendant who was also on this flight.

"No, no! I'm proposing to that woman over there." I pointed at Mary.

"Oh, that's sweet! I don't know whether he'll do it, honey, but we'll ask him. We'll let you know."

Half an hour later, we were climbing to thirty thousand feet. The pilot's voice filled the cabin. "Good afternoon, ladies and gentlemen. We apologize for the delay."

He proceeded to describe our flight path, the weather in Chicago, and our expected time of arrival. I waited anxiously. Was he going to read my note? Finally, he continued. "I have a special message from one of our passengers. 'Macy Kane, since we met, you have taken my life to new heights and destinations. Will you marry me?'"

Damn, my penmanship! I thought. My *r*'s often looked like *c*'s.

Mary looked at me puzzled. "Who is Macy?"

The ring in my lap was all the reply she needed. She let out a shriek.

Before she could say "yes", she found herself surrounded by a pack of women passengers. They crowded around her seat and craned their necks, oohing and aahing over the ring. For a few minutes, the ring was the center of attention; I was just the delivery boy.

Eventually, my two flight attendants shooed the passengers away and served us champagne. Mary raised her glass. "Yes, Tom, I would love to marry you."

The following summer, with our families gathered around us at my parents' Rhode Island summer home, we declared our wedding vows. We were madly in love.

THOUGH I STILL wore the pants at the wedding, I otherwise fulfilled the roles more conventionally associated with the bride. I planned the wedding, sent out the invitations, and arranged the catering. I scripted the ceremony and managed the

With Mary at Wedding

rehearsals. On the morning of the wedding, while I made final preparations, Mary, her sister and her children toured the mansions of Newport. "Just make sure you're back in time for the ceremony!" I hollered after them.

I wasn't able to dress the part I wanted to play that day, but that didn't mean that I couldn't live it. Perhaps, I thought, I just needed an outlet for expressing my nurturing side. Mary clearly loved that part of me. Maybe things would work out.

LATE-TRANSITIONING TRANSSEXUALS who have married are often asked two questions: Were you honest with your partner? Do you think you were fair to marry them? These are questions that haunt us. But there is a problem with them: they are asked with the benefit of 20-20 hindsight.

I was as honest with Mary as I was with myself. At the time of our wedding, I felt confident that I would be able to manage this problem. Nobody marries their loved one planning to hurt them.

Evelyne and Mary had brought a whole new dynamic into my life. They were surrounded by friends. They were sociable and sweetly loving. They drew me out of my cocoon and surrounded me with a ready community. I had fun socializing and didn't need to study the sports page to do it. I was confident that all these new forces in my life were going to heal me.

Meanwhile, I considered it my job to keep my issues to myself. One of the expectations that our society tends to press upon fathers and husbands is that they are there to protect their family. They should admit vulnerability only as a last resort—when they know of a certainty that they will not be able to insulate their loved ones from something dreadful. Until then, it is their job to take the body blows. I had disclosed my struggles to Mary and Evelyne. Now it was my job to shut up about them.

TWO YEARS AFTER I WED MARY, Sally approached us. Would we allow her and Bob to move with the children to another state so that she could pursue a career opportunity? We agreed and went one better: we would move too.

I did not want Haley and Cam to grow up living between two cities. Mary and I considered it more important to stay near them than to remain in Chicago. Besides, as consultants, we spent most of our time traveling. We decided to relocate to the same town in New Jersey that Sally and Bob planned to move to.

We were welcomed into our new neighborhood as soon as we arrived. During our first week in Chatham, our neighbors happened to be holding a block party. Mary enthused as she introduced us. "Wow. You guys are amazing! We've never had a whole neighborhood throw us a welcoming party before."

In short order, Mary became the de facto social chairman of the neighborhood. Our friends nicknamed her the Mayor of Chatham Heights.

We settled into our new life. Most of the next ten years were idyllic. We vacationed all over the world—to Latin America, the Caribbean, Europe, Africa, and Hawaii. We went skiing and kayaking and took up golf. We enjoyed cocktail hours and barbecues with our neighbors. We watched our children grow and two new grandchildren enter the world. Life was good.

BUT AS BEFORE, our good times were punctuated every year or two by visits from my hidden side. Though I tried to keep my dressing private, it proved impossible. This was hard on Mary.

I didn't just dress differently, I shaved my body. Mary couldn't understand my need to do this and hated it. At night, she loved to rest her head on my hairy chest. When my hair was gone, it was as though I was, too. "Couldn't you dress up without shaving? Couldn't you do that for me?"

But shaving wasn't something I did as an aesthetic act. When my feminine side surfaced, she (this other part of me) was mortified to find her body matted with hair. My arms felt vile and disgusting. I hated the site of my chest; it looked repulsive. Until I removed my hair, it took over my thoughts, gnawing at them like an itch. Even a casual glance at the back of my hands nauseated me.

Knowing how Mary felt, I tried to fight the urge. But each day, my feelings of revulsion intensified. Finally, I could take it no longer: I pulled out my epilator.

An epilator looks like an electric razor. But rather than cut the hairs, its rotating disks pluck them from their root beds. It can uproot several hundred hairs in a minute. With a beard as dense as mine, the process was excruciating. But I had to have that hair gone! Shaving would clear the hair for a day; epilation would eliminate it for a couple of weeks.

Mary tried desperately to look past this.

October 2002

My Dearest Tom,

I am writing this to try to put into words how I am feeling right now. I am so afraid of losing you. I love you more than I love myself. I'm afraid that you're changing into someone else, something I don't know how to deal with. I don't want to be without you yet I'm having trouble being close to you right now.

I tried touching your arm last night and it freaked me out, I just wanted to go to my side of the bed and curl up in a ball. I hate that feeling! I want to be close to you, feel your touch, my touching you, your kisses, your arms around me ...

I just don't know how to get past this right now. ... It makes me so sad I just burst into tears. I wish I could just put it out of my mind and just love you for you, but I'm sorry Tom I just don't know how. I can't even fathom living without you and yet I'm so scared of what's happening right now that I actually think about leaving to get away. I have always been one to run away, if I don't see it it's not real. Please help me by loving me. ...

Your loving wife.

Whenever I shaved, it transformed the atmosphere in our home. I rose early and collected my clothing for the day. I showered and dressed in another part of the house. At night, I changed in one of the other bedrooms. No matter the temperature, I slept in long-sleeved pajamas in order to cover my body. Mary no longer slept in my arms. The heat from her body no longer soothed my belly. We slept on opposite sides of the bed.

IN THE SPRING OF 2002, my dressing went into remission again. My situation was a bit like the wolf man in reverse: when my body hair returned, my world filled with sunshine.

Mary and I cloaked ourselves in a mutual amnesia. Our laughter and intimacy returned. That summer, we attended her thirtieth high school reunion in Richmond, Michigan. Mary was so happy to be able to introduce the man she loved to her childhood friends.

Our next eighteen months were a joy. We watched Evelyne graduate from Interlochen. We bought a time-share in Mexico. We vacationed in Puerto Rico and Costa Rica.

There was something a little manic about periods like this. We celebrated our life together so joyfully because we knew that these moments would not always be there. At some point, the hair would disappear again. The dresses, makeup, and heels would come out of their boxes.

IN THE FALL OF 2004, the urges did return, this time with greater strength than before. For the first time, I gave my feminine side a name, Tina. I wrote in my journal, "I'm not sure why. I just like it."

By now, I had concluded that this wasn't something that would ever go away. After thirty years, I finally gave up on my strategy of repression. That had accomplished nothing. In fact, it had only led me into deeper despair and self-loathing. I opened my mind to a new tactic: containment. Perhaps I had a legitimately feminine side. If so, I needed to make space for her. I wasn't clear how large a part of me she was, but she was there. "Hello, Tina."

Evelyne was now living in Europe, so I co-opted her closet and gave it to Tina. This was partly a matter of convenience. It had been an annoyance to have to continually box and unbox her things, to cart them to and from the attic, and to lock them in a trunk each time I wanted to let this side of me out.

But the real reason I took possession of the closet, I think, was to legitimize Tina's place in our household. I was tired of my cycles of shame. I was tired of feeling that I had to sneak around my own house. I had become more concerned about my deepening episodes of depression than about my dressing. Perhaps, if I didn't try so hard to repress my feelings, they would moderate. I needed to find a way to be happy again.

I started to experiment with laser treatments and electrolysis. I wanted to permanently reduce my facial hair. Shaving left a five-o'clock shadow; epilation was terrible for my skin. Getting laser and electrolysis treatments was an acknowledgement that Tina was here to stay. I was beginning to incorporate her into my life.

Permanent hair removal takes a long time. Electrolysis (regarded by the FDA as the only permanent method of removal) typically involves 100 to 200 hours of treatment spread over one to three years. After only thirty minutes of treatment, my face was welted with sores. These formed scabs that could take several days to heal. While my face was healing, I could not wear makeup.

As a result, I could not possibly get electrolysis while going through my Tina phases. The scarring and lack of makeup would make me look even more outlandish. I had to do it when I was most comfortable as Tom. This fact introduced a new dynamic into Mary's life: Tina was now encroaching on my everyday world. With each passing cycle, Mary was seeing less and less of Tom and more and more of Tina.

AS A GESTURE to Mary, I decided not to eliminate all of my facial hair. Instead, I sought to thin it enough to make occasional removal less of a chore and to minimize my five-o'clock shadow. When I wanted to, I was still able to sport a goatee. In fact, in between Tina's appearances, I tried to keep one going for Mary. It was my visual reassurance to her that Tina was gone for the time.

This token did little to soothe Mary. Each time I epilated my face, she grew furious. "It makes you look ridiculous! Do you honestly think you look like a woman?! For God's sake! Just look at yourself."

It was one of the rare occasions when she used words in an effort to hurt me. Her outburst delivered, she stormed out of the room to the furthest reaches of the house to cry. Alone at my end of the house, I cried, too.

IN 2003, J. Michael Bailey published, *The Man Who Would Be Queen.* In it, he argued that transsexualism represented a sexually motivated preoccupation with having a female body. Borrowing from Ray Blanchard, he labeled this *autogynephilia.* When I read the book, I wondered: is it possible that he is describing me?

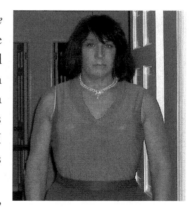

I hated Bailey's thesis. If he was right, my condition was little more than a sexual fetish. According to him, this was my way of internalizing my attraction to women—of giving myself the most intimate partner imaginable.

Bailey emphasized the erotic aspects of crossdressing. Is that all this was? Was I putting Mary through hell for a stupid bit of kink? The possibility gnawed at my conscience.

Much as I hated Bailey's thesis, I reasoned that I owed it to my family to consider the possibility. Autogynephilia was a tempting if distressing explanation. Yes, at times there was something erotic about dressing up. I couldn't deny that. I agonized: is that why I did it? If Bailey was accurately describing me, I needed to know.

Bailey's book drew heated criticism from many in the transgender community. Detractors labeled it pseudo-science that was "influenced by academic racists and others in the neo-genetics movement." They filed lawsuits claiming academic misconduct and data fabrication.

I eventually came to agree with Bailey's critics. It *is* a disastrous theory. Its only merit is that it acknowledges a truth that many of us prefer to gloss over: when you are trying to repress your feminine identity and are raging with testosterone, a part of you is almost certain to find something erotic about women's clothing. How else is your testosterone to make sense of what you are doing?

Bailey's thesis implied that I was crossdressing as someone not me. But he was wrong. The one time when I felt myself was when I was cross-dressed. I didn't do it as a joy ride. In fact, the male side of me hated it. It unmanned me without resolving my underlying anxieties. As a woman, it left me feeling a mere caricature of myself.

Bailey's observations were not only unscientific, they confused symptom with cause[1]. I was becoming increasingly aware that I had a genuine feminine part to me, one that I had been repressing. Wasn't it more accurate to say that it was she who wanted to dress up? Now that Tina had finally emerged into my consciousness, she and Tom were engaged in a pitched battle for my soul. My body, my marriage, and my closet were their battleground.

IN THE EARLY 2000s, I had yet to work out all of these distinctions. I only knew that I had finally begun to accept the idea that I had a feminine side. Part of me clung to the hope that I would finally find a way to contain it.

---

[1] The debate over Bailey's methods is beyond the scope of this book. See "An Investigation into the Publication of J. Michael Bailey's Book on Transsexualism by the National Academies" by Lynn Conway, 2008.
(http://ai.eecs.umich.edu/people/conway/TS/LynnsReviewOfBaileysBook.html)

I determined to learn everything I could about this topsy-turvy gender world. On the Internet, I discovered a cottage industry of magazines, boutiques, and discussion boards. I learned about drag queens, crossdressers, transsexuals, and fetishists. Many of them seemed to have found a way to take joy in their strangeness. Could I do the same?

If I could not rid my life of these feelings, perhaps I could find a way to make peace with them. Could I, like these other people, take the strangeness in me and celebrate it? After all, what was the harm? If nothing else, I might dampen my intense, emotional swings.

On the Internet, I found many examples of transvestites who had incorporated their feminine side into an otherwise conventional life. I learned about support groups like Tri-Ess, Renaissance, and The Beaumont Society. They offered a variety of programs to support crossdressers and their spouses: chat rooms, monthly get-togethers, and occasional retreats. Their goal was to create a safe and private environment where people could be themselves. It was also a place where spouses could offer one another support.

I also discovered the International Foundation for Gender Education (IFGE). Their promotional statement grabbed my attention:

We advocate for freedom of gender expression and promote the understanding and acceptance of All People: Transgender, Cis-gender, Transsexual, Crossdresser, Agender, Gender Queer, Intersex, Two Spirit, Hijra, Kathoey, Drag King, Drag Queen, Queer, Lesbian, Gay, Straight, Butch, Femme, Faerie, Homosexual, Bisexual, Heterosexual, and of course—You!

Wow. Surely I fit somewhere in their gender bestiary. But where?

As luck would have it, IFGE would shortly be holding a three-day conference in nearby Philadelphia. Next to the Internet, transgender conferences were the most important source of information in our community. They offered seminars on a range of topics: advances in scientific research, training in feminine deportment, surgical and non-surgical feminization techniques, how to transition at work, how to cope with family rejection. Vendors rented booths to advertise their merchandise and services.

But it was the opportunity to meet the entire gender spectrum face-to-face and side-by-side that drew me to the conference. I had felt alone all my life—a one-person freak show. I longed to meet others like me. Which among IFGE's alphabet soup of gender outlaws would I identify with?

I was especially interested in understanding whether I was a transvestite or transsexual[2]. I was aware that these two groups were considered different but wasn't sure that I understood the distinction. Transvestites, as I understood the term, were heterosexual men who liked to dress up as women. But for what reason? Were they celebrating a feminine side that our macho society denied them? Or were they engaged in a crass, sexual self-gratification that debased womanhood?

The Oxford Dictionary defined a transsexual as *a person who emotionally and psychologically feels that they belong to the opposite sex*. What did that mean? There seemed to be so many types of transsexuals out there: post-op, pre-op, non-op. Some claimed to be heterosexual, others homosexual. Some transsexual women said that they loved their penis. Others hated it. I was baffled. What lay beneath these differences? Where did I fit in?

AT ABOUT THE SAME TIME that I was preparing to attend IFGE, I happened across a book by Lannie Rose, a transsexual woman. She titled it, *How to Change Your Sex: A Lighthearted Look at the Hardest Thing You'll Ever Do*. In it, Lannie addressed the question of gender identity

---

[2] In this book, I have used the terms that best capture Mary's and my state of mind at the time. Today, *crossdresser* is generally preferred to *transvestite*, as the latter has often been used with negative connotations. In addition, some consider it inappropriate to use *transsexual* as a noun. They recommend that it be used only as an adjective (e.g., *transsexual man, transsexual woman*).

with an analogy: How would you decide if you wanted to become a firefighter?

The only effective way to figure out if you are a transsexual is [by] trying on different roles and seeing which ones feel like they will fit you best. It's the same for finding out anything about your true self.

What if, Lannie supposed, you thought you wanted to be a firefighter? Yes, you might read a few books to test your interest. But even if the books made firefighting look appealing, you would hardly commit yourself to a lifetime of firefighting on that evidence alone. You would follow a few firetrucks to see what it was like to put out a fire. If it still looked interesting, you might get to know a few firefighters. If you felt a kinship to them, you might next enroll in firefighting school. Finally, you would try the job for a while. Only then would you really know whether you were born to be a firefighter.

I don't think that Lannie was suggesting that gender identity is something you choose. She simply meant that books — including hers — cannot tell you who you are. Nor can scientists. You have to figure it out by experience; and you are better off doing it in little steps.

Why hadn't I thought of this before? We all tend to learn who we are by experience. We try out different role models and mix with different groups. Children and teenagers do it all the time. I needed to expose myself to these gender alternatives and to try them on for size.

There was just one problem: I wasn't a teenager. I was a middle-aged business professional and a family man. How was I to examine these alternative identities? I decided that my first step would be to attend the IFGE conference.

❧

TO MY SURPRISE, Mary agreed to attend the conference with me. She wasn't looking forward to it, but was as desperate as I for information. She hoped for a peek at what I might become. Was it something she would be able to tolerate?

I dressed for the event in women's business and weekend attire. Attendees who dressed in similar attire probably accounted for

With Mary at IFGE

half of the conference participants. A quarter dressed in provocative clothing: deep-vee blouses, stiletto heels, and mini-skirts. The remaining quarter arrived decked out for a weekend of fantasy play: Raggedy Anns, sorceresses, serving wenches, dominatrixes, and submissives.

It relaxed me to think of myself at the conventional end of a spectrum for a change. Did Mary notice it too? I hoped that she might find relief in the notion that she was married to a transvestite with sensible taste in clothing.

IN ADDITION to experiencing the full variety of the gender spectrum, Mary and I absorbed a lot of new information. For Mary, the most important event of the weekend was a seminar that explored the science of gender dysphoria. The lecturer presented the results of studies that compared the brain scans of transsexual women to those of cis-women and cis-men[3]. It revealed that the studied areas of the transsexual women's brains resembled those of cis-women more closely than they did those of cis-men.

---

[3] *Cis* essentially means *non-trans*. It is a prefix referring to someone who has always identified with the gender they were assigned at birth. It comes from a Greek root meaning "on the same side". Where gender is concerned, your mind and body are on the same side.

The presenter explained that the emerging consensus among gender specialists was that transsexuality develops in the womb, shortly after conception. All mammals start their fetal development from a female template. If, at a  critical stage, the fetus is exposed to certain hormonal signals, it shifts tracks and starts to develop a masculine anatomy. It is as though the body were traveling down a train track and a switch is thrown: once the body heads in that direction, it continues along that track for the rest of its life. (This part of the science is well established.)

The problem, he said, is that, in some mammals, humans among them, the brain develops several weeks after the sex organs do. If the brain is exposed to different hormone signals than were the sex organs, it will head down the opposite track. The cited brain scan study supported this theory.

For Mary, this was manna from heaven. At last, she had a way to understand and explain what I was going through. She still felt distressed. But she no longer blamed me for it. Never again did she criticize me for removing my facial hair.

Studies like this one have been repeated many times. Unfortunately, the sample sizes are so small, the results so variable, and the measurement instruments so grainy that it would be unfair to call the evidence conclusive. But, for the two of us at the time, it was a lifeline. I felt relieved of a crushing sense of guilt.

But knowing of these studies didn't solve anything. We still needed to figure out how we were going to live with my condition. I also needed to determine where I fell on this gender spectrum that everyone kept talking about.

MAKING DISTINCTIONS between transvestites and transsexuals is a sensitive topic in our community. As I navigated the conference that weekend, the tension between the two groups was noticeable. Some of the transsexuals I spoke to expressed open disdain for the transvestite attendees. They hated being lumped into the same group, especially when debating public policy issues such as access to bathrooms. In an award speech, a prominent transvestite complained that she felt treated like a second-class citizen by her transsexual sisters. She felt that they regarded transvestites as unfinished business—people afraid to take the final step of self-realization. She concluded her speech, declaring that she was happy as she was.

The controversy depressed me. Here we were, begging the rest of the world for tolerance. But we were finding it difficult to show the same consideration to one another.

I had attended IFGE praying that I would find myself at the transvestite end of the spectrum. Crossdressing was something that I could manage and contain. It was something that Mary and I could negotiate. As a result, I spent most of my time at IFGE in the company of crossdressers.

Those that I spent time with were wonderfully gentle and kind. Contrary to what certain feminist writers had led me to believe, they weren't trying to make a mockery of womanhood. They were trying to express an important part of themselves. In contrast to what Bailey had led me to expect, I found little in our conversations that was sexual or erotic. Crossdressing seemed to give these people a sense of peace. It allowed them to access a part of themselves that was otherwise unreachable.

Bailey had been criticized for working with a biased sample. He drew heavily for his research on people he had met at certain bars. To be fair, my IFGE sample was probably oppositely biased. I spent most of my time at the convention with the half of attendees who dressed as I did. Some of the other crossdressers clearly had a sexual agenda—they told me as much. But I could not say what lay behind it. I didn't try to mix with them.

FOR MY PART, I was particularly moved by a seminar that was open only to couples. Most of the attendees were middle-aged pairs who had been together for at least a dozen years. Like Mary and me, they were struggling with the husband's desire to express his feminine side. A few were struggling with their children's gender-variance. In all, about thirty people gathered for ninety minutes of facilitated discussion. Each couple took a few minutes to share their story.

As we went around the room, all I could think about was the poor wives. Most of them said that they felt uncertain about the future of their marriage. A few declared their determination to stick it out. But even among these women, I could detect neither pride nor happiness. At best, they seemed to be enduring. Was that the future I was condemning Mary to?

One male participant particularly troubled me. He explained that he and his wife had come because they had a nephew who was planning to become their niece. He said that he had come to the conference, hoping to learn enough to become more accepting. He was really having trouble with this.

Then he dropped his bombshell: He—the uncle—had been born a she. He had transitioned in the 1970s and had so acclimated himself to his male identity that he could no longer empathize with what his nephew / niece was going through. While I applauded his honesty, I was stunned by his admission. How could anyone who has struggled with their gender be so insensitive? Were the rest of us as self-absorbed as he was?

I recalled the tense feelings between the transvestites and transsexuals. Were we all incapable of seeing beyond our own agenda? Of all the people I had met at the conference, the wives in the couples' session seemed to be the only ones who were making an effort to reach beyond themselves. Did we deserve them? Did I deserve Mary?

MARY AND I RETURNED from the weekend exhausted. But where Mary had found some cause for solace, my worries intensified. I was especially concerned about the impact I was going to have on my family if I continued on this trajectory. I didn't want to fall into the trap of self-absorption.

Mary's Reflections on IFGE

I decided to attend the IFGE conference because I was hoping that it would help me to understand what Tom was going through. I felt that I was losing him and needed to understand where his life might be headed. How could I help him? And, frankly, what did I need to do to protect myself? Was this a life I wanted to be part of?

Walking through the hotel on the first day was a shock. An elderly, bearded man was casually roaming the hallway dressed in women's clothes. No makeup, just some clothes. Another man, middle-aged and overweight, was whirling about on an oversized tricycle. He was dressed as Raggedy Ann, complete with rainbow lollypop. I kept asking myself, "What is going on in their heads? Do they really think they look good or passable?"

But later, during the dinner, speeches and dancing I saw smiles on these people that would make anyone smile back. They were so happy to be able to dress as they wanted. It was something I never expected.

Being surrounded by hundreds of crossdressing men was at first overwhelming. But as I settled into conversations with them, I found it so easy talk to them. Their stories fascinated me. Their sorrows won my compassion.

I found it impossible to fully transfer my empathy to Tom, however. It wasn't anything that he said or did. I just couldn't bear the thought of losing him.

SOMETHING ELSE worried me after IFGE. It was the dawning fear that I might, in fact, be a transsexual. While I had enjoyed the time I had spent with the crossdressers at IFGE, I left the conference with the nagging suspicion that I wasn't one of their tribe. Their chemistry felt different. But perhaps, I thought, I was experiencing beginner's jitters. I had, after all, spent a lifetime repressing this side of me. It wasn't likely to resolve itself in a weekend.

For months after the conference, I continued to focus on the transvestite end of the spectrum. Crossdressing was clearly the least destructive solution for my family. Maybe I needed to give it time. Maybe, too, I needed to get to know some crossdressers better.

I looked into local chapters of Tri-Ess and Renaissance. I read articles and books by and about transvestites. I visited a crossdressers' club in Manhattan where a group of men had rented out an apartment. Each of them paid a monthly fee for a key, a clothing locker, and some closet space. They used the apartment as a safe place in which to dress. They met regularly for a night out on the town. They went out to dinner, attended theatre performances, and visited dance clubs.

Aside from their ability to afford this arrangement, the membership had little in common. There were business executives, burly union workers, and balding accountants. As at IFGE, I found them to be sweet, personable people who had struggled most of their lives to conform to society's rules. They just wanted a place where they could relax and be themselves.

As Lannie Rose had instructed, I let experience be my guide. My crossdressing friends were all very nice. But the harder I tried to be one of them, the more I realized that I was once again trying to be someone I wasn't. Attempting to be like them left me feeling fake.

I noticed something else: the more that I embraced my womanhood, the less I found anything exciting about dressing up. I just wanted to dress on the outside as I felt on the inside. I felt less like I was pretending to be a woman and more like I was pretending to be a man.

BUT ONCE AGAIN, my cycles intervened. In the autumn of 2007, Tina went back into hiding.

I never could figure out what made these cycles come and go. I suspect that it had something to do with the amount of energy they consumed. Dealing with my feminine side was exhausting. I could only take it for so long. Dressing helped to lighten my mood for a time, but it didn't resolve my underlying anxieties. The secrecy and shame was especially draining. I suspect that the person inside me, feeling unfulfilled and fatigued, eventually retreated back into my subconscious.

Proud Father: Haley's Graduation

The most wonderful part about Tina's absences was that they enabled me to focus my energy on the world around me. I lived for such times. During this particular cycle, for example, I got to watch Haley graduate from high school. She had won one of her school's most coveted trophies, the Bell Award. At her graduation, I showed up with a dozen custom-made nametags pinned to my lapels. Each carried a different picture from her life. I proudly identified myself on each one: "Haley's Pit Crew".

Mary and I vacationed in Charleston, South Carolina, then Spain. We attended my youngest brother's wedding. During the weekend, people repeatedly photographed me together with my two brothers, David and Graham. Seeing the three of us together comforted me. We had grown up separated by our ages. Now, at middle age, life was finally sorting us into the same cohort. We had wives, teen-age children, and gradually expanding waistlines. I looked forward to aging gracefully with them. I pictured the three of us as a new family fixture, a trio of uncles with a taste for Scotch and a penchant for corny punch lines—chips off the old block.

My greatest joy continued to be that of being a father. But, as my children entered their teens, this source of happiness became more and more difficult to access. It wasn't that my children were becoming self-absorbed jerks. Far from it. Haley, Cameron, and Evelyne continued to amaze me. So, too, did my stepchildren, Nathan and Lindy.

There was the time, for example, when Cam was about fourteen. One afternoon, he approached me, a tone of hesitation in his voice, "Dad ... could I talk to you about something?"

"What's up, Sweetie?"

"I was wondering ... I was wondering if you could help me with some money."

Oh, God, I thought. What does he want to buy? Probably a video game. "What do you need help with, Sweetheart?"

He proceeded with caution, "Well ... I've decided that I want to learn Mandarin. But they don't offer it in our school. I found someone who could tutor me. I can pay for half of the cost with the money I earn teaching violin. I was wondering ... could you help me with the other half?"

He didn't see it, but I started to cry. "Of course."

What a kid.

No, my problem wasn't that my children were becoming less lovable. My problem was that I was finding it harder and harder to impress them. A case in point was my adventure with Cam to the Canadian Maritimes.

I HAD MADE IT A TRADITION that, when each of my children turned fifteen, I took them on a weeklong trip to a place of their choosing. We would do whatever they wanted. I had taken Evelyne to southern California and Haley to Argentina. Now it was Cam's turn.

Unfortunately, I broke my cardinal rule. Rather than wait to see the sort of trip that Cam might design, I lobbied for a weeklong trek in the wilderness. "Why don't we go to St. John's, Newfoundland?"

Ever since I was a child, I had wanted to go there. When I was Cam's age, I had read about it in the *National Geographic*. The magazine had described the island as remote and exotic. Cam was very safety-conscious. Unlike other destinations I had considered, he wouldn't have to worry about getting lost in a dessert or fending off grizzly bears. Wouldn't it be cool for my budding young man and me to discover this Acadian paradise together?

It wasn't just the camping that attracted me. The wilderness was the one place where I had always felt free of gender conflict. It was the place where I felt most manly. I knew a lot about hiking, camping, and orienteering. I loved the vigor of a challenging trek. If there was anywhere that I could share my manhood with Cam, this would be it.

Unfortunately, I little appreciated the terrain of St. John's. It was a quagmire! Beneath our feet, craggy boulders alternated with deep crevices and gluey peat bogs. Everything was covered by the same thin layer of moss. As a result, we could never be certain what we were stepping on or into. One minute, Cam was balancing atop a slippery toehold of sponge. A second later, he was sinking, waist-deep into primordial ooze. This, I knew, was not his idea of fun.

Camping with Cam

On our second afternoon, I exulted: I had found a glorious campsite for the two of us. It was a soft, green field of moss in an open clearing. It was situated in the middle of a cascade of gentle rapids whose sound filled the air like a melody. I felt as though we were standing in the middle of a Thomas Kinkade painting.

A camera lens might have found the site idyllic. But for Cam and me, it proved to be anything but. The bed of moss looked soft and inviting. But to sleep on it was to balance on a saturated sponge. If we lay perfectly still and distributed our weight, it was wonderfully soft. But at the tiniest movement, our elbows, legs, and buttocks sank into cold, clammy depressions. Only a thin layer of plastic beneath our tent kept us dry. I don't know about Cam, but I barely slept.

The adventurer in me loved the uninviting terrain. So long as death didn't threaten, I enjoyed making my way through nature's mazes and unexpected barriers. Each conquered inconvenience confirmed my virility.

But the father in me cringed in horror. This was hardly the week I had planned for my son. I was pretty certain that he was miserable. Thankfully, his good nature prevailed. He quietly and politely endured the week. To my eye, it was a slow-motion train wreck.

DURING THIS LATEST CYCLE, I decided to take advantage of Tina's absence in another way. I investigated an idea that had occasionally sprung to mind in the past, but that I had heretofore dismissed: was it possible that my gender confusion was the product of repressed homosexuality?

I had never found men attractive. But I reasoned that I might be repressing something. Could that explain my feelings? If I was going to cure my gender, I had to consider every possibility, even this one.

The idea that I might be a gay man was easier to deal with than the thought that I might be a transsexual woman. Being gay had by now become more socially acceptable. Though it would certainly affect my relationship with Mary, she would probably find it less embarrassing. It would also affect my relationship with my children a lot less than would being a woman.

As a gay man, I could look forward to a huge support network. Gays were achieving new levels of affluence in America. Transsexuals, on the other hand, were stereotyped in the press as mentally unstable, homeless, and unemployed. Being gay was easier to hide. It would be far less traumatic for everyone in my life—especially for me.

STILL, this was an odd thing for me to consider. Years before, I had been confronted by homosexuality in a very personal way. It had happened during my sophomore year at Princeton. I was rooming with three other underclassmen at the time, one of them a political science wonk named Mike.

Mike's mother and father had died when he was a child, so he grew up in Philadelphia with an uncle who suffered from a mild mental handicap. During fall break, I invited Mike and another friend, Steve, to come to Washington D.C. We would stay with my family. Mike and Steve would attend some political meetings while I caught up with friends from high school.

On the way to my house, we stopped in Philadelphia for a day. There, we met Mike's uncle. He was mentally slow, but was a gentle and loving soul; we liked him. He seemed to be a little embarrassed on Mike's behalf, but we thought nothing of it. We traveled on to D.C. and enjoyed a week of politics and parties.

At week's end, we returned to Princeton, stopping in Philadelphia long enough for Mike to pick up some fresh clothes. While Mike and Steve went upstairs, I drove to a gas station to fill up the tank. Fifteen minutes later, I returned to Mike's apartment building, pulling up behind an ambulance and a police car. Mike's door was open. Oh my God! Had someone fallen? I ran upstairs to find Mike, watching in silence as paramedics transferred his uncle into a body bag.

Mike didn't tell me what had happened until a week later. His uncle, it turned out, had left a suicide note. In childlike scrawl, he explained that, when he saw Mike together with Steve and me, he realized what a burden he was. The note ended, "You will be better off without me."

Far from being better off, Mike fell apart. He felt guilty and alone. A few weeks after the incident, he reached out to a girl in our class, Kim. They had gone to several campus events together. Mike declared his love for her and asked if she would date him. Kim responded that, while she regarded Mike as a very good friend, she did not consider him a love interest.

Given that I was his best friend and one of his roommates, I felt that it rested with me to be there for him. Most nights, after hitting the books in Firestone Library, Mike and I met up at the Chancellor Green Pub. It was our habit to grab a pitcher of beer before knocking off for the night.

On one of these nights, we returned to our dorm after our usual round of books and beer. The centerpiece of our living room was a pair of tattered armchairs. They had clearly seen better days: green stuffing sprouted from the arms like rotting broccoli. Rusted coils peaked out from underneath.

Normally, Mike and I sat across from each other and rounded out our evening with some quiet bullshitting. I sat down in my accustomed chair. But tonight, rather than collapse into the chair opposite me, Michael pitched himself onto the arm of my chair and, with a yawn, stretched his frame across the back. The hair on my neck stood on end. I knew that move from high school!

I leapt out of the chair and spun around to face Mike. "What the hell is going on?!"

I loved Michael dearly as a friend. If I thought I could be gay, I would probably have tried to be there for him. But I wasn't and I couldn't. I delivered the same let's be friends speech that Kim had delivered only a short time before. I worried that I might send Mike spiraling further into depression. But what could I do?

At the end of the semester, I left school for a year. I wasn't angry with Michael. I just didn't know how to manage the boundary between friendship and romantic love. What is more, I was terribly confused about myself. I needed space, lots of it. I spent the year teaching at The Heights and camping in the Rockies.

So here I was, twenty-five years later, questioning myself. Was I gay? And if I was, what kind of a shit friend had I been to Michael? Had I been a sham? Could I get nothing right? God, what a mess life can be.

I DIDN'T TRY to explore the possibility that I was gay by pursuing relationships with men. I was happily married to Mary. I was, in fact, still head-over-heels in love with her.

But I did try to look at men differently. While walking to work, I glanced up at billboards of male underwear models. Did I find them attractive? When Mary and I went to the movies or watched television, I studied the male leads a little more closely. Was I repressing some reaction? Tennis and soccer players were known for being sexy. Did I feel anything when I looked at them? When Mary and I socialized with gay friends, I considered: do I feel more at home in their company?

Nope. Nothing.

This strange exploration only confirmed my lack of attraction to men. Try as I might, I could not dredge up any feelings. And why, I considered, should I? Men represented everything that I hated in my own body: they were hairy; they had a penis; they were clumsy. They made a game of farting and belching. Gross!

I was attracted to women. But I was attracted to them in a weird way. I didn't want to romance them. I wanted to be one of them. I was as confused as ever.

A part of me was relieved that I wasn't gay. It meant that I hadn't betrayed my friendship with Mike. But another part of me was sad.

The fact that I had tried to be gay is a sign of how desperate I had become. I was now attempting to manufacture feelings that I had never experienced. Like all of my theories before, this one went nowhere. On went the cycle of ups and downs. Each time, the ups were a little less up and the downs were a little more down.

❧

TINA RETURNED A YEAR LATER—earlier than Mary or I had expected. But this time, I decided to handle it differently. I would finally explore the one possibility I had been avoiding: was I a transsexual? I reached out to a Manhattan therapist who specialized in gender dysphoria (GD)[4].

Out and About in NYC

Dear Dr. Rachlin,

I have spent most of the past 40 years alternately struggling with and eagerly exploring my gender identity. I have progressed as far as I can on my own and want very much to seek personal counseling.

At this point, I am thoroughly convinced and accepting that I am very transgendered. I have attended TG conventions, started electrolysis, and often present as a female at home (2-3 days a week). I have occasionally shopped and traveled as Tina but otherwise continue to present as a pretty stereotypical male.

I accept who I am. Though I have had episodes of severe depression, I don't think I have ever been what you would call suicidal.

Nonetheless, I seem to be moving closer and closer emotionally to that precipice of gender reassignment. My issue (I think) is figuring out where I want to go from here. I want a professional who can help me to think this through very carefully. While I want someone who is open to gender

---

[4] At the time, it was generally referred to as *gender identity disorder* (GID). Today, *gender dysphoria* is the preferred term. To call it an identity disorder is to impose a value judgment—much as when the medical establishment regarded being gay as a mental disorder. Our disorder isn't our gender identity. It is the intense discomfort we experience when our body and identity don't match.

reassignment, I want someone who will really help me to consider alternatives.

… My wife, Mary, is aware that I am seeking this counseling. She is naturally stressed and confused, but otherwise very supportive. She remains my best friend.

I look forward to talking with you.

When I researched transgender therapists on the Internet, I got the impression that most were there to help patients on their journey toward womanhood. But I wasn't there yet. I continued to hope that someone specializing in my disorder might help me to explore less drastic alternatives. Dr. Rachlin made it a point in her advertising that her goal was to help patients explore alternatives in order to choose the best path. That sounded perfect! I started to meet with her weekly.

So began my serious examination of what it might mean to be a transsexual woman.

EARLY IN OUR WORK TOGETHER, Dr. Rachlin suggested that I attend some group meetings with others who were struggling with the same issues. I started to attend a weekly walk-in clinic for transgender women at an LGBT center in the New York City metropolitan area. Typically, these meetings drew a gathering of 25 to 40 people. For ninety minutes, we crammed ourselves into a tiny room and formed a circle of chairs.

I vividly recall my first meeting. Each attendee introduced himself / herself and briefly described their current situation. I say "himself / herself" because the first thing each person declared to the group was their pronoun of preference. "Hi, my name is Tina and I prefer *she*." Most declared for *she*. A few were still at a stage where they felt more comfortable with *he*. Few, if any, described themselves as crossdressers. Most were people who, like me, were struggling with the inescapable feeling that they were women.

I looked around at the strange assemblage. Every point on the gender transition spectrum was present. There were women who had clearly transitioned years ago. They looked beautiful, poised, and feminine. Their bodies were soft and curvy. Most of the walk-ins were in some in-between stage of androgyny. Their budding signs of womanhood competed for attention with their masculine shoulders and brow lines. Then there were those in the early stages of exploration. They still presented as men at work and at home. Most of these had just come from their office. Their clothes said "man", but the lipstick and earrings they had put on as they entered the room hinted at things to come.

I would like to say that my first reaction was to appreciate the beauty in the room. It wasn't. "Holy cow!" I thought. "I am in a freaking leper colony!"

But just as quickly, I completed my thought: "And I have never felt so at home. This is me. Oh my God, this is me."

I listened as each attendee described their situation. Most had horrifically sad stories to share. They had been disowned by their families. They had lost their jobs. They were struggling to find anyone who would employ them. Many had been evicted from their apartments. Shelters had refused them. Some were living on the street.

I was roiling inside. The Tom side of me was horrified: Is this what I have come to? Could I possibly fall any further in life? What will I tell Mary? What will I say to my kids? How will I face anyone?

Meanwhile, the Tina in me was elated: I am finally face-to-face with people I understand. I am in a room full of others who know what it is to be me. I am not alone anymore. Thank God, I am not alone.

Though I had met many transsexuals at the IFGE conference, I had largely avoided them. At the time, I was just dipping my toes into the shallows of the gender pool. The transsexuals were swimming at the deep end. Now, here I was, way over my head, trying to stay afloat with everyone else in the room. Where was my horizon?

It was a confusing night. I didn't know whether to weep for joy or sorrow. On the drive home, I had to pull over to a side street. I leaned on the steering wheel and began to sob. "I have found a home! I have found a home!"

But, God, what a home. It was in the middle of a war zone. I wept for fifteen minutes more. What was I going to tell Mary?

I CONTINUED TO ATTEND these meetings each week. A month into the process, I sent Mary an email.

Darling,

I miss you. I am so sorry that you have to put up with this. What with all my meetings, I feel that I hardly see you these days. So I wanted to give you an update.

These group sessions are the hardest homework I have ever had to do. I went out with the girls after our meeting tonight. We share a common wound—but very little more[5].

I find myself constantly staring at their hands. Even the most passable girls have muscular forearms and big hands. I find myself wondering: is this the freak I was born to be? I try so hard to get rid of these feelings, but nothing seems to work.

Though they stand by their gender, none of the girls seems happy with her life. Most are jobless and alone. Most live with constant danger and rejection. They would give anything (except their gender) to escape this. They are struggling to survive. The evening wasn't exactly a night of fun. I keep hoping that their experiences will chase my feelings away. But they only seem to confirm who I am. Damn!

I love you lots. —T

It was when I met these wonderful women that I started to organize my thoughts around the notion of "the person inside". Some of us may not be very attractive superficially, I thought. But if the world

---

[5] As an employed, upper middle class, middle-aged white person, I was a bit of an outlier in the group. When we discussed gender, we had a lot to share. But beyond that, our life experiences could hardly have been more different. We enjoyed one another's company, but as though speaking to each other over a fence.

would only look beyond its stereotypes and our appearance, it would discover some beautiful souls.

I recalled the words of a forgotten philosopher: "It is the wounds of our youth that give us our humanity." Like bits of coal, our childhood pains are transformed over time into the diamonds that grace our spirits in middle age. We are able to empathize with the hurts and misfortunes of others because we know something of their pain. If this notion was true, our walk-in clinic was afire with sparkle. I was surrounded by diamonds, not lepers.

Sadly, our group contained some broken souls as well—broken not by their gender but by the hatred, prejudice and indifference with which they had had to contend. When treated with pressure, coal can harden into something beautiful and enduring. It can also crumble into dust.

MARY WATCHED WITH GROWING SADNESS as my therapy progressed. She had been able to cope with my crossdressing. But now I seemed to be exploring far more consequential options. She couldn't abide the thought of losing Tom forever.

One night, over dinner, she sat quietly, playing with the food on her plate. She looked across at me, "I was wondering: Have you ever considered … Could you … er … Couldn't you take drugs for this?"

"Huh? What do you mean?"

"Well, maybe you just need more testosterone. Have you ever thought about that?"

I never had. Just the thought made me anxious. Testosterone felt like poison to me. It filled my head with uncomfortable thoughts. I couldn't imagine taking more of it.

"I don't know," I said. "I'll ask my therapist."

Mary could sense my discomfort. Her eyes started to water. "I … I just think that we need to think of every possibility. That's all."

"Of course, Dear. I'll ask. But I've got to be honest: I'm scared of what it might do to me."

"Well, what about antidepressants—those sorts of things? Have you ever considered them? Lots of people take them. If your problem is how this makes you feel, maybe they would make the feelings go away."

She started to cry. "I just want my Tommy back! I just want my Tommy back!"

I felt deflated. I had spent a lifetime hiding my true self in order to make everyone else around me comfortable and happy. Now I was on the verge of discovering who I really was. And Mary, the one person who had stood by me, was asking me to consider a lifetime of self-medication in order to keep the genie in her bottle.

Yes, my dysphoria made me miserable. But at least I was me. Would drugs condemn me to a lifetime living in fog? Was I going to become Mary's anesthetized hand puppet?

But I understood her grief. And I shared her fears about my future. Did I really want to follow my sisters at the clinic into homelessness and unemployment?

"I'll look into it," I said.

WHEN I BROACHED THE TOPIC with my therapist, she immediately dispensed with the idea of taking testosterone. "It's been tried. Trust me, it will only make you feel worse."

I felt a tremendous sense of relief. "What about drugs for managing mood?"

She outlined my options and laid out the pros and cons of each. There were antipsychotics, antidepressants, and anti-anxiety drugs. Yes, they might help my mood, but they wouldn't cure my gender dysphoria. That would still be there. One of her concerns was that they might cloud my judgment. She pointed out that someone in my condition needed to be constantly alert to social cues. She added that some of these drugs posed serious medical risks: they could bring on thoughts of suicide. She considered this a particular concern in my case.

Some of the drugs were addictive. I would have to let someone else control my access to them and would have to submit to regular monitoring. Yes, the drugs might alleviate some anxiety, but they also might interfere with my ability to work on my real issue: my gender dysphoria. She suggested that we not rush into this. I agreed.

At home, I turned to medical references and to the Internet. *Transgender Care* supported my therapist's point of view: "Medication is best reserved for serious mental illnesses, such as schizophrenia, major depression, and panic disorder."

I considered my own mental state. Aside from my gender dysphoria, my mental health was great. Except when coping with GD, I was a happy, optimistic, and energetic person. I easily engaged with others and had healthy, loving relationships. At work, I was a high performer. Antidepressants could substantially alter my mood and thinking. Did I want to put all my positive qualities at risk?

I turned to the transgender discussion boards. One participant posted the question, "Have antidepressants helped you?" The responses were an almost unanimous "No."

> *They make me more stable, but overall, worse, even more depressed. ...*
> *No, they made me suicidal. ... More than anything, they harmed me. ...*
> *Oh God, I used to be on that crap. I stopped being able to function.*

One respondent pointed out that the drugs could help if you had an underlying problem with your brain chemistry. But if your problem was depression brought on by gender dysphoria, your only solution was to deal with the dysphoria itself.

I reported my findings to Mary. She dropped her gaze to the floor. "I guess that's that."

∾

BUT MARY'S CAUSE was not without hope. My masculine voice wasn't quite done. It ventured one last possibility: What if Tom has a deeply wounded psyche? What if Tina was that part of Tom that had a healthy connection to her feelings and to the rest of the world? What if she could teach Tom how to access those feelings? If Tom couldn't save himself, maybe Tina could.

Dunking on Stepson, Nathan

I decided to take a risk. I would let Tina take control for a while. I would observe her emotions and learn from them. As Tom, for example, I felt very uncomfortable when it came to sex. It seemed dirty and wrong—even when it was consensual. I knew that this was silly, but couldn't escape the feeling.

As Tina, I didn't feel that way at all. Consensual sex was a perfectly natural and healthy form of expression. Why shouldn't I feel comfortable telling my partner how good it felt? Tom could never do that. Was it possible to transfer Tina's feelings to Tom? Could I make her the teacher?

Tina was more at ease than Tom in conversation. She spoke freely about her emotions. She didn't beat around the bush or waste time choosing words. She said what she was thinking and it worked. Why couldn't Tom do that?

In some respects, I didn't feel any difference between Tina and Tom. In either case, I had the same career ambitions. I had the same political views and moral values. But socially, I felt more at ease and less inhibited when I presented as Tina. Why?

It was an awkward experiment, largely because it involved a lot more time living as Tina. I started to commute to therapy sessions and to attend group meetings presenting only as Tina.

This proved to be a logistical challenge. I couldn't go to the office as Tina. However, my therapy sessions and group meetings were far closer to work than to home. Where was I going to change clothes? How was I going to get into and out of the city? My train was generally full of neighbors from home and colleagues from work.

Rather than ride the train to work, I drove. I parked in Midtown in a shadowed corner of a self-park garage and walked the mile to my office. At the end of the workday, I trotted back to my car. I slid into the passenger seat, locked the doors and, in near darkness, changed clothes. I styled my wig, applied makeup, and checked myself in the mirror. … I'm ready. Take a deep breath.

I exited the car and headed downtown. Sometimes I walked, sometimes I took the subway. In either case, I kept a constant watch on the faces around me. Was there anyone from work who might recognize me? What would I do if they did?

For that matter, what would I do if I was harassed by a complete stranger? Was anyone taking notice of me? I imagined a teenager snatching my wig and sprinting into the night shouting, "Mother-fucking faggot!" All the way downtown, such possibilities turned themselves over and over in my mind. What could go wrong? What would I do? Would anyone help me?

On one occasion, I had to walk past a row of construction workers near Penn Station. As I passed each one, he called to the others and pointed a finger at me, "Dude walking!" Their chorus of laughter followed me down 7th Avenue. I tried as best I could to hide my shame and become invisible.

Another time, after a therapy session, I decided to treat myself to dinner at an outdoor café in Chelsea. I wanted to stop feeling so afraid of the world. What better way to do it than by sitting out in the open air? Chelsea was known as an LGBT-friendly neighborhood. It was a safe place in which to stage a trial run. As my waitress took my order, she shot me a knowing grin. I winced. But she was otherwise very nice. I decided that I could live with that.

After dinner, I headed up 8th Avenue toward the parking garage. As I crossed 29th street, a wino, stone-blind drunk, hollered after me, "Hey! I hope you're robbing a bank in that disguise!"

His brain was so addled that he could barely stand upright. But when I looked in his direction, he wagged his index finger at me and cackled, "Hah! I made you smile!"

He collapsed into a series of sniggers. Ah well, I thought, he was right. He had made me smile. I was disappointed that someone who could barely walk straight could so easily identify me. I realized that everyone I had been passing that day must either have been too busy to notice me or too polite to register a reaction.

But I *had* smiled back at the wino. I thought to myself: I can handle even the worst public ridicule with dignity. I might be a gender freak, but I'm a goddamned strong one.

BY APRIL of the following year, I was starting to feel a sense of hope.

Dear Mary,

I had some great discussions with Dr. Rachlin today. She said that it seemed pretty clear that I had grown up with a wounded masculine identity. I seem to be able to tap into a lot of feelings as Tina that I can't as Tom.

I don't want to give you false hopes. It is still quite possible that I am inherently transgendered. But it is also possible that my real issue is a deeply wounded male psyche. Tina may be a way to express feelings that I don't feel I have the right to express as Tom. ... I think it important to continue to allow Tina to surface. It seems to bring out a lot of contrasts between Tina and Tom that are useful for me to examine.

I want you to know that I am trying my hardest to repair Tom. He certainly deserves better (from himself).

Love,

I continued my experiments. To the world, I presented most of the time as Tom. But inside, I tried to live every moment as Tina. What did I see as her? What did I feel? Why?

One day at work, for example, I stepped into an elevator. I was dressed in a suit and tie. As the doors closed, two Otis elevator mechanics joined me. They were massive, standing well over six feet tall. Their linebacker proportions dwarfed our tiny compartment. It wasn't often that I got to experience what it was like to feel so small in comparison to others. I stood in the back of the elevator and let Tina take over. What did she feel?

She felt unashamed. They were cute—really cute. She would have loved to be held by one of them. It would have made her feel so womanly. She liked the idea of feeling safe in a man's arms.

The elevator ride lasted for less than a minute, but the memory lingered for weeks. If Tina could so enjoy the thought of being held by a man, why must Tom feel so guilty about holding a woman? He shouldn't. His amorous feelings toward women were no more inappropriate than were Tina's feelings toward men. If Tina could enjoy her thoughts, why couldn't Tom enjoy his?

When I wasn't thinking about systems integration projects, reorganizations, and household chores, I was engaging in similar mental experiments. Gradually, Tom began to channel Tina. By September, I was certain that I had the problem licked.

My Darling Mary,

... You probably don't appreciate all the progress I have made [in therapy] and what I have learned. ... I am pretty confident that you need never worry about Tina again—no matter what you do. I am a man. ... I love you so much Darling. I value your happiness above all else. I cannot wait to see you.

I had won! After forty years of trial and error, I had finally beaten this godawful affliction. I was immensely proud. I had gone face-to-face with one of the most threatening notions a man could confront. I had allowed myself to be unmanned in public places. I had displayed my most feminine side in the heart of New York City. I had silenced my ego and had permitted a woman to school me.

I was a real man now! I started to fantasize about the book I would write and the movie offers that would follow. I was going to help a lot of unhappy people.

MARY AND EVELYNE shared my certainty. Later that fall, with my therapist's assent, I ended my sessions and stopped attending the walk-in clinic.

To commemorate my victory, I joined the Centercourt Athletic Club. I hired a tennis pro and registered for the inter-club league. I hung out in the men's locker room and joined in the early-morning bull sessions. I entered my scores into our club's rating system and tracked my competitive progress.

I also started to hang out with the other fathers in my neighborhood. We went out for beers together. I invited them over to my fire pit for drinks. There, we drank cocktails, exchanged small talk and humored each other with our feeble jokes. In the winter, Mary and I went on a cruise. In the spring, we took Haley and Cam to watch Evelyne graduate from Oberlin.

Life was wonderful. Several months after declaring victory to Mary, I wrote to my therapist:

Dear Kit,

I have been looking forward to telling you how wonderful life is and how grateful I am. I don't feel a need for our talks but miss them. . . .

You would laugh at my progress. I have gotten very involved in an early morning tennis league (40 men, 2 women). I think I described them to you as a bunch of would-be high schoolers howling at the moon. They are a wonderful group. Behind their rough exteriors, they are a sensitive and caring community.

We communicate a lot by email. About half of the emails are trash talk, potty humor, and ribaldry. But there are also many that raise awareness for local charities and that seriously discuss political issues.

I think I told you that I had always felt like an outsider with big groups of men—and that I found it easier to connect with women than with men. That seems to be resolving itself. If my time with you was focused on repairing my inner connections, I think my more recent theme has been to restore and repair the outside ones. And with very nice results. . . . Thank you VERY, VERY much.

Tom

৵

ON THE EDGE

Night time sharpens, heightens each sensation
Darkness stirs and wakes imagination …
Close your eyes and surrender to your darkest dreams
Purge your thoughts of the life you knew before …
In this darkness that you know you cannot fight
The darkness of the music of the night

— From "Music of the Night", Phantom of the Opera

ONE NIGHT, I was at my tennis club, locked in an especially tight match. My opponent, Tony, and I hated losing to each other. We never said so, but you could tell it by the way we never spoke. We just grunted and grinded our points out, lonely gladiators in an empty arena. 15-love. 15 all. 15-30. 30 all. Lob. Pass. Drop-shot. Lob. Cross-court. Lob. On and on we played. The only evidence that we were there was our labored  breathing, the sound of our sneakers digging into clay and the rhythmic thud of the ball against our racquet strings. We battled on in grim silence.

On the court next to us, four women were enjoying a game of doubles. In tennis, opponents switch sides every other game. Each time the women exchanged sides, they gathered at the net, sipped water from their bottles and chatted.

"I couldn't go to yoga today. Little Mike had the flu."

"Oh, the poor dear! Is he getting any better?"

During the next change of sides, I learned that Amy and her husband had recently returned from a wonderful vacation in Aruba.

"Did you two wear sunscreen?"

"Of course!"

"Good, sun is so bad for you."

Two games later, the women resumed their chatter. "Did you hear about the Township proposal to install a new sidewalk on Pine Street?"

"Oh jeez! There go our taxes again."

As the night progressed, I listened to the women with growing interest. Why couldn't I be playing with them? It wasn't that their conversation was particularly interesting. It just felt like my home. I don't even remember how my match with Tony ended that day. I wasn't really there anymore.

I DISMISSED THE EVENT as an off night. These things were bound to happen. Man up, for God's sake!

But episodes like this started to repeat themselves. At neighborhood parties, I became more observer than participant. I found it difficult to fit in with conversations. The men's ribald humor and preoccupation with sports appealed less and less to me. The women welcomed my company, but as a man.

One of the things I enjoyed about being with women was that they tended to be more interested in discussing feelings. But I was pretty sure that these women wouldn't be interested in hearing what I was feeling just then.

What I was feeling was the returning presence of Tina. Once again, she was re-entering my life, as always, on tiptoe. I became preoccupied with my weight. I grew distracted when dressing. I started to frown at the hair on my arms.

Tina began to show up at work as well. When the guys went out for drinks, I passed. I wasn't interested. When some of my women friends went out for lunch, I wanted to join them. But I didn't dare. I worried that it would only draw comment. Besides, as with my friends at home, I couldn't share how I really felt inside. So what was the point?

I was alone again. I felt crushed. I had thought that I had vanquished my demons. When I had told Mary that she had her Tommy back, I had meant it. But I realized now that this wasn't true. I had simply carried myself through another cycle. I had thrown everything I could think of at this problem. Now I had nothing left with which to fight. I lost all hope.

MY BOUTS OF DEPRESSION intensified. I sat in the dark and brooded. In an effort to silence my mind, I listened almost constantly to podcasts and audiobooks on my iPhone. Mary had a running joke: if she wanted to reach me across the room, she had only to dial my mobile number.

On weekends, I distracted myself with projects—big ones. I built ponds, retaining walls and a gazebo. I carted three tons of topsoil into our back yard. Wherever there was sunlight, I planted flowers and bushes. I patched our neighbor's driveway. Landscaping brought me a measure of peace. It was genderless, involved no other people, and provided a physical outlet for my frustration.

On some nights, Mary woke at one or two am to find my side of the bed empty. Inevitably, she located me somewhere in the house, listening to podcasts as I painted a wall, built a cabinet or pressure-washed the garage floor. She appreciated my contributions. She knew that it was, in part, my silent apology for who and what I was. But she worried that I was working myself to exhaustion.

I had no choice. At times like this, it was only through exhaustion that I found a few hours of sleep.

WHAT WORRIED ME more than anything was that I had started to think about suicide. I never made specific plans and never researched it. But I had moments that were so profoundly painful that ending my life seemed an inviting alternative. I imagined a dark, peaceful void that offered escape from my pain. Peace. Everlasting peace. That's all I longed for. I was fifty years of tired.

I began to consider the possibility that Mary and the children would be better off without me. Mary, I knew, would never leave my side. She was too loving and loyal. I wanted her to be able to move on in life without all the tears. Haley, Cameron, and Evelyne were such incredibly wonderful people. They were making their way in the world with great success. They didn't deserve the burden of having a gender-freak for a father. It would dog them for the rest of their lives. My words from years before returned to me: *Why don't you just crawl into a hole and die?*

So long as I had been able to maintain the presence of the likable Princeton graduate, everything had been tolerable. My family, I felt, could be proud of me. I was an asset.

But I could no longer keep up this charade. Earlier, when I had thought of myself as a damaged male, it wasn't a pretense. I was genuinely trying to be the best man I could be. But now that I understood myself differently, presenting myself to the world as Tom grew more and more difficult. Now I *was* faking it. I couldn't be false to those I loved.

ONE NIGHT, I arrived home, filled with especially dark thoughts. Haley was there. Put on your winning smile, I told myself. Gut it out. Your role is to be there for your children. Just be there.

I couldn't do it. At some point in the evening, I bolted to the bathroom and locked the door behind me. I collapsed onto the rug and started to sob uncontrollably, "Why me, God? Why me?"

This was the night when life as I had known it ended. I had organized my adulthood around being the best semblance of a father and husband I could manage. Those two roles remained my deepest sources of joy. And now I knew that I could no longer sustain them. My children were about to lose their father, Mary her husband. I lay there and bawled. Outside, I could hear Haley crying. "What's happening to Daddy?"

I cut back on tennis. I grew quiet at parties. I withdrew from the family, preparing myself for the inevitable return of Tina. Another year of shame and isolation. Another year of pain and disappointment for Mary. And now I had infected the children.

Days passed. I waited.

IT ALL CAME TO A HEAD a few weeks later. Mary was asleep when I arrived home. It had been a long, stressful day at the office. I drew myself a warm bath, lit some candles, and turned on Pachelbel's Cannon. The gentle chords had always brought me peace. I just needed to sit in the candle-lit shadows and relax my mind. I was not putting an end to my life. Not yet anyway.

I was just beginning to unwind when the door exploded. It slammed against the bathroom counter. Mary fell into the room, screaming and sobbing. "No! Don't! No!" she wailed. I had never seen her face so contorted. She collapsed onto the floor beside me and cried.

She had wakened to the sound of running water and had leapt to the certainty that I was putting an end to my life. We sat together holding hands over the edge of the tub and let our tears fall. "I don't know if I can keep this up," I choked. "I just don't know."

Up until this year, I had always tried to approach my problem as a man confused with gender. But I had lately begun to entertain the possibility that I really did have the mind of a woman. What did that mean, "to think like a woman?" I wasn't sure I knew.

But it captured my experience perfectly. I had always found it difficult to identify as a man of any sort. I had always felt most at home in the company of women. My male body felt alien to me. I only found peace as Tina. Most of the time, I had only managed sex by imagining myself as a female. Womanhood was the only way I was capable of relating to the world.

I had spent the last few years walking on eggshells. How would my transvestite friends feel when I said that I wasn't one of them? How would I explain myself to feminists? What about all of my male friends: was I betraying them? Was I taking something away from my children or giving them something better?

I told myself: You are trying to take on the burdens of the world, Tina. And yet you are barely alive. Maybe you should focus on being yourself. Let everyone else work out their own issues. Feminism isn't valid if it cannot accommodate your reality. Let them work it out. Your responsibility is to let people know who you are.

THE NOTION that I was repressing the true me went a long way towards explaining my deepening depression. I had lately been possessed by a recurring thought: What if I continue to hide this person inside me? When my parents die, they will do so never having known who I was. When I die, my children will live on, forever ignorant of the person who had loved them all those years from behind her barricade. If I should live, never having allowed another soul to know or to touch me, could I say that I had lived? No.

I also finally understood why my efforts to have a conversation with God had always ended in failure. It wasn't that he wasn't there. It was that I wasn't. If you are not in the room with someone, how can you hold a conversation with them? You cannot. By hiding myself in shame, I had made myself invisible even to God.

Now that is being alone.

I was well aware that many conservative Christians took issue with gender-variance. In their minds, to dress as a woman was to violate the norms that God had set in place since Adam and Eve. To surgically alter my body was to desecrate his gift to me.

But wasn't it a greater sin to hide my soul from God? If my soul was that of a woman, didn't I owe it to God to accept his gift with gratitude? Perhaps my greatest sin all these years had been to silence and shame this even more precious gift from him. In the Bible, the Lord explains to Samuel,

> *The LORD seeth not as man seeth; for man looketh on the outward appearance, but the LORD looketh on the heart (1 Samuel 16:7).*

I looked into my own heart: it beat with the soul of a woman. For the first time in my life, I wasn't ashamed. I realized, in fact, that it was my duty to God to reveal myself to the world for what I was—and to be proud of his creation:

> *Neither do men light a candle and put it under a bushel, but on a candlestick; and it giveth light unto all that are in the house. Let your light*

so shine before men, that they may see your good works, and glorify your Father which is in heaven (Matthew 5:15-16).

If others wanted to think of my genitals as my most defining creation, let them. I was pretty sure that God cared more about my soul.

∾

HERE, I THINK, is why so many transsexual men and women from my generation transition later in life: We spend decades pursuing every explanation and remedy that we can think of. Every explanation save one. And why not? When we were growing up, the thought that we didn't match our birth certificate was beyond comprehension.

But eventually, we see our time running short and our list of alternative explanations running out. Exhausted and demoralized, we look at last to the one door we had never opened. Open it. Or die never having lived.

And so we open it.

THE REALIZATION that I wasn't living my identity was the turning point in my life. I finally understood where my thoughts of suicide had been coming from. They had sprung from my own actions.

I had been complicit in my own, slow-motion murder. The true me had been buried alive when I was a child. And it was I who had done the spadework. Suicide was simply the logical conclusion to everything I had been doing to myself. Why not finish the job?

I thought back to my college roommate, Michael. His uncle's suicide had certainly not given Mike any peace. After that incident, I had always grown angry when I heard that someone had attempted suicide. How could they be so selfish? How could they be so cruel?

Now that I was facing it myself, I began to understand it differently. I had always thought of suicide as something you could control. I now saw that, once you allowed yourself to cross a certain point, you were no longer the master of your emotions. Your mind became clouded. It was reeling in pain and desperate for relief. It could imagine but one path to release: permanent rest.

Having ventured a couple of times into this no man's land, I knew that the only way to avoid suicide was to make certain that I never returned to that place of darkness. But how to do it? In thirty years, I had never found a way to stop these cycles. In fact, with each repetition, they had only gathered in strength. Each time, I seemed to fall into a deeper void.

FOR SEVERAL WEEKS following the bathtub incident, I more or less limped through each day. I was a beaten dog. My spirits sank lower. At work, my boss worried. "Is everything OK, Tom?"

"Mary and I are just struggling. That's all."

That was an understatement. Mary was frantic. Hearing of our situation, Evelyne flew home from Belgium to spend a week with us. My parents and siblings started to visit on weekends. They did this partly out of concern for my safety. But they were also worried about Mary. It was crushing her to see me brought so low.

And I was ashamed of my weakness. How could I even think such thoughts? It was pathetic. It was disgusting.

But I was not alone. A Virginia study of 300 transgender people found that 65 percent had contemplated suicide. Studies in other geographies yielded comparable findings—far higher than the eight percent of the general population who had ever contemplated suicide. Another body of research focused on suicide attempts. Among transgender populations, findings ranged from 18 percent to 41 percent, typically falling in the low 30s. The average for the general population in the U.S. is less than three percent.

What struck me as I read these grim statistics was that they were based on surveys of people who were still alive to respond. How much higher would the numbers be if they included the voices of those who had silenced their souls forever?

I WRACKED MY BRAIN: how could I avoid becoming a statistic?

One night, while ruminating in the dark, I had an epiphany. My problem wasn't my gender. My problem was me. I had always described myself with words like "freak" and "leper". I realized: I am as transphobic as the rest of the world. I am the one inflicting the damage on myself. I am the bigot in the room.

I had to change my attitude, and change it fast. Victory didn't lie in conquering my gender. It lay in accepting the one I had been given. More than that, it lay in learning to be grateful for it. My gender was God's gift to me. I had to learn to love myself for who I was. I had to learn to see the beauty in people like me. If I couldn't see it, how could I expect anyone else to?

THAT WAS THE DAY that I emerged from my shadowland. From that day forward, a load was lifted from my shoulders. I didn't have a plan yet, but I had a conviction. Even if I didn't understand it, I was going to accept my womanhood. I would follow this conviction wherever it led.

I was still filled with anxiety. But it was different now. Heretofore, my worries had come from within. They were an artifact of my own self-loathing. Now they were coming from outside: "What will the neighbors say?" "Will I lose my job?" "How will my children react?" "What will Mary do?"

These were crushing problems in and of themselves. But they were nothing as compared to self-destruction and self-hatred. I still had a steep hill to climb. But where I had been climbing my entire life in darkness, I was now doing so by daylight. At least I could now see the obstacles around me. I felt a new sense of determination take hold.

My euphoria was short-lived. I had many life-shaping decisions to make: What did I plan to do to myself medically? How was I going to explain my actions? What were my plans for my family, my career, my marriage? I had to make these decisions quickly. Once word got out that I was transitioning, things would move

Brussels 2011
One of Last Traditonal Poses

rapidly beyond my control. In putting my plans together, I had to consider three major constraints: medical, legal and professional.

THE MEDICAL CONSTRAINTS were imposed by the standards of care established by the World Professional Association for Transgender Health (WPATH). WPATH had been founded in the 1970s by Dr. Harry Benjamin, one of the first physicians to focus on gender-dysphoric people. The majority of medical professionals serving the transgender community abided by its standards. If I wanted feminizing hormones and surgeries, I would have to follow WPATH guidelines.

These guidelines required that I get letters from two licensed therapists confirming that I suffered from gender dysphoria and that the situation warranted medical intervention. In order to qualify for certain surgeries, I would also have to live as a woman and take hormones for at least a year. These were minimums. For certain procedures, doctors recommended at least two years of hormone therapy.

Some transgender people consider these standards restrictive and demeaning. I thought they made sense. My greatest fear was making a bad and irreversible decision. The intent of the standards was to give people like me ample opportunity and professional support to confirm our gender identity and to adjust to our new role before we did something we couldn't undo.

That didn't mean that I liked the standards. They did feel demeaning. Here I was, a middle-aged adult with children and grandchildren. I had been making my own decisions for years. I had advised senior executives on multi-million dollar initiatives. Now I was the ward of a team of medical specialists. Would my doctors grant me permission to be myself? What would I do if they didn't? What if I picked a therapist who had their own agenda? I had read several stories about therapists who practiced conversion therapy. Rather than help their patients to find their authentic selves, they attempted to brainwash them to conform to community standards.

Following the WPATH standards meant that I was going to have to live with a lot of embarrassment and vulnerability. I was going to spend a year presenting myself in public as a woman even though I still sported muscular shoulders, a five-o'clock shadow, and a masculine brow line.

THE SECOND CONSTRAINT I faced was the need to establish my new legal status. At a minimum, I would need a new passport, driver's license, and social security card. But before I could get these, I had to obtain a court-ordered name change and a medical letter from a qualified physician.

Once I got my new identity documents, I would have to move quickly to change everything else in my documented life: my employment records, college transcripts, credit cards, medical insurance, life insurance, wills, property deeds, bank accounts, and retirement accounts to name only a few. If, for example, my employment and social security records did not match, my employer might face an audit from Immigration Services. The mere notion that I could be declared an illegal alien was mind-blowing. Where would they send me?

Without all of these documents, I could not easily hold a job, drive a car, or own a home. I could not get credit cards or bank accounts. I might not receive medical attention. I would find it difficult to pay utility bills, own a phone or purchase things online. Without a change to my gender marker, I was at risk any time I went to the bathroom or interacted with a law enforcement official.

It can be very scary, I realized, to live in a world where your legal documents put you at risk. For the first time, I began to appreciate the deeper aspect of cultural privilege. In the past, if I thought about cultural privilege at all, I had thought about it in terms of preferential treatment. Did I, as a white male, get promoted faster and paid more than others who were equally qualified? This, I now saw, was the tip of the iceberg.

The most damning aspects of cultural preference run much deeper. As a cultural elite, I had always taken my legal status for granted. I didn't think twice before entering a bathroom. It never occurred to me to hesitate before approaching a police officer. As long as I was a law-abiding citizen, my country was there to protect me.

Once I crossed the gender line, however, this would no longer be true. In many states, lawmakers have written their laws to explicitly deprive transgender people of the basic protections that every other citizen in America enjoys. In some states, I can be fired for coming to work each day in a dress. I can be evicted from an apartment for wearing lipstick. And I have no legal standing on which to challenge such actions.

I would spend the rest of my life feeling as one who is hunted: Is it safe for me to enter a convenience store at night? Will somebody beat me up for using the bathroom? If I am attacked, will the police protect me? If I have to go to the hospital, will doctors admit me?

When I had enjoyed cultural privilege, such questions never crossed my mind. Now that I was losing it, they were in my head all the time. A visit to the zoo, a stroll through the park, an errand to buy postage stamps—even the simplest events in life began to strike a menacing note.

I finally appreciated the scene from a movie that another transgender woman had shared in her blog. Two cops, one black and one white, are driving in their squad car. The black policeman asks, "Do you ever think about the fact that you are white?"

"No. Why the hell would I do that? I'm a person like everyone else."

"I think about being black every single day."

A 2011 study of gender non-conforming people, *Injustice at Every Turn*[6], found that 19 percent of respondents had been refused medical care because of their failure to conform to gender norms. Of those who had been forced to seek refuge in a homeless shelter, 29 percent had been refused access because they were transgender. Another 25 percent were evicted after revealing their transgender status. Why? What threat were they posing?

THE THIRD CONSTRAINT that I had to plan around was my company. My employer, Pfizer, Inc., purported to support transgender people in the workplace and had earned a score of 100 in HRC's Corporate Equality Index (CEI) for ten years running[7]. At the time that I was planning my transition, a company had to include transgender colleagues in its non-discrimination policies and insurance programs in order to score 100.

But the CEI measures policy, not practice. I wasn't aware of any transgender workers in our midst. To my knowledge, no one had put our policies and leadership to the test. How could I know what my company would do? Mary and I had come face-to-face with many transsexuals who had shared depressing accounts of their experiences at work. Many had been fired. Others had been shunned, harassed, or marginalized.

Twenty-six percent of the respondents to the *Injustice at Every Turn* study reported that they had lost a job because of their gender variance. Fifty percent had suffered harassment at work. Almost three quarters reported that they were trying to hide their gender variance from

---

[6] *Injustice at Every Turn: A Report of the National Transgender Discrimination Survey*, National Center for Transgender Equality and National Gay & Lesbian Task Force (Washington D.C., 2011)

[7] As of this publication, Pfizer has scored 100 thirteen years in a row.

coworkers. This only heightened my alarm. Presumably, the reported rates of discrimination would be higher were it not for efforts to live in stealth.

Even the most enlightened companies, I learned, often imposed strict guidelines where transgender issues were concerned. It wasn't a matter of prejudice; they were protecting themselves from lawsuit. Gender dysphoria is a diagnosed medical condition. As a result, it is subject to federal regulation under HIPAA.[8] That means that any discussions of gender identity are legally treated as patient-confidential. As a result, corporations are advised to maintain control over workplace transitions. Among other things, they need to make certain that none of their leaders makes inappropriate comments or disclosures. The consequences to the company, if they do, can be significant.

Most of my transgender friends advised me: until you are ready to come out of the closet, don't discuss your gender with anyone at work. It could put your job and benefits at risk. Don't consult Human Resources until you and your medical team have a clear plan. When you do consult them, bear in mind that they will almost certainly want to control the process as work. I took their advice to heart. I didn't even dare to search Pfizer's intranet to see what our policies were. As far as I was concerned, they were top secret.

TAKEN TOGETHER, these three constraints put me in one heck of a bind: I had to figure out a way to satisfy the year-as-a-woman requirement without revealing anything at work. I wasn't ready to go to work as Tina: I still had a lot to learn before I could present myself credibly as a businesswoman. People relied on my advice and analysis for important decisions. If I wanted to keep my career, I had to protect my professional reputation.

---

[8] Health Insurance Portability and Accountability Act.

Nor was I about to approach Human Resources. At the time I made my decision to transition, I wasn't certain that I would have a job at the end of the year. A few months before, Pfizer had eliminated my job as part of a general downsizing. My employment had been extended for a year only because someone realized at the last moment that I was playing an important role on a critical project—rebuilding our key account sales force. They extended me for the project's duration—another twelve months. Under the circumstances, the last thing I wanted to do was to approach someone in HR.

A couple of things played to my advantage. I was in a role that supported colleagues all over the country. We were used to working without face-to-face contact. I had recently received a glowing performance review and enjoyed my boss's complete confidence. I discussed the situation with my therapist. We agreed that I would live 24/7 as Tina except for the times that I had to go into the office.

So began what I came to refer to as my year of living dangerously.

AT HOME, the first thing I did was to swap closets. Tina was now my daily routine. Tom had to settle for the spare closet. I packed all but a few of his belongings and stored them in the attic. Mary was outwardly supportive but clearly distressed. Things were now moving very fast.

Each morning, I dressed as Tina and prepared to work from home. If I had to go to the city for something unrelated to work, it was Tina who joined the other commuters on the train. If there was a local errand to run, Tina ran it. The neighbors were still unaware of my plans, so I had to shop at stores in other towns.

Still, I had always to be ready to switch back to Tom at a moment's notice. I might plan the day as Tina, only to learn that a last-minute meeting demanded my appearance in New York. Or Mary might get a call from a neighbor who was stopping by to see her. This constant back-and-forth could be very confusing.

It also created some amusing situations. One day, I had to go to the city to meet with my therapist. Since I was presenting as Tina, I couldn't go to the office. But I had to run several meetings that day. What to do?

After taking the train into New York, I went to a Starbucks near Penn Station. I bought a large, decaf coffee, secured a table, and fired up my computer. I connected to the Internet and launched the meeting using our company's virtual conferencing application.

Visually, I was presenting to everyone in Starbucks as a woman. I was wearing a blue, Ralph Lauren sheath dress, conservative makeup and a carefully arranged wig. To everyone on the conference call, I was presenting as Tom. All that they could detect was my familiar, masculine tenor.

I tried to focus on running my meeting. But I could not help but be aware of the stares from the patrons around me. Perhaps they had seen someone like me on stage or in the street, but I was pretty sure that this was the first time they had seen a man in a dress discussing project deadlines and user acceptance testing in a coffee shop. Throughout the call, I sustained an inward chuckle. If I ever wanted to test a colleague's powers of concentration, I decided, this was how I would do it.

On other days, I was rushing out the door for a Tom-day at the office. Mary's shout caught up with me, "Honey, have you checked your face this morning?"

Thank heavens she was there. It would have been embarrassing to arrive at the office adorned with the remnants of mascara and foundation. I started to keep make-up removal pads in my briefcase. Even so, I occasionally goofed. One day, my boss, Matt, interrupted a progress review. "Tom, were you painting or something this weekend?" He gestured to the flecks of red that clung to a couple of my fingernails.

"Huh? … Oh, that. … Yeah, I guess I was."

BUT MY MAKEUP was the least of Mary's concerns. She was far more worried about my safety. Each day that I went into the city as Tina, she found it impossible to fall asleep until I returned home. I still didn't pass very well in public. I passed no better, in fact, than I had a year before when the wino and construction workers had serenaded me through Midtown.

Mary's greatest fear was that, if someone attacked me, no one would come to my aid. She was terrified that one night, she would receive the dreaded phone call: "Ms. White, we found your husband beaten and raped tonight. I'm afraid that we found him in a dress and women's underwear. Could you come down to the station? We have some questions for you."

It wasn't that I looked like a transvestite out on a lark. Far from it. I took great pains to look put together and professional. But I still had broad shoulders and masculine facial features. My cheeks and chin often bore the telltale marks of electrolysis.

The most frightening situations were those when I returned from the city on a night when the Knicks or Rangers were playing at Madison Square Garden. Penn Station was situated directly beneath the arena. On nights like this, I generally had to stand on the train for an hour, shoulder-to-shoulder with dozens of young men who were heading home, buzzed on adrenaline and alcohol. I made myself as invisible as I could. If I was lucky, I found a seat. I buried my face in my computer and kept my eyes pointed down. I was terrified what these late-night inebriates might do to me.

AS I BEGAN my transition, transgender safety was getting a lot of press. The stories that appeared in the news alarmed me. The world seemed to find sport in our disposal. According to statistics from the FBI and estimates by the Harvey Milk Institute, when I had decided to live according to my gender, I had increased my odds of being murdered by a factor of 1,500.

I looked at a list of transgender homicides from the previous twelve months. We had been clubbed to death, burned to death, shot, and stabbed. Our bodies had been dismembered—our eyes, hands, feet, and genitals removed. We had been raped, asphyxiated, stoned, and strangled. We were disposed of in trash bags, dumpsters and sewage gullies. No one seemed to care. Why? Where was this rage coming from?

One source of unrest was the public toilet. I watched on YouTube as a church leader in Pennsylvania proudly informed his congregation that he kept a bat in his car for people like me. If he ever saw one of my kind coming out of a woman's room, he would take his stick of white ash to their head. That, said this man of God, is what people like me deserved. I read about a mother and daughter who had viciously attacked a transgender woman in a Baltimore McDonalds while she was going to the bathroom.

If I were a pervert, I thought, the last thing I would do would be to call attention to myself by dressing as a woman. And I certainly wouldn't wear heels. That would be asking for trouble. Besides, what was to stop a pervert from preying on little boys? Didn't they deserve protection too?

But public prejudices saw things differently. Under the circumstances, I did everything I could to avoid trips to the women's room. When I had to use one, I did it quickly.

My worries about safety followed me wherever I went—on the train, to the grocery store, to the mall, even to our local Dunkin Donuts. Mary offered to run errands for me, but I insisted on doing them myself. If this was to be my lot in life, I had better find out now.

BEYOND SAFETY, there was the issue of shame. In a shoe store one day, I approached a clerk. "Do you have sling back sandals like this one in a size x?"

"I don't know, *Sir*." She gave me a withering look and walked away. At a grocery store, I could not, for the life of me, figure out where pine nuts were shelved. Ordinarily, I would have asked a clerk. But dressed as I was, I wandered another twenty minutes until I found them. When I arrived home, Mary was annoyed: "Where have you been? I was worried!"

I stopped at a local gas station one day to fill up my tank. As I lowered the window, I handed the attendant my credit card. "Could you fill it up with regular, please?"

He snatched the card from my hand. His eyes burned with a malevolence the likes of which I had never seen before. I rolled up the window and locked the doors. Were I not at a busy, daylight intersection, I would have feared for my life. He really looked like he wanted to do something violent.

A few weeks later, I stopped at another gas station. This attendant, a man of about fifty, gave me a friendly smile.

Thank God, I thought. "Could you fill it up with regular?" I handed him my card.

"Of course!" he replied. He activated the pump and returned to the window.

"You're very pretty. I like your kind of person. Why don't you come back later today?"

He winked at me and licked his lips. Oh, for God's sake, I thought. I just want to buy some goddamn gas. Can I do it without becoming an object of hatred or lust? Can I just get treated like a human being?

Meanwhile, the news media continued to debate the threat that people like me posed to public safety and righteous living.

THERE WERE OTHER MOMENTS, though, when even I had to laugh. I was visiting, Christie, my voice therapist one morning while presenting as Tina. Her office was in a high rise near Wall Street. Upon leaving my lesson, I headed to the bathroom. I sat down in a stall and waited for nature to take its course.

After a few seconds, I looked down. In the stall to my right, I noticed a pair of dusty, men's construction boots. Yikes! I had entered the wrong lavatory. I inched my high heels as far to the other side of my stall as possible and waited for the owner of the boots to finish.

He must have eaten a lot of starch the day before. For fifteen minutes, I had to listen as every imaginable sound tooted from his orifices. Grunts, groans, and rumbles were punctuated by sighs of relief. I grinned. This would make for a great sitcom scene.

Finally, Mr. X finished his business. I prepared to leave.

But I was too slow. Just as Mr. X exited, half a dozen male voices crowded in. They were on break from a meeting. As they went about their business, they engaged in small talk. I made myself even more invisible. My legs were now hiked in the air, my purse and briefcase piled on my lap. I grinned: This was expanding into a mini-series!

When the men finally left, I flew out of that bathroom. I was not going to get caught again. Unfortunately for me, just as I opened the door from my side, the janitor was opening it from his. "Hi!" I smiled. I shot past him and flew down the hall.

I have never used the wrong bathroom since.

STEREOTYPES OF TRANSGENDER women notwithstanding, I did not find it a joy to dress as a woman each day. As far as I was concerned, I was girding for battle. I was preparing for a daylong inspection by a hundred unforgiving eyes. Everyone seemed to feel that I was fair game for instruction and critique.

Wig Fitting

CONSIDER THE SIMPLEST OF OUTFITS, running attire. One morning, I decided to take a quick run to the nearby Passaic River. I put on a running bra, some black running pants, a tee shirt, and a runner's jacket. I checked my makeup and wig. Everything looked fine.

I headed out the door, up the hill and around a curve. One of the neighbors who knew of my transition was walking her dog[9]. When she saw me approaching, she immediately reversed direction. I waved a hello as I jogged past. Later that week, I was told that she had reported to others on my poor presentation. "A real woman would never go running without putting her hair in a ponytail!"

Evidently, she did not understand that you cannot put a temporary wig into a ponytail. Unless you glue the wig to your scalp, the lining will show. Given that I had to put the wig on and take it off once or twice a day, glue was not an option. But my excuse didn't matter. My critic was a cis-woman. She held the scorecard. I had been dealt another black mark.

ANY WOMAN who wanted to could easily poke holes in my presentation. I learned not to argue in such situations. I politely thanked them and took mental notes: had they said something useful? I had to suck it up and learn what I could from the encounter.

But it was hard. People could be very preachy. They critiqued my wigs, my make-up, my eyeglasses, and clothing. They offered advice about my voice, my diction, my posture, and walk. "Try moving with a little more sway. Straighten your back. Move your feet as though walking a tight rope. Put your heels down first."

The day after I received this coaching, I watched the women of New York navigate its streets and sidewalks. None of them walked that way. These were the days when I wanted to scream. Why did everyone assume that I wanted to look like Barbie and act like Princess Diana? Why was everyone else so obsessed with my appearance?

Welcome to womanhood, Tina.

PERHAPS IT WAS KARMA giving me my comeuppance. A year or two before, I could justly have been blamed for fostering these

---

[9] This was about seven months into my year-long trial. I had, by this time, become known to a few of my closest neighbors (described later in this chapter).

impressions. The truth is, many transgender women play a role in contributing to our stereotype as would-be Barbie dolls. Earlier in my transition, my daughter, Evelyne, had met with my therapist. One of the issues they discussed was my focus at the time on makeup and clothing.

"I told her that I feel like I'm talking to my kid sister," Evelyne reported to me. "I get sick of hearing about clothing and makeup. And the things you pick out are either juvenile or hyper-feminine. I've already got a kid sister. You're supposed to be a dad!"

Thankfully, Dr. Rachlin offered Evelyne a helpful perspective: "Did you go through a similar phase when you were young?" Evelyne admitted that she had. "Well, your dad is just going through that phase, too. He never got the chance. Don't worry. It will pass."

The early stages of transition are especially weird. Even I was aware of it. For about a year, I had an inexplicable fascination with the color pink, with Laura Ashley quilts, stuffed animals, and trendy nail polish colors. Part of me was horrified by this fascination. But, for some of us at least, it seems to be an unavoidable rite of passage. It is as though we are compelled to capture all of the lost experiences of our youth. When we were teenage boys, we had to sit on the sidelines and watch as the other girls tried silly fashions and over-applied makeup. Now it was our turn.

I am still not certain what motivates this preoccupation. Perhaps we are trying to create a shared past with other women. Perhaps it is how human beings learn. It may be that the little girl inside us just wants a chance to express the childhood she had been denied. Whatever it is, I often found myself wishing that I could retreat to a special farm until this fever had passed. I was as happy as anyone else when it finally did.

AS MY THERAPIST FORETOLD, I quickly outgrew this phase. I was now dressing by choice as a normal adult. I was more interested in mastering a five-minute makeup routine than in trying a new perfume. I wanted to get on with my day. I had projects to run.

But I still had to contend with my critics and tutors. Even if I didn't want to think about fashion and female decorum, they did. I realized that the only way to stop these impromptu lectures was to prove that I knew more about everyday fashion and beauty than did my instructors. Unfortunately, I had missed out on forty years of training and socialization. I had a lot of catching up to do. I channeled my annoyance into education.

I watched DVDs on feminine movement and posture. I attended a class on feminine deportment. There, I learned that women fill their forks differently than do men ("don't let me see you go past the front third of your fork, ladies!"). I was told that, unlike men, women hang their coats around the outside of a chair. ("It's all in the details, Tina.")

I watched YouTube to learn how to roll curlers for different effects, how to apply eyeshadow for the daytime, and how to contour the cheekbones for evening. I subscribed to a half-dozen video blogs that offered career women tips on office fashion and everyday beauty shortcuts. I downloaded PDF documents. One illustrated three ways to tie a scarf. Another shared home remedies for removing stains and for making blouses their whitest.

I flirted briefly with mainstream women's magazines, like Vogue, Marie Claire, Vanity Fair, More, and Shape. But I found that I preferred web sites that focused on the science behind beauty products. Paula's Choice produced Beautypedia (the "number one source for reliable, evidence-based skincare"). The Environmental Work Group published SkinDeep, an online database that profiled the toxic chemicals in 80,000 cosmetics products. I didn't want a new mascara each week. I wanted to find one that I knew to be safe and effective and to stick with it.

By the end of the year, I had gained a lot of confidence. Gradually, the tide began to turn. Women complemented me on my outfits ("Where did you get that skirt, Tina? I want it, too."). They asked me for instruction ("I like the way you've tied your scarf. How did you do that?"). They asked for my product recommendations ("What's a safe product for coloring my hair?"). They still offered impromptu tips of their own, but now it was a two-way conversation. I felt on equal terms.

❧

AT THE SAME TIME, I was learning things that were much more important than deportment and cosmetology. In particular, I was learning to forgive myself. In February, I described my efforts in my journal:

For me, the past year has been less about transition. It has been one long apology to the person inside me—a quest for forgiveness and healing.

Every day, I am nursing that child back to health. I play with it, protect it, and listen to it. Miraculously, she is responding. She is becoming joyful, exuberant, and happy. I don't know if I have fully earned her trust and forgiveness. But she is a kind and loving person. I am hopeful that I will.

This is an element of transition that few outside our community appreciate. Now that Tina finally had a voice, she had a lot of pent-up anger to express. I am not sure that I understand the nuances behind ego, id, and superego, but there was a continual conversation going on inside my head.

As far as Tina was concerned, some part of me (let's call him Tom) had been in control for forty years. As she saw things, he had screwed up colossally. In fact, he had tried to kill her. He had made her life a joyless darkness. Why should she ever trust him?

Throughout the year, those who were aware of my transition asked me, "What about Mary?" "What about your kids?" I never shared my inner response. But, silently, I raged, "Yes, but what about Tina? Why doesn't anyone give a damn about her? What about what she's been through?"

People are right to say that, early in our transition, we are somewhat self-absorbed. But it isn't necessarily born of an exuberant sense of self-declaration. We are in the act of recovering our lost self. For the first time in my life, I was listening to the voice that I had so willfully silenced. I was seeking her forgiveness; I was trying to win her trust.

If you could hear the conversation inside my head during my first year living as Tina, here is what you might have heard. ...

Do you really need to buy those shoes, Sweetheart? Well, OK. You have been through a lot. I'm sorry I never listened before. ... Yes, I guess you deserve them. I am really here for you this time. Trust me, I won't let you down again.

A bit silly and indulgent, I know. But I felt as though I were nursing an abused child back to health.

I WAS ALSO PROTECTING HER. Tina was far from perfect. I knew that. But if she was going to make it in life, I had to stop apologizing for her existence. She needed someone to believe in her. That someone had to be me.

This wasn't easy to do. Even as I was figuring out who Tina was, people were putting her under a microscope. What did Tina think she was solving? Did she really think that she was convincing as a woman? Why didn't she let others who were more experienced pick out her clothing? Did she understand that she was going about her transition all wrong? Everyone questioned her competence.

I could have taken the easy way out and passively accepted all of this instruction. But the most important thing I was doing this year was to allow this fragile being inside me to come out of her shell. She was new to this. She was going to screw up. It was hard for the fifty-year-old parent in me to keep quiet. But if this little girl was going to master the game of life, I had to let her play. I had to silence all of her coaches on the sidelines. When I did, they didn't always like it.

ANOTHER IMPORTANT THING that I was learning was what I might expect my career to become.

When I was young, women had been told, over and over, that their place was in the home: They were intellectually inferior to men. They lacked the spirit and aggression to function as competent leaders. Their presence was a disruption to high-functioning executive teams.

As I surveyed the popular media, I found that transgender women were now subject to the same nonsense. At best, we were portrayed as damaged goods: we were to be pitied, tolerated, and protected. More often, we were presented as willful oddities—as dancers, sex workers, and performance artists. Sure, a few of us managed to shunt ourselves into the margins of mainstream society—as beauticians, waitresses, and secretaries. But we reportedly did that in order to support our makeup habit. We had, it seemed, inherited the fifty-year-old stereotype of womanhood. Was this to be my future?

I began to scour the Internet for examples of transsexual women who had carved out successful careers in my areas of interest—in business, technology, science, and academia.

Most of the profiles that popped up in my early searches conformed to stereotype. I found many examples of women in entertainment with erotic pictures and exotic life stories to share. That was fine for them, I thought, but not very relevant to my life.

I quickly learned that my search results had more to do with the limitations of search engine algorithms and with the fact that most trans women with families and conventional jobs prefer to guard their privacy—as do most people. The few who were willing to acknowledge their transsexual status, preferred to be known for their technical accomplishments. As one of them explained to me, "Tina, I transitioned so that I could finally put my gender behind me. I want to be known for what I contribute to society, not for what I do or don't have between my legs."

But as I continued my search, I found one example after another of transsexual success stories. The first thing that struck me was the breadth of careers represented. There were, of course, singers, dancers, models, and actresses. But I also found lawyers, doctors, physicists, university professors, accountants, police officers, pilots, and journalists. I unearthed elementary school teachers, surgeons, therapists, ministers, truck drivers, and real estate agents. And I found lots and lots of business executives, consultants, marketers, information architects, software programmers, and project managers.

To be sure, all of these people reported having to contend with a great deal of prejudice and discrimination. But if I was willing and able, I realized, I could aspire to be just about anything.

The second thing that struck me was the extraordinary level of accomplishment achieved by many transsexual women. At the time, Margaret Stumpp was in her eighteenth year as the Chief Investment Officer for Prudential Financial's $80 billion investment management subsidiary. Megan Wallent was leading a division at Microsoft. She had earlier reported directly to Bill Gates while she oversaw two releases of Microsoft Windows. She was still living with her wife and their three children[10].

Lynn Conway, a former executive at Xerox, Memorex, and IBM, had been a key architect of the Department of Defense's Strategic Computing Initiative. She had also been elected to the Electronic Design Hall of Fame. Amanda Simpson, previously the Deputy Director of Advanced Missiles and Unmanned Systems at Ratheon was now a presidential appointee in Washington.

I also found impressive leaders in science, medicine, and academia. Dr. Rebecca Allison was serving as the Chief of Cardiology at CIGNA. Joan Roughgarden, a recently retired evolutionary biologist, had taught at Stanford University for almost 30 years. Rachel Padman, an astrophysicist, was a lecturer at Cambridge University. Deirdre McCloskey, a globally recognized thinker in my own field of economics, had just won an award from the Competitive Enterprise Institute for her studies of human prosperity.

---

[10] Megan recently re-transitioned back to Michael. She explained that she did so only because she learned that she has a genetic condition that makes it very risky to take estrogen. She said that she had no gender regrets and that she was simply bowing to the logic of science. She still considers herself to be a part of the transgender community.

These examples transformed my outlook. Yes, my future was going to be a difficult one. But it didn't have to be bleak. In fact, it might prove to be pretty interesting. Who, in their right mind, I thought, wouldn't want to hang out with women like these?

ॐ

MARY HAD WITNESSED my struggles and understood that this wasn't a matter of choice. She knew how desperately I had tried to avoid this next step. She loved me and stood by me. Nonetheless, during the first year of my transition, she wept almost daily. She was losing the man she had cherished above all others; she was disconsolate.

I tried to be there for her. I tried to comfort her. But she only pulled away. I didn't know what to do. And then one day, she finally made me understand.

She was having another crying fit. "You don't understand!" she wailed. "I lost my last husband to another woman. It was so painful— so demoralizing! And now I am losing the love of my life." She sucked back several sobs and tried to catch her breath.

"And, once again, I am losing him to another woman. But … but this time it's worse: The bitch wants me to be her best friend!"

She collapsed into another string of sobs.

Wow.

I finally understood what several friends had tried to explain to me: I, of all people, could not fix this. All I could do was to give Mary and those around me the time and space to pick up the pieces and reorder their lives. I needed to honor their grief and to respect their decisions. I could continue to care for them if they would have it. But I was no longer the family problem-solver.

One of the more frequent questions people ask me is what it felt like for me to lose my manhood—by which they mean my male anatomy. Losing my anatomy was never an issue for me. Losing my identity as family problem-solver was devastating.

THE THOUGHT OF LOSING MARY was another source of distress. Mary and I had never doubted each other's constancy. But nor did we take it for granted that we would stay married in light of all the changes I was going through. I couldn't imagine my life without Mary in it: she was my soulmate. Every day, she stood up for and defended this bitch who had taken her husband from her. How often in life do you find someone with such character and fortitude?

But I was changing with each passing day. Who would I be and how would I feel five years from now? Did we belong together? Was it selfish for me to want to hold on to her?

I thought back to a movie I had seen in high school, *A Touch of Class*. George Segal played a married insurance executive who was going through a mid-life crisis. Glenda Jackson played his clandestine lover. The two had agreed to have a romantic, no-strings-attached fling. But then they fell in love. As the relationship developed, George struggled with what to do:

> *I went to a shrink five times a week to hear the same questions.*
>
> *"Do you love your wife and kids?"—Of course I love them!*
>
> *"Would you give them up for the girl?"—Hell, no.*
>
> *"Would you give the girl up for them?"—I can't. I love her.*
>
> *Thousands of dollars later, he [the shrink] came to the key question: "Do you love her enough to give her up?"—That's the one that pinned me to the rack.*

I, too, felt pinned to the rack. Did I love Mary enough to let her go? She was so fiercely loyal; would I have to push her away for her own good, as George had done to Glenda? With my future such a question mark, would Mary be wiser to cash out now? Many of our friends certainly thought so. Mary shared some of their tidbits of advice:

> *You should divorce his ass! Get out now, while he still has money. ...*
> *You don't owe that selfish bastard a damn thing. ... Mark my words: he*
> *has a five-year plan worked out. And you're not in it.*

Mary didn't just have to worry about her relationship with me. My transition threatened to damage her reputation and to unsettle her relationships with everyone else in her life.

Was our marriage now a liability to her? Would her coworkers label her a lesbian?[11] Would her friends look down on her as someone too desperate to fend for herself? Would she be ostracized for being too different? By supporting me, Mary risked moving from the height of respectability to becoming an object of pity and derision.

And then there were the "simpler" issues. If we split up, what would happen to her relationships with the rest of my family? If we stayed together, how would her friendships have to change? Would I expect to be added to her circle of girlfriends? Would they even allow that? If I started to spend more time with transgender friends, would I expect her to come along?

Even if Mary supported me in principle, did she want all of these changes in her life?

ONE MORNING, I broached the topic over scrambled eggs and coffee. "You've always wanted to return to Chicago. ... The only reason you moved out here was to let me follow the children. You can do your job from anywhere in the country. Why don't you start spending a little time in Chicago every month? It will give you the space to explore what you want for you. It will give you an opportunity to see what it might be like to return to single life. You used to love being single. Let's get you a place in Chicago."

---

[11] Mary wouldn't have cared about being labeled a lesbian had she felt that it described her. Like me, she wants to be known for who she is.

Mary shook her head. "No. I'm staying here with you while you go through this. I'm not interested in dating. And I certainly don't want to train another husband! If I move to Chicago, it will be with you."

That was that. When Mary made up her mind, it stayed made.

I TRIED TO THINK of little ways to express my appreciation and to demonstrate my commitment to our marriage. Although she hated the task, Mary had always managed our bills and taxes. I now took these on. When she commented on the poor state of our sundeck, I sanded and stained it.

She had always wanted to redecorate the children's rooms. So, one weekend, I tore out the carpets, installed floorboards, and repainted the walls. She loved the transformation.

When Mary noted that the running boards on our SUV were rusting through, I bought new ones and installed them. Mary had been raised in a family of autoworkers, whereas I had rarely tinkered with anything bigger than an oil filter. But I was determined that no one was going to call me a Barbie want-to-be. I was proud of the grease and dirt that had collected under my coral fingernails.

MARY APPRECIATED my efforts. But still she struggled. Her carefree laughter of old had become a stranger in our house. We continued to spend most of our free time in each other's company, but it was different now. She was having a difficult time with all of the change in her life.

One day, for example, we went shopping for clothing at Kohl's. Mary had never liked to shop. When she buys clothes, Mary knows what she wants even before she leaves the house. She makes a beeline to the appropriate rack, scans the labels for her size, and marches her quarry to the cash register. Mission accomplished.

I, however, was still learning about clothing. Early on, I had made the mistake of buying clothes online. If they looked pretty on the models, I reasoned, they would look good on me. I quickly learned that this was not a good way to shop for women's clothes. I found, for example, that, while dainty blouses with peter pan collars and cap sleeves might look good on women with small frames, they looked hideous on me. They accentuated my broad shoulders and masculine forearms. My body shape looked better in deep V-necks and asymmetrical half-sleeves.

I converted the department store fitting room into my study hall. There, I learned how to better present myself using techniques like color-blocking, A-line silhouettes, and diagonal ruching. Though I purchased relatively few items, I tried a lot of things on.

It wasn't that I was obsessed with feeling feminine. Dressing had long since ceased to be a source of novelty. Rather, I had come to learn that I would be judged by my appearance, especially by other women. I wanted to feel confident that I could present myself well. I wanted to look sharp.

So there we were at Kohl's on a busy Sunday afternoon. As usual, Mary had dispatched her own shopping list in a matter of minutes— crew socks and a pair of white, summer shorts. Meanwhile, I had disappeared into the fitting rooms to examine half a dozen new dresses. Bored, Mary seated herself in the waiting area. On either side of her, sullen husbands passed the time playing video games and checking email on their iPhones. Mary pulled out her own iPhone and dialed her daughter.

"Gee, Mom," Lindy teased, "when you married Tom, did you ever imagine that you would be sitting in the waiting area with all the other husbands, while he tried on dresses?"

WITH TIME, Mary and I began to establish routines that worked for us both. Since she hated to shop, I switched from buying clothes for me to becoming her personal shopper. I got to continue my education and she was relieved of a major headache.

One day, we went to the mall to buy her a pair of shoes. During the drive, she explained what she was looking for. "I just want a black ankle boot to replace my old ones. I want a slight heel—but they can't pinch my toes."

As soon as we entered the store, I helped her to locate a pair of shoes that matched her criteria. Then, while she was trying them on, I scoured the aisles for other prospects. Would she like a pair with elastic gores for comfort? What about a wedge instead of a heel? Did she prefer something plain? Would she consider something with harness straps? What about brown instead of black? What outfits was she planning to wear?

In minutes, I returned, my arms loaded with plunder. She tried on each selection, letting me know what she liked and didn't like.

If I sensed that Mary had any energy left, I encouraged her to try something new. At first, she resisted my entreaties. But with time, she grew to trust my judgment. Today, she boasts that she practically lives in a pair of herringbone ballet flats that I had first pressed her to try on.

Then, too, there were times when Mary turned the tables on me. Her favorite shopping trip was almost certainly our visit to the mall to have my ears pierced. For half an hour, I had to stand in line behind three nine-year-old girls. All the while, Mary stood by my side, sharing our rite of passage with the girls' mothers. "Yes, this is Tina's first time, too. She is so excited. ... Aren't you Honey?"

SO IT WAS that we gradually renegotiated our daily routine. We adapted our behaviors and expectations a little at a time. The only constant was our commitment to communication. What was she worried about? What could I do to help? What was I struggling with?

I marked our turning point around another of Mary's crying episodes. "Sometimes I think that this is God's way of punishing me for my two earlier divorces," she wailed.

"Did you ever consider that you might have it backwards? You've put up with three husbands. Maybe God decided that it was time to give you a wife."

This time, she laughed. She let go with a deep, joyful guffaw.

It didn't occur to me then, but I was gradually negotiating my way back into being the family problem-solver.

DURING THAT FIRST YEAR, the one thing that made me more anxious than my relationship with Mary was my relationship with my children. I had recently watched a video, *Trans*, which included an interview with a transsexual woman a year after her sex-reassignment surgery. All she could talk about was her kids (who, like mine, were in their 20s). They had pretty much stopped talking to her. ...

> *I miss my kids. I never realized that it would end up like this. I thought it would be tough, but I thought that they would keep talking to me and that we could work through it. ... It hurts most at night. I just wish I could reach out and fix it. I've always fixed everything. ... I can't fix this.*

In my case, it appeared that bringing my children along was going to be the easiest part of my transition. When they learned of my plans, each of my children found a way to express their love and support. Shortly after I informed her, Haley sent me the following email:

> *Dear Dad,*
>
> *I love you too. The other day I was reflecting on how, my whole life, I could sense there was something else going on inside your head because you would throw yourself into work, pick-up a new hobby, or just have very pensive days. If it counts for anything, learning more about what you are dealing with has helped me understand that, in those moments, you were trying to shield us from more complexity, which was a tremendous act of love. I think it is amazing and beautiful that you are trying so hard to take care of all of us as you grapple with such great challenges. I don't know if I've ever felt more loved in my life. Whenever you're having a low moment, please remember that, no matter who you are, you succeeded as a parent at making me feel very loved.*

I thought to myself: this transition is the most wonderful thing I've ever done. I don't know why I doubted that I would be loved. As I had done years before with Haley and Cam's drawings, I carried a printout of Haley's email with me wherever I went.

I WORRIED ABOUT MARY'S CHILDREN as well, especially her daughter, Lindy. When Mary and I telephoned her to break the news, I was prepared for the worst. Lindy and her family were devout Christians who interpreted the Bible literally. Lindy generally dressed according to the dictates of the Bible, rarely wearing pants. She and her husband, Jeff, forbade their children to read *Harry Potter* because it contained sorcery.

A few years before, Mary and I had attended a service at Lindy's church. The minister delivered an impassioned sermon that day, *Fifty Reasons I Hate Stinking Liberals*. He bellowed out reason number thirteen: "Rush Limbaugh is a stinking liberal!" Reason number twenty-two faulted liberals for trying to save the ozone layer.

Given their conservative religious convictions, I worried that Lindy and her family might disavow any relationship with me. I worried, too, that they might disown Mary for standing by me. I could ask a lot of things of Mary. Giving up her children wasn't on that list.

Neither of us had ever shared anything about my gender issues with Lindy and Jeff. How were we going to tell them? We called Lindy one night and said that we needed to talk. "I'm listening!" she smiled.

We hemmed and hawed our way through my story. I explained my history. Mary described our struggles. I announced my plans. When we had finished, Lindy didn't skip a beat: "You two do whatever you have to do. We love you no matter who you are. We mean that."

She went on to apologize if her earlier interpretations of Christianity had made her seem unapproachable and judgmental. She didn't say that she approved of or understood what I was doing. But she felt that God's command to love trumped everything else. It wasn't for her to judge me. She ended the call with the usual, "I love you", and her reminder that we were in her prayers.

I felt humbled. Here I had been so worried about Lindy's judgment of me. Apparently, it was I who had been guilty of judging her. I was finally showing the courage to live my truth, I thought, and this was God's way of letting me know that everything was going to be OK.

That spring, I also decided to come out to our closest friends in Chatham. I was terrified. Most of them were political conservatives. Their jokes at our cocktail parties tended to come at the expense of Democrats, minorities, and welfare programs. Still, I knew them to be people with a generosity of spirit. We had been friends for over a decade.

More important, I reasoned that I owed it to Mary to talk to them. She had become so isolated by my need for secrecy and needed some people that she could turn to for support. The problem was that she didn't know how to broach the topic with our friends. I decided that the responsibility for breaking the ice lay with me.

I was also concerned that most of these friends had young children. I felt that I owed it to the parents to give them a chance to absorb my news and to consider how they wanted to handle it within their families.

One night, I tested the waters with my closest friend over a pair of porterhouse steaks and a bottle of cabernet. I don't recall the details of the evening. Too many thoughts and emotions were swirling around in my head. I only remember that he was wonderful with his love. Yes, he was shocked. He didn't know what to say or do. But he let me know that he was there for me.

A few weeks later, I decided that it was time to face the music with our other close friends. All four of the families in question lived on the road that circles the top of our hill. Proceeding in a clockwise direction, I called on the three remaining couples. I figured that news of my transition would travel quickly in our tightly knit group. I was hoping to catch all of them on the same day so that they could hear the news directly from me.

Walking into someone else's home and announcing that you are in the process of becoming a woman is terrifying. What the hell was I expecting them to think, say, or do? I rang each doorbell. "Are both of you home? Can I talk to the two of you ... alone?"

With that, I sat them down and trusted whatever came from my heart.

Not surprisingly, they greeted the news with shock. This was probably the last thing they had expected to hear from me. But their responses were affirming. One neighbor said, "All that I've known of you, Tom, is your constant care for the comfort of everyone else in our community. How can you expect any less in return?" Everyone I visited made it clear that they loved Mary and me and would be there to support us.

HERE I HAD BEEN ASSUMING that no one would love the real me. And yet everyone I had spoken to had expressed their unconditional support. If they could love me, perhaps it was time that I did the same. In May, I sent an update to my family:

Dear Family,

I know that all of you have been so worried about me. Thank you for your love. Since I have decided to accept myself, life has been a joy that I have never known before. ... I still don't know who or what I am. But I am content with that admission. And I am happy for the first time in my life.

Perhaps the Velveteen Rabbit had it wrong. It isn't others loving your bumps and scratches that makes you real; it is when you can fully embrace those bumps and scratches yourself. Other people loving you is a wonderful gift. But it is an empty gift if you don't love yourself.

Love to you all,

T

ॐ

IN JULY, Evelyne asked if she could finally meet Tina face-to-face. We planned a night out together in New York City and agreed that she should bring her friend, Peter, just in case she needed a buffer. The three of us met on the corner of 5th Avenue and 14th Street. Evelyne was a little nervous at first, but gradually relaxed. Having Peter with us proved a smart thing to do. As appetizers were served, he and I did most of the talking. This gave Evelyne a chance to catch her breath and to take it all in.

Dining with Evelyne

Two hours later, we said our goodnights. Evelyne and I headed to Penn Station to catch a train home. It was late and she was tired. A few minutes out of the station, she fell asleep, cradled in my arms, her head resting on my breast. This is so wonderful, I thought. I finally get to hold one of my children as I had always imagined it. Though my arm had fallen asleep, I didn't move. I wanted this moment to last forever.

But a couple of days later, everything changed. Evelyne and I were talking on the phone when she began to sob. "I'm sorry. ... I just can't do this!" she choked. "I've got to go." She hung up.

I felt shaken. My daughter found the mere thought of me so mortifying that she could not even complete a conversation. I wrote to Mary, "I am so depressed: when my children see me, they look away in horror. I feel like the elephant man - hideous to some and a curiosity to everyone else."

That weekend, Evelyne sent me an email:

I didn't expect my reaction the other night - it honestly came out of nowhere. All of a sudden, I burst into tears and couldn't breathe. ... I am just ... devastated. ... The devastation hasn't come until very recently, when it started to sink in that my dad is gone. ... On top of all this, I'm just plain mad. I didn't have my dad growing up, then I got him, and he became everything I wanted and then some. Now he's gone again. That is a very deep wound. ...

Then there is the fact that we just aren't compatible. ... Tina doesn't want to talk about the same things I've spent years talking [to Tom] about. Tina is not the stable rock I've been so grateful to have in my life. Tina is so completely consumed by her own transformation (understandably). ... I feel like I'm spending time with my sister a few years back, not with my dad.

It's not that I need our conversations to be focused on me. ... I don't need to talk about my job, my life, boyfriends, etc. I just want to talk to Tom. Being Tom makes you sad and depressed. Meanwhile, talking to Tina ... makes me sad and depressed. I am happy for you. ... But for the time being ... I need some space to mourn and move on.

Ouch.

THIS PROVED to be the start of a general trend. At about the same time as the incident with Evelyne, Cameron invited Mary and me to have breakfast with him in Princeton. He said that it was OK for me to come as Tina. As Evelyne had done, he brought along a friend to serve as a buffer.

Mary and I had a wonderful time getting to know his roommate, Joe. But Cameron, usually so relaxed and glib, was on edge during the entire meal. When breakfast was over, we walked the two boys toward campus. As we parted, Mary hauled Cam in for her usual bear hug. He extended a tentative wave in my direction and turned towards the safety of his ivory towers.

After that, all three of my children became noticeable by their absence. We rarely spoke or corresponded. We never got together. And who could blame them? Evelyne had been right: they didn't just have to deal with the death of someone. They had to contend with a walking reminder of the father they had lost. Was I about to suffer the fate of that poor woman on *Trans*? She was right, I thought, I can't fix this.

FOR THOSE OF US TRANSITIONING, the event marks the start of something wonderful. All my life, I had navigated the world, walled off from humanity. I had been screaming as one buried alive. But no one could hear me. Now I was free. I could breathe. "I'm here!" I cried. "I'm here!"

But to our loved ones, we are as the walking dead. They have lost something that was precious. Someone who was once a rock of stability in their lives is now but a shadow.

Every memory and plan that these loved ones had anchored to that rock has suddenly been cut adrift. Perhaps they had looked forward to introducing future boyfriends and girlfriends to their cool dad. Perhaps they had fantasized about the day when their father would walk them down the aisle. When times were tough, they had known of a certainty that there was one safe harbor that they could count on for shelter—Dad.

We who transition have found sunshine. Now it is our loved ones who are lost in shadow. When thrust into darkness, the human impulse is to run to daylight. Escape the darkness. Run! Run! Run!

It is a healthy instinct. But for the recently out transsexual, it feels dreadful. For the first time in my life, I felt capable of giving and receiving love with nothing to filter me. It was right there in front of me! And yet, those who I most desperately wanted to hold close to me had turned away—how far and for how long I couldn't be sure. Now it was they who had vanished into shadow.

Mary wrote to reassure me. ...

Sweetheart,

I know that this is difficult for you. It is difficult for all of us. You have to be who you are. ... Know that I will always be there for you. You are my best friend and we will get through this together. I think the kids just need some distance from Tina right now. ... You can be whoever you need to be with me and I won't look away.

THINGS WENT NO BETTER on Mary's side of the family. Her sister, Leslie, had always been sympathetic and supportive of me. She had, in fact, been visiting our home during the depths of my depression and knew what I had been struggling with. But listening to Mary cry each day had begun to wear on her. That summer, when we visited her home in South Carolina, Leslie told Mary that she thought I was being selfish. Didn't I understand the pain I was creating for my family?

I said nothing. Instead, I vented my anger in my journal,

> ... *It is they who are being selfish. Everyone wants me to conform to their norms for their comfort. I am finally giving myself life. No—selfish is expecting me to suck it up and eat away at my soul just for everyone else's comfort.*

Later that month, Mary and I visited Lindy and her family in Michigan. It was the first time that they were meeting Tina face-to-face. They were loving and polite, but reserved. To my distress, they insisted on addressing me as Grandpa. I think that they thought this the right thing to do for my soul. They were genuinely worried for my sanity. Perhaps if they re-grounded me in my true nature, it would bring me back. I just needed someone to hold a mirror in front of me.

I tried to endure it. I knew that they intended it as a loving act. Give them time, I thought. Be patient. They will eventually see that I am not crazy.

But every time one of my grandchildren called me Grandpa, I writhed in pain. I felt humiliated and enraged. I wanted to scream. I wanted to run away. Instead, I quietly sulked. I spent most of my time reading alone in my bedroom or taking long walks in the forest.

One morning, we went to watch my granddaughter, Rosie, ride horses at a nearby stable. One of the boys beckoned to me, "Hey, Grandpa Tom, come over here!"

Now I wasn't just angry and hurt, I was frightened. We were in the Bible belt of rural Michigan. And here was my family, calling me out in front of all the other riders, their parents and the stable hands.

Perhaps it was another part of their therapy, but I was having none of it. I recalled the video of the church leader with his baseball bat. I retreated to the far end of the stable, as far from everyone as I could get. It was the only place I felt safe.

That night, I cried myself to sleep. I felt so helpless and alone.

BACK IN CHATHAM, things were also taking a bad turn. It had been my strategy to give our close friends a heads-up and then to step away in order to give them the space and time to absorb my news. I had invited them to call on me any time they wanted to talk. In the meantime, I continued to present in the neighborhood as Tom. I thought that I was being respectful. I thought that I was creating a space in which Mary could establish a support network without my influence.

But my strategy did not work out at all as I had intended. From my friends' perspective, it must have felt as though I had gently dropped a dog turd on each of their doorsteps and tiptoed away. News of my plans and Mary's despondency began to dominate their cocktail hours and barbecues. Mary's transparency, usually such an asset, began to wear on people. She let all of the tears she had bottled up for so long come flooding out. "Why don't you just divorce him?" they asked.

I was never present for these conversations. It pained me each time Mary when shared them with me. But I had been the one to set this in motion, hadn't I? I had wanted her to have her own support network. If that was the advice they had to offer, I needed to respect it. And perhaps they were right. The idea that she should divorce me had certainly occurred to me.

Over time, a vicious cycle developed. Neighborhood parties and social get-togethers had always been occasions for relaxation. Now, thanks to me, they were anything but. Yes, I had respectfully quarantined myself at home, but my shadow continued to stalk the neighborhood.

With each passing week, I felt that my friends were turning on me. I was told (through emails and the grapevine) that I was selfish, deceitful, and thoughtless. One of the few people to visit me said that they had been teased by one of my friends, "Are you going over to Tina's to play dress-up?"

Rather than do anything about it, I retreated further into my hermetic domain. I went for walks in the neighborhood only under cover of darkness. One of the reasons for my total retreat was a paranoia that I might be outed at work. All it would take was one mention of me at a party or in an email that connected to someone in Pfizer. That would have put my career, my family, and my future in even greater jeopardy. My number one priority had to be to keep anything from escalating.

Meanwhile, none of my friends came to visit. Apparently, as far as they were concerned, this problem was of my making. It was mine to fix. I drafted a letter of apology and asked one of my friends to review it. They promised to do so but never responded. After that, I gave up. Mary and I had a lot on our plates. I decided that I needed to focus my energy on my wife, my children, and my career. Friendships would just have to wait.

At LEAST, I consoled myself, I have my trans community to fall back on. They understand me. I was so excited, therefore, when I was invited to speak at a Trans 101 workshop at Columbia University. Though I was not yet out at work, I wasn't worried. I was going to present to the students under my alias, *Tina*.

I showed up for the workshop, proud of my womanhood. I arrived in a blue dress, a red car coat, and a pair of black pumps. I had carefully prepared myself to bare my soul and to defend my gender. I had been labelled a *he*. I was now most emphatically a *she*—a *transsexual she*.

I could not have dressed nor prepared my notes more inappropriately. The students were polite, but they clearly considered me an oddity. It wasn't that I was transgender. Quite the opposite: It was that I was so conventional. As they put it, I was too *binary*.

Where my generation of transgender people seemed to worry over the distinction between *transvestite* and *transsexual*, these kids questioned the concept of gender altogether. They wanted to do away with binary pronouns like *he* and *she*. "I prefer to be referred to as *ze*," one of them explained to me.

They didn't care what my gender was. To their way of thinking, by declaring myself a woman, I was promoting an outmoded concept. Why should my gender matter? As far as these students were concerned, I was as much a part of the problem as was the rest of my generation.

Most of the attendees described themselves as genderqueer. As I looked at their disheveled clothing and compared it to mine, I confess that the older generation in me was thinking, "Ha! More like gender grunge!"

Their clothing aside, it was refreshing to see their energy and earnest search for truth as they saw it. I left wondering if I could ever adapt to their ideas. But isn't that what I was asking everyone else to do for me? If I wanted others to be open to my experience of gender, didn't I need to be open to this one?

It was a nice learning moment—but a poorly timed one. I was feeling fragile and alone. I had gone to the seminar hoping, in part, to hear a few of my comrades applaud my bravery and to wish me Godspeed. But once again, I found myself on the outside looking in. Except for Mary, I felt alone in the world.

AFTER SEVERAL MONTHS living as Tina, I began to feel confident in my ability to navigate public spaces. Whether I passed or not, I was now comfortable asking directions, making purchases and eating in restaurants. I was at ease dealing with salespeople, waiters and waitresses, tradesmen, and cashiers. Through these interactions, I had learned a valuable lesson: my

In Line for Jimmy Buffet

attitude mattered a lot more than my ability to pass. If I projected confidence and warmth, most people responded in kind. If I was hesitant and shy, they were likely to look upon me with suspicion.

But I had yet to venture beyond midtown Manhattan and my carefully choreographed errands near home. Would I survive in the wider world? How would Mary handle it? In the summer of 2012, we decided to find out.

Mary and I were long-time Jimmy Buffet fans. We had collected his albums all the way back to *Down to Earth* and had attended several of his concerts. In August, we bought tickets to his show in Atlantic City. This was a big step. We would be in close quarters with thousands of people. But if there was any crowd I felt safe in, it was an arena full of Jimmy Buffet Parrotheads. Their brand of rowdiness was one of fun-loving celebration.

On the day we arrived, Mary and I wandered the casinos, the Boardwalk, and beaches. At first, we kept a constant watch on the people around us. Were they pointing or staring at me? Were they making remarks? I always kept my eyes trained in front of me ("never let them see your fear"), but Mary occasionally spun around to check on the people behind. We need not have worried. But for a few glances, everyone was too absorbed in their own diversions. After an hour, we relaxed our vigil.

By concert time, I was revved up. I loved Jimmy Buffet. I loved even more the thought that the real me was about to experience him. What would it feel like? As Tom, I had always turned to his music when I wanted to feel happy, spontaneous, and exuberant. Tina was good at spontaneity on her own. How would the music affect her?

As we stood in line, Mary snapped a picture of me on my iPhone. We looked at it. "I have never seen you so happy," she said. She was right: I was positively incandescent.

Mary and I wandered to our section of seating and grabbed a couple of chairs. Everyone around us was giddy. I forgot about my gender.

We weren't men and women, boys and girls. We were ten thousand party-happy Parrotheads and the party was about to begin.

Most of the people around us were young, heterosexual couples. But, shortly after we arrived, a group of women filed into the row behind us. When they started to give us high-fives, we caught on: they understood us to be fellow lesbians. I was tickled to be included in their celebration, but I looked over at Mary. She had said that she did not want people to mistake her for a lesbian. Would she tense up? No, she, too, was a Parrothead tonight. We sang and danced our hearts out.

THE DAY FOLLOWING the concert, we went for a walk along the beach. To our left, a small parade had begun to form. We approached. It was the Annual Atlantic County Puerto Rican Parade. Mary and I gathered with the other spectators in front of a bandstand at the end of the parade route. Mary nudged me and pointed to my right. "You should talk to her!"

I looked. A foot away from me, another trans-woman was watching the parade with a friend of hers. I grimaced. She was in her early twenties. She was wearing black leather fetish wear and sported piercings everywhere on her face. Where she wasn't sheathed in leather, she was coated with tattoos.

I didn't mind any of this. To each their own. What I minded was Mary's notion that, just because the two of us were transgender women, we ought to be talking with each other. I was pretty sure that we didn't have much in common beyond our struggles with gender. Under other circumstances, I would have been happy to talk to her. But I was annoyed: Why does everyone seem to assume that our gender is all that defines us?

"No!" I hissed to Mary.

❧

IN SEPTEMBER, Evelyne's younger sister, Angela, contacted me. "Tina, would it be possible to use your house in early October for Mom's fiftieth birthday party?" They were planning to invite about fifty guests and were organizing the evening around a private performance by Christine's favorite folk singer, Patrick Fitzsimmons. Our home, she said, offered an ideal layout.

"Of course!" I replied. "Bring them on! You just need to understand that they will be visiting the home of Tina and Mary, not Tom and Mary."

"We wouldn't have it any other way," Angela replied.

At the time that I agreed to throw the party, my main thought was that, in addition to being a nice gesture to Christine, it was the perfect chance for me to see what it was like to play hostess to a crowd of strangers. Nobody attending would know me or travel in my professional circles, so I wouldn't have to worry about repercussions at work. I assumed that everyone attending would know that I was trans. Christine wasn't the sort to hold back details.

On the day of the party, Christine and Mikel arrived to help us set up. As they organized the kitchen, they talked about the people who were coming that night. As I listened to the names, it dawned on me: at least half of these people weren't strangers. I had met them before as Tom. In fact, Mary and I had been guests in one of their homes.

"What did they say when you told them about me?" I asked Christine.

"I didn't tell anyone anything." she responded absently. She was busy arranging flowers on the kitchen table. "Why should it matter? You are you. What business is it of theirs?"

"But ... but ..." I was speechless. She had a point. Why did I have to apologize for or explain myself? It was my house. They were my guests. Still, I worried that things might get awkward.

Earlier in the day, I had debated whether to wear a dress or slacks and a blouse. At the last minute, I went with the dress, a simple black sheath with white piping. As the guests started to arrive, I stationed myself near the door in order to greet them and take their coats.

Among the first to arrive was Christine's cousin, John, and his wife, Karen. It had been they who had hosted Mary and me in their home a few years before. John was a big, friendly bear of a man. As I opened the door, he stepped in and extended a handshake. "Tom! How the … What the …? What is this? … Is Halloween early this year?"

He let out his friendly roar and prepared to join me in my strange idea of a joke. Christine stepped in. "She's not dressed for Halloween, John. Didn't you see the invitation? This is Tina and Mary's house. Tom is Tina."

"You're kidding … right? This is a joke … right?"

John looked back and forth, first to me, then to Christine, then back to me. He waited for one of us to crack a smile and let him in on our merry little prank. It finally dawned on him that Christine was serious. His pale complexion took on a beet-red glow.

John wasn't registering any sort of transphobia. He was just embarrassed and hurt. "Why didn't someone tell me ahead of time? I just made a complete fool of myself." He smacked his forehead. "I can't believe I said those things. … But … But … how was I to know?"

"I know, John," I responded. "I'm really sorry. Don't feel bad. It's pretty funny when you get down to it. Can I get you a beer?"

OTHER GUESTS started to file in. I greeted each of them, introduced myself, and took their coats. They passed me with a mixture of puzzlement and discomfort. Apparently, no one had forewarned them about their new hostess. No one said anything unpleasant, but as I circulated through the house, I felt as though a ten-foot buffer zone circulated with me.

Don't push it, I said to myself. Everyone needs time. Give them a chance to take it all in. Just be your confident self. I made myself busy refilling drinks, pushing hors d'oeuvres, and cleaning up empty dishes. After a while, I went upstairs for a breather. I'll give them a little time without me, I thought. While I was there, I decided to change from my dress to my slacks and blouse.

As I returned to the party, one of the women approached me. "That was a smart thing to do," she said nodding at my outfit. "You look so much more approachable in those slacks. That dress was kind of intimidating. Now you are part of the party."

I had known that women are more thoughtful about their clothing. But I hadn't appreciated that dress could so influence social dynamics.

Whether it was the change in clothes or the passage of time, the rest of the evening went smoothly. Gradually, the women drew me into their conversations. We talked about the birthday gifts, family politics, vacation plans, and spouses. Having spent so many years among the husbands, I knew what the men were thinking: "look at them in there, clucking away like nobody's business."

Well, I mused, I am finally a part of the hen house. And I love it!

HALFWAY THROUGH THE EVENING, my reverie was interrupted. One of the guests was describing a piece of jewelry her husband had given her. "He usually has such good taste—but I don't think he did such a good job this time. ... What do you think, Tina?"

She thrust her arm into the middle of our circle. I panicked. Oh, my God, what's the right answer? Do I go with, "No, it's gorgeous!" or, "Oh God, you're right. He really screwed up!"?

The women waited for my response. I bit my lip. "I'm sorry, girls, I'm new to this. What's the right answer?"

Everyone laughed. My inquisitor winked, "I'm such a bitch, aren't I, Tina?"

We huddled closer and continued our conversation. Apparently, I was still part of the brood.

A little while later, my friend with the jewelry pulled me aside. She gestured toward me and smiled, "You know, Tina, I'm a conservative, blue-collar Republican. I don't normally approve of this sort of thing, but I've got to admit, I really admire the way you are going about all of this. You're alright!"

It struck me as an odd political characterization, but for the rest of the night I walked on air.

❧

NEAR THE END OF OCTOBER, Mary and I visited Evelyne in Brussels and made a side-trip to Venice. I flew as Tom but otherwise traveled as Tina. Venice was beautiful. But it was a difficult experience. Everywhere we went, I seemed to draw as much attention from passersby as did the buildings and canals. The young men—those who took our tickets at museums and who waited on us in sidewalk cafés—seemed to find my presence particularly offensive. As they took my money, they looked me in the eye, "Thank

In the Piazza di San Marco

you, *Sir.*" They delivered the "Sir" with an unmistakable note of contempt. "You're not fooling me," they seemed to be saying[12].

One waiter took his contempt a step further. Mary and I had been enjoying a glass of wine on the embankment along the Grand Canal. "We don't accept credit cards, *Sir.* You will have to pay in cash."

I ignored his jab and wandered off to find an ATM. When I returned fifteen minutes later, I found Mary in a state of agitation. "You won't believe what that jerk said!" she blurted. She pointed across the embankment towards the waiter.

"What?"

"He asked me why I was wasting my time with you. He told me to come back to his place tonight and he would show me what a real man

---

[12] Only recently did Mary confess to me: "I hated it whenever you asked me how you looked in an outfit. You looked horrible! But what could I say?"

is like. How can people be so low? I'm married, for God's sake! ... Let's get out of here!"

I paid the check without a tip.

This seemed to be a recurring theme. The world considered me objectionable. But who was behaving badly? Who was mistreating women?

During our stay in Venice, my favorite spot to relax was the piazza outside St. Mark's Basilica. At the end opposite the church, the city had erected a massive silk-screen photograph of transgender super model, Andreja Pejić. At the time, Andreja was all the rage in Europe. At moments when I was feeling especially low, I parked myself on the bench across from her and quietly took her in. Together, she and I owned the piazza. We knew what those waiters could do with themselves.

BRUSSELS PROVIDED much-needed relief. I don't understand why, but no one seemed to notice me there. I rode the trams and buses, shopped the malls, and enjoyed the sidewalk cafés without incident. I don't recall anyone staring at me.

On Friday night, Evelyne took me to an Irish pub in her neighborhood. As we entered, my spirits withered. Televisions lined every wall—each one tuned to rugby, soccer, or Australian rules football. The bar was packed with hulking men who alternately nursed their pints and cheered their teams on. This is not going to end well, I thought.

As it turned out, Evelyne and I had a wonderful time. Everyone in the pub quickly figured out that I was trans. But they didn't care. In fact, they delighted in my presence—especially when they learned that I was there with my daughter. "Wicked cool!" We struck up one conversation after another and ended up staying until the pub closed at 4 am.

In Venice, I learned to look past others' prejudices. In Brussels, I learned to look past my own.

BUT OUR OCTOBER wasn't over yet. Shortly after returning to New Jersey, Mary and I boarded a flight to Chicago. We wanted to see our old gang again. We had already exchanged heartfelt emails with them regarding my transition, so I wasn't nervous. In fact, I was looking forward to seeing everyone.

On our first night in the city, several of us met up at a bar on North Clark Street. We were a few blocks away from the pub where, fifteen years before, they had given me their unanimous thumbs up. "You know," I teased them, "this is all your fault. You were the ones who approved me."

"And we still do!" they cheered.

OUR LAST TRIAL RUN came in January. Mary and I were to travel together to the Grand Canyon. For the first time, I planned to fly as Tina. Since my job involved occasional air travel, I reasoned that I needed to be certain that I could handle it.

As I approached the security checkpoint at Newark Airport, I pulled out my driver's license, my boarding pass, and a letter from my therapist. The letter explained that I was under a doctor's care and that I was following medical advice. Although I was now presenting as a woman, my license continued to present me as a man.

I handed my boarding pass and license to the agent. He looked down at the license. ... He looked up at me. ... He looked down at the license again. Just as I was getting ready to pull out my medical authorization, he stamped my boarding pass and waved me on. "Thank you. Have a nice flight. ... Next!"

Phoenix didn't go as smoothly. I had to pass through security again. Although I made it through the scanner, the agents said that something in my luggage had set their equipment off. They escorted me to a side station for a detailed luggage inspection and a pat-down. I wasn't too worried: the agent patting me down was a middle-aged woman who seemed, if anything, to find this boring. I was pretty confident that she wasn't doing this for a thrill. I decided to stay calm.

Mary did not. I could see her standing twenty feet away, on the other side of the security zone. She was complaining to anyone who would listen, "I can't believe you all are doing this to her! It's a disgrace!"

I felt so loved and cared for at that moment. Mary was truly my guardian angel. But a part of me wished she would shut up. I didn't see anything to be gained by harassing a federal agent. A few minutes later, the inspection complete, the agent wished me a good day and waved me on. We made our connection with a minute to spare.

Twenty-five years before, Sally had braved the depths of the Grand Canyon with me. We had spent a week roughing it in a pup tent. Together, we had watched snow fall on the plateau above, even as we hiked in balmy sunshine below. A few years later, now a single father, I had taken Haley and Cam for hikes along the rim of the canyon and into the surrounding dessert. Cam scoured the countryside for deer and other "naked animals". Haley managed our maps, our food supply, and me.

On the present trip, Mary and I sipped white wine spritzers and viewed the canyon from our private balcony. We shopped nearby towns and went on guided tours. Three experiences of the canyon— three experiences of Tina White. Life, I mused, is what happens while you are making other plans.

Our travels were going well. At home, I looked forward to Christmas and New Year's. The kids would be coming home. One of the families we had been close to had invited us to their Christmas party. New Year's would bring with it a new milestone in my life: I had decided that, beginning January 1, I would no longer present as Tom with our friends. Seventh months, I felt, had been plenty of notice.

Christmas 2012

Christmas was going to be my first opportunity in a while to get some quality time with my children. I missed them desperately; I longed to feel close again. I thought back to the Christmas years before when I had introduced Ebenezer and his presents into our household. Could I come up, once more, with something inspired and creative?

I had once collected the artifacts from my years with Angela in a box. These included my boutonniere from her high school prom, her letters to me, and our tickets to the National Zoo (our first date). I had gathered them and placed them in a miniature sea chest. Once in a while, I pulled out that box to remember the experiences we had shared. I called it my Ange Box. Why not create a Tom Box for each of my children?

I went to a craft store and purchased four unfinished boxes made of birch wood. I bought a quart of dark brown stain, some glue, a foam brush, and a can of lacquer. I returned home and rooted through my collection of photographs. I found lots of photos of me with each of the kids. There we were camping, kicking soccer balls, and shooting baskets. We read books, posed at Disney World, and swam at the beach.

I cut each of these photos and glued them to the inside and outside of the boxes, forming three-dimensional collages of our lives together. I wanted my children to know that, as far as I was concerned, Tom remained a part of our family. I cherished all of our memories together.

I wanted them to know that I wasn't going to be the sort of person who announced to everyone that "Tom is dead."

I thought that this might be a place where they could store some of our memorabilia. I knew that my transition was going to be tough on them and that it might be nice for them to have this keepsake to pull out on occasion. Once again, this was me, the problem-solver, at work.

JUST AS MY MOTHER had done years before when she had given me *Our Bodies, Ourselves*, I watched expectantly as they peeled back the wrapping of their boxes. I was so certain that they would mark the gesture as another example of my creativity and thoughtfulness. This was going to be magnificent.

It wasn't. The kids recoiled in horror. What I had considered a keepsake, they apparently regarded as a coffin. They couldn't get away from those boxes fast enough. Boy, did I call this one wrong!

I have replayed that scene over and over in my mind. Some of my friends defend me, saying that it was a very thoughtful thing to do. But I'm not sure that the gift was the only issue. I was trying to solve a problem that, so far as they were concerned, had been of my own making. I was the last person my children wanted to help them to deal with their loss of Tom. As Mary had explained months before, I was now the bitch who had taken him away.

A FEW DAYS after the children left, Mary and I attended our neighbor's Christmas party. It was a sumptuous affair. Our hosts knew how to cook and entertain like nobody's business. Each room had been set up with several food stations. There were sausages, seafood, pastas, vegetable dishes, and garlic bread. The dessert stations offered pies, pastries, and sweets. This was the neighborhood's favorite feast of the year.

I wanted this evening to go perfectly. I hadn't told anyone, but it would be my last event in the neighborhood as Tom. I was so nervous that I made it a point not to drink any alcohol. I wanted to be as clear-headed as possible.

At one point in the evening, someone confided something to me and warned me not to discuss it. But I misread their facial expression. What they had intended as a serious directive, I took to be a mischievous goad—as in when someone says to you, "whatever you do, don't …"

Trying to fit in with the levity of the evening, I did exactly what they had told me not to do. I shared the comment with my very dear friend. I had expected some sort of sarcastic reply and a laugh, "Yeah, right! Screw you! Now get me a refill."

Instead, on my last night out as Tom, I hurt the last person I had wanted to—the friend who had first expressed love and support for me. I had hurt him deeply. Oh well, I thought, I guess it's as good a time as any for Tom to exit the world. He seems to be losing his touch.

WHERE FAMILY AND FRIENDS were concerned, I ended 2013 feeling about as low as was possible. To be sure, I was luckier than were many other transsexual women. Most of my family continued to support and engage with me. Several of my neighbors had sent me beautiful letters of support at the end of the year. But those I had most expected to stand by me had distanced themselves. They were hurt and annoyed. In each instance, they made it clear that my gender wasn't their issue. It was me.

Ouch.

CROSSING OVER

Sunset and evening star,
And one clear call for me!
And may there be no moaning of the bar,
When I put out to sea.

...

For though from out our bourn of Time and Place
The flood may bear me far,
I hope to see my Pilot face to face
When I have crost the bar.

— From Alfred Lord Tennyson, Crossing the Bar

EVEN AS I WAS VENTURING out into the world, I was also beginning my medical transition. In June of 2012, I started to take hormones under the guidance of an endocrinologist.

FrankensTina

Some people describe our physical transition as though it were a medical wave of the wand: Your fairy godmother enters the operating room in her white lab coat. She waves her hands and says, *Abracadabra.* Poof! You are a woman. A few weeks later, you make your television debut: "So, Ms. White, how does it feel?"

If only it were that easy.

In fact, the process has all the charm of a kitchen-remodeling project. You live for months in a half-finished shell as strangers traipse into and out of your home. They tear off the roof. They change the plumbing, knock out a wall, and rip up old flooring. All the while they are there, you dare not invite company in. Meanwhile, your carpenters, plumbers, and roofers assure you that everything is going to be "just great".

During the balance of 2012, I invited about a dozen specialists to examine the middle-aged body that was my home. Each presented me with a long list of options, decisions, and considerations. They reduced my person to so many pieces of anatomy and their procedures to a production schedule.

ONE OF THE FIRST specialists I consulted spent several minutes examining my head. She penciled a few notes, put down her clipboard and looked me in the eye. Her recitation went something like this:

"Well, Tina, your brow line protrudes a lot more than is typical for a female. I would recommend that you remove some of the bony mass on your forehead. The problem is that, in your case, I would recommend removing quite a bit. That makes it a more complicated and risky procedure. It involves cutting your skull open and sawing away some of the bone. There is a cavity behind there. If it isn't closed properly, you could end up with chronic sinus infections. Those can be serious. There are few surgeons in the world that I would recommend to perform such a procedure. I am not one of them.

"I would also recommend a scalp advancement. Look up here." She held a mirror in front of me and continued. "Most women's hairlines extend further into their face than do men's. What we do is to cut an incision in your head. We start behind your left year, follow your brow line and continue down and around behind your right ear." She traced the path with her index finger.

"Then we pull your scalp forward an inch or two and staple it back together. This will sever many of the nerve endings on top of your head. It may take a year for them to grow back. In the meantime, you may feel a constant numbness up there. That's normal. It usually disappears.

"Personally, I would also recommend narrowing your jaw. Your surgeon will stick a saw inside your mouth. He will cut away some of the thickness in each jawbone. You will almost certainly want to reshape your nose, too. It's quite masculine. You'll want to make it a little smaller and to point it up a little. Of course, if you do all of these things, your surgeon will have moved so much around, you will need to tighten the skin around your eyes. You are going to need an upper and lower eyelift.

"These are just my recommendations based on how I would think about this. But this is a very personal decision. The good news is that you won't need to have your trachea shaved. You don't appear to have a prominent Adam's apple."

I wasn't talking to my fairy godmother. I was talking to a mad scientist! And this was only the first of several procedures I was considering. Every medical transition is unique. Some people decide that they need few, if any, interventions beyond hormones. Others sign themselves up for a long series of procedures.

I was evaluating six major procedures: facial surgery, sex reassignment surgery, breast augmentation surgery, vocal surgery, hair transplants, and electrolysis. As I weighed each of these, I focused on three questions: What do I need to do in order to pass in public? What do I need to do to feel safe using the bathroom or a fitness center changing room? What do I need to do in order to see myself in the mirror? I also considered cost, coverage, and risk.

But, as I learned more about these procedures, I realized that I had left out a major factor: time. Even if I did only two or three of these, I was committing my body to a long-term renovation project. When I wasn't working, I would be spending the next few years of my life on a medical assembly line.

I would have to sequence these procedures and schedule each one months in advance. I had to space them far enough apart to allow my body to heal. Before and after each surgery, I would have to alter my diet, my exercise, and medications. I would have to undergo regular testing to control the risk of blood clots and hemorrhages.

When I finally selected a doctor to perform my facial surgery, I learned that it would involve eight hours in the operating room and eight weeks of recovery time. Bone takes a long time to heal, so I would have to wait another nine months to see the final results. Time proved to be a recurring theme with my doctors.

MANY MALE-TO-FEMALE TRANSSEXUALS, especially those who transition later in life, decide that they need to get hair transplants to fill in their receding hairline. It isn't a matter of vanity so much as a question of passing. A receding hairline is one of the most visible cues for gender and one of the most difficult to hide.

It is hard for someone who is looking you in the eyes to miss your hairline. You can tell when they have stopped listening to you: their eyes continually wander to your forehead. Cis-women complain of men who ogle their breasts. One of the banes that transsexual women face is people who continually stare at their scalp.

I visited with a couple of hair transplant specialists. The first thing I learned was that I would need to wait for about a year after my facial surgery to get a transplant. I would need to allow all of the blood vessels and nerves in my skull to heal. Then, I would have to wait another nine months after the transplant in order to see the outcome.

Immediately after my transplant, the affected area would be mottled with hundreds of bright red dots. That's not good, I thought. Each dot represented a new hole in my head, the site of a newly embedded hair follicle.

After a week, the redness would be gone. That's not bad, I thought, I can handle that. But then I learned that the newly transplanted follicles would be gone, too. A week after the procedure, my bald spots would be back, just as before. That's not good, I thought.

All of my new hairs would fall out of my head. The roots would stay, but I would have to wait three months before they produced anything. Then I would have to wait another six months for these wisps of baby hair to mature into the real thing. Both of the specialists I consulted warned me that they could not guarantee results, particularly in light of my facial surgery. The scalp's ability to support hair is heavily dependent on the local blood supply. My facial surgery might compromise that.

I LOOKED NEXT into sex reassignment surgery[13] (SRS). At least this will be less noticeable, I thought. I can get the surgery and recover behind the

---

[13] I prefer the term *Gender Confirmation Surgery* (*GCS*) but am using the more familiar term.

privacy of my clothing. I won't have to share my recovery with the rest of the world.

This turned out to be partly true. SRS does afford more privacy. But it makes up for this in other ways. For several months before the surgery, I would have to submit my most private area to the pain and indignity of repeated electrolysis. Someone would have to permanently remove all of the hairs on and around my penis with an electrified needle and tweezers. What many people misunderstand about male-to-female SRS is that the surgical team doesn't remove your penis. They turn it inside out. You don't want all of those hairs growing inside you!

But the electrolysis was nothing compared to what I would have to endure for the year following my surgery. When someone gets an ear pierced, they need to keep something inside the hole for a period of time in order to prevent it from closing. To keep my vaginal sutures from closing up, I would have to do 30-minute "stretching" exercises five times a day every day for six months and then three times a day for several months more.

Nursing mothers complain of the indignity of having to find a place to nurse their baby while at work or on errands. Like them, I would have to find a discrete way to work my medical follow-up into my daily routine—five times a day. I tried to envision what this might be like: "Excuse me, can I reserve this office for today? ... No, I'm sorry. I can't share an office with someone. ... No, I'd really prefer not to explain. It's considered patient-confidential information under HIPAA."

EACH TIME I MET with a specialist to discuss a procedure, they started our meeting with the same question: "how long have you been on hormones?" Since I had started to take hormones in the summer of 2012, the earliest I could schedule my first surgery would be the late spring of 2013. Depending on my choice of surgeries, I might have to schedule them into 2015 and beyond. And that's if I was aggressive.

Fortunately, things were going well at work. I had received a rare (at Pfizer) *exceeds expectations* performance rating. In the fall of 2012, I managed to convert my one-year employment extension into a full-time position in a new department. My first responsibility would be to manage a major software development initiative. I did a little calculating: in order to keep my project on schedule, I would have to plan my coming out for either April or November.

I could not imagine surviving another seven months living as Tina while working as Tom—especially while managing such a visible project. Living a double life was taking a toll on Mary and me. It was also unrealistic to think that I could keep my secret for that long. I would have to make April work. That meant that I would start my software project as Tom and finish it as Tina.

OF ALL THE MEDICAL INTERVENTIONS I considered, the one that worried me the most was changing my voice. I had always been uncomfortable with my body, so I didn't find the thought of changing it to be a problem. I had only to manage the pain, the medical risks, and everyone else's reaction.

My voice was a different matter. Some of my fondest memories at home were of reading to Haley and Cam and of reciting poetry with Evelyne. At work, my voice was instrumental to my job: I persuaded clients; I coached and directed colleagues; I provided advice and counsel. One of the reasons that I was effective in these roles, I felt, was that I had a voice that conveyed gentle authority. As one colleague put it, I had "a good bedside manner."

When I looked at myself in the mirror now, I saw Tina. But when I listened to myself speak, I heard Tom. If I raised my pitch, I heard Robin Williams' Mrs. Doubtfire chirruping back at me. How could I hope to keep my career if every word I spoke was so off key?

Unfortunately, forty years of testosterone poisoning had left their mark on my body. The drug had permanently enlarged my chest cavity and thickened my larynx. Female hormones would do nothing to fix this.

I had two options. The first was to undergo a risky surgical procedure. Aside from a catastrophic risk, like loss of voice, my chief concern was that the outcome was difficult to predict. I could end up with a high squeal or a smoker's rasp. I might lose the ability to project to a large audience. I would likely lose some of my vocal range.

I had spent the last fifty years in a body that felt foreign to me. That had made me miserable. I did not want to spend my remaining decades listening to the voice of a stranger. I opted for the second alternative: voice training. It takes a lot more work, but its overall impact can be more dramatic since it addresses more than pitch. The results are also easier to control. I could always consider surgery later on.

On YouTube, I found many before-and-after examples of transgender women who had successfully retrained their voices. Though some had developed voices that were too girly for my tastes, I was encouraged by their examples. That winter, I started to work with a professional voice therapist.

WE MET FOR AN HOUR each week. Christie gave me thirty minutes of daily homework. Each day, I started my exercises with shoulder rolls, lip puckers and nose scrunches. I moved on to sixty seconds of exaggerated chewing and lip trills. Once I had loosened my muscles, I practiced my scales using a variety of syllables: "hee, hee"; "hoo, hoo", "mee mee", and so on. The goal of these exercises was to warm up my voice as I gradually raised my pitch by about an octave.

But pitch is a small part of the equation. For most male-to-female transsexuals, the more important and more difficult challenge is to change the way their voice resonates. Men tend to have voices with much richer, boomier resonance. They are like a cello, women a violin. You can get a cello to play pretty high notes, but it still sounds like a cello.

The trick is to retrain your body and mind to produce sound from the front of your face instead of from the back of your throat. This creates sound from a smaller chamber.

It was a lot more difficult than I had expected. I had to breathe differently. I had to push air from my body more forcefully. I had to quiet the muscles in my throat and to activate those in my mouth. Meanwhile, I had to stretch my lips and jaw and to exaggerate each articulation. While focusing on all of these new mechanics, I had to remember what it was that I was trying to say.

I spent the bulk of my thirty minutes practicing strange combinations of words, most of them beginning with the letters *m* or *n*. These consonants are easier to focus from the front of the face and hence provide a good opportunity for practice. To keep things interesting, I converted Christie's word lists into nonsense verse. I must have sounded like a transsexual parody of Edward Lear:

> *Many merry mindless, muscular monkeys kneel 'neath nameless national monuments, madly mixing my Momma Melissa Mooch magnificent, mushy, moldy mango-magnolia muffins, measuring marmalade margarine most mysteriously, never missing Monday morning mid-day make-up meals nor nineteen-minute nickel-napkin naps near noon.*

I repeated phrases like these a dozen times.

In addition to a higher pitch and smaller resonance, there are other skills to master. Women tend to pronounce their syllables and sentences more fluidly than do men. They vary their pitch and pace more often. As a man, I had been trained to speak with a steady, reassuring tone—to be grounded. As a woman, I was having to learn to become an aerial acrobat!

Rather than raise my voice, I might soften it in order to get someone to lean in and listen more closely. Rather than punch each word for emphasis, I might slow my pace and use more dramatic pause. I wasn't just changing the way I spoke. I was having to rethink the way I expressed myself for specific effects.

THE BEST WAY I can describe all of this skill-building is to compare it to learning to play the violin. Anyone who has heard a first-year violinist knows how awful the sound can be. But if the player is seven years old, you smile at how cute they are and pray that they practice in private. But here I was, a fifty-year-old adult who had to master my new instrument in public for all the world to hear. There were no do-overs. I was practicing on stage 24/7, aware that, to everyone else's discerning ears, I was missing a lot of notes.

Christie kept the exercises fun and always managed to lift my spirits. Nonetheless, I found voice training a continual struggle and cause for despair. I wasn't at all confident that my voice would be ready for prime time when I came out at work—this, even though I had been interviewed on National Public Radio for a segment about women and voice.

The problem was more mental than physical. I was struggling to let go of this part of my history. I had often fantasized about gentling myself into old age reading to my grandchildren, much as I had read to Haley and Cam. I sometimes found myself crying as I listened to Judith Owen sing *My Father's Voice*.

> *Oh my father's voice / Was a very special thing.*
> *And when I went to sleep at night / I knew I'd wake to hear him sing*
> *…*
> *Oh my father's voice / Was a very healing thing*
> *And in our house of mirrors / There was safety it would bring …*
> *But he doesn't seem to understand / The pleasure that it brings …*

My body was one thing. But how could I take my voice away from my children?

AS 2013 APPROACHED, I considered one more frontier: the Internet. As Tom, my identity was all over the place: in email, Facebook, LinkedIn, and Google⁺. I belonged to a variety of online professional and social communities. How was I going to establish Tina's Internet presence and integrate her into these networks? And, if I started to give her a presence now, how was I going to keep anyone from linking my two profiles until I was out of the closet at work?

In our hyper-connected world, this proved a lot more challenging than I had anticipated. Take a simple text message. In August, when Mary had snapped the picture of me at the Jimmy Buffet Concert, I decided to share it with my close friend back in Chatham. I texted it to him. Several days later, I started to worry: why hadn't he replied? Was it too-much, too-soon? Was he annoyed?

As it turned out, the picture had gone to his mother in Italy. This caused a bit of confusion and consternation in his household. I had selected my friend's name from my iPhone directory. But when his mother had been visiting the U.S. several months before, I had recorded his phone number against her name. Somehow, my text crossed over to the wrong contact. I felt terrible on behalf of my friend. Here he was respecting my secret and I was outing myself to his mother halfway around the world. Not cool, Tom.

After that, I became paranoid. If I could slip up so easily with a simple text message that I controlled, what chance did I have with Facebook, LinkedIn, and Google+? It didn't take long to find out. Shortly after opening my Tina Facebook account, I got my first stalker message. An elderly gentleman named Albert thought I was really cute. Would I be his friend? I immediately learned how to maximize Facebook's privacy settings.

A FEW DAYS LATER, I got a note from my daughter, Evelyne. "Dad, are you aware that you are now listed as my mother on my Facebook page? Do you think that's such a good idea?" Apparently, when I had tagged Evelyne as my daughter on my Tina profile, Facebook looked at my gender marker and automatically adjusted Evelyne's profile to match. As far as Facebook was concerned, I was now her mother. Did I want everyone connected to her to be aware of my transition so soon? It was another example of unexpected consequences in our integrated world. After this and the texting fiasco, I decided to minimize Tina's virtual presence until I was out at work.

IN EARLY MARCH, Mary and I attended another transgender conference. I was getting close to my planned date for coming out at work. Was it safe, I wondered, to venture out? What if someone recognized me?

But the Keystone Conference offered a great opportunity to meet with leading surgeons and with transgender women who had already transitioned on the job. This was

At Keystone 2013

a great opportunity to road-test my transition plan. Besides, I thought, we'll be in Harrisburg, Pennsylvania. Whom could I possibly run into from Pfizer?

On the very first morning, Mary and I were having breakfast with the Lori Fox, the president of Lori Fox Diversity Consulting and a board member at Out & Equal Workplace Advocates. Lori was an expert in workplace transitions and had offered to give me her counsel.

As we sat at breakfast, James, my electrologist from Buffalo, New York wandered into the room and sat at a table to my right. A few minutes later, the Boston surgeon I had selected to perform my facial surgery entered with his staff and sat at a table directly behind Lori. With Mary sitting beside me, I was now surrounded by all of my caretakers. I thought to myself: This is a hug from the universe. How cool is that?

At that instant, another familiar figure entered the room. Oh, crap! It was a consultant whom I had worked with at Pfizer. He wasn't here for the conference; he was breakfasting with his daughter. As fate would have it, the hostess seated them immediately to my left. I ducked behind my menu. I could hear the universe snickering at me.

I don't know whether it was because he was uncomfortable with the transgender presence in the room or impatient with the slow pace of service, but after a minute of looking around, my consultant friend gestured to his daughter, and they left. Whew!

I LEARNED LATER that he was at the hotel because his daughter was competing in a regional hockey tournament for young teens. As things turned out, this tournament provided an amusing backstory to our conference. About 500 transgender women and a handful of transgender men were staying at our hotel that weekend. The other half of the hotel's capacity was filled by a similar number of hockey parents and their children. All weekend long, hockey sticks and ball gowns stepped gingerly past each other in a waltz of the uncomfortable.

A part of me empathized with the hockey parents. This was obviously the last thing that they had expected that weekend. They had brought their children to Harrisburg to compete in an important tournament. But the mischievous side of me took delight in their predicament.

On the second afternoon, Mary and I were sharing an elevator with two costumed crossdressers, a couple of hockey moms and their two boys. The mothers had backed themselves into the rear corners of the elevator, where they pressed their sons against them. As Mary and I prepared to exit, I turned to her and said loudly, "I talked to our accountant this morning. I think our investments earned another $1 million in income last week."

If they were going to think of us as freaks, I thought, at least we could be rich freaks.

BUT MY CONSULTANT FRIEND was only the first of my surprises that weekend. On the second day of the conference, Mary pulled me aside. "Did you know that one of your colleagues from Pfizer is here?"

"What the ..."

My head began to spin. Oh my God, I've been found out. The one thing that I didn't want to happen has just happened. "Who are you talking about? … What are they doing here?" This was a disaster.

But then it occurred to me: wait a minute, if they are here, they must be in the closet too. Maybe it won't be so bad.

As it turned out, Alaina and I had worked together on an organizational restructuring a few years before. When we finally connected that afternoon, I suspect that we were both a little freaked out to see the other so transformed. I know that I was. It was karma again: we were getting a taste of the medicine we would soon be giving to all of our associates.

Alaina was about a year behind me in terms of her plans to transition at work. But she was far more knowledgeable than I was about the relevant policies and processes at Pfizer. She, Lori Fox, and Victoria, another woman I met at the conference, provided me with invaluable coaching and encouragement. Once again, I thought, I am getting a hug from the universe.

Over the course of three days, Mary and I met with several surgeons and attended a number of career-focused workshops. We learned a lot. My plan was now set.

But we were appalled by the stories that many of the women shared about their transition experiences at work. Some had been fired from their jobs without cause. The lucky ones had merely been shunned or transferred into roles with minimal human contact. Few enjoyed insurance coverage. Those who did, found it difficult to have their coverage honored. Mary and I wondered: would I suffer the same fate?

BY SUNDAY MORNING, we were conferenced out. I reflected: when I had attended IFGE several years before, I had kept to the shallow end of the pool, spending all of my time with the crossdressers. At Keystone, I had dived into the deep end and stayed there. I felt far more at home at the transsexual end of the spectrum.

I thought of the old joke about the difference between the pig and the chicken at the farmer's breakfast table. The chicken is involved (an egg) but the pig is committed (a sausage). I still didn't understand where my gender identity came from, but I was now fully committed to it.

On Sunday morning, as we packed our suitcases to head home, I turned to Mary. "So, what did you think?" I expected her to tell me that she had seen and heard enough to last her a lifetime. It had been an intense few days.

"I just want to get involved in fighting workplace discrimination against these people! I was disgusted to see how society treats them!"

Not for the first or last time, I thought to myself: Is my wife amazing or what?

IT WAS A LOVELY SPRING DAY. I had just arrived at Penn Station and was getting ready to hike the one-and-a-half miles across the city to my office. On the way into New York, I had made a decision. Today was to be the day: I would contact a senior executive in Human Resources whom I knew. I would set up a meeting to discuss my situation. While sitting on the train, I sent him a quick email:

Dear Chris,

I could use your counsel on an important career issue. It doesn't involve leaving the company and doesn't involve any complaints. It's just a bit personal. I would be happy to meet in Chatham over coffee or breakfast if that better suits you.

Thanks — Tom

Twenty minutes later, as I was making my way across 6th Avenue, my iPhone began to buzz. It was an email reply from Chris: "I am heading out of town for a couple of weeks. If you want to talk, it will have to be now."

Oh well, I thought, at least this will be interesting. I dialed his number.

And so, on a bright, sunny morning, surrounded by a throng of Midtown pedestrians, I revealed my lifelong secret to someone in my company: "Hi, Chris! ... I know you're in a hurry so I'll get right to the point. There is something that I have been struggling with all my life. You see ... I am ... er ... I am a transsexual. Mary and I have been wrestling with this for years. We have finally decided that it is time that I come out of the closet and be who I am. I could use your advice about how to handle this at work. You are the first colleague I have ever discussed this with."

Chris paused for only a second. "Tom, first of all, let me say that I am deeply honored that you trusted me enough to approach me about something so personal. ... Wow. ... Thank you. I'm really floored." His personal preamble delivered, he moved quickly to more practical considerations. We talked a few minutes longer and laid out some next steps.

TWO WEEKS LATER, I scheduled a similar meeting with my boss. I was terrified. Matt was a conservative Christian from South Carolina who loved few things more than church, family and football. He had just brought me onto his team to run a project that was critical to them. He had basically saved my job, and here I was showing my gratitude by dumping a hefty headache onto his lap: in a matter of weeks, I planned to change my gender and to take an eight-week leave of absence. Though his conservative background gave me pause, my instincts told me to trust him.

As I entered his office, I didn't make eye contact. I was shaking. I hemmed and hawed. In fact, I started to cry. But eventually I got it out.

I explained my history, my situation at home and my plans. I paused for Matt's reaction.

"Tom, thank you for coming to me about this. I can see that it is difficult. Let me start by making one thing very clear: Not only am I glad that you joined our team, I consider it providential. You are going to find that you have joined a team that will be very welcoming. They are a wonderful group of people who embrace diversity. They will be excited to welcome Tina."

He went on to explain that, yes, this was new and different territory for him. But he viewed it as an opportunity for him to grow in his faith even as he supported me. He was grateful. Of the many scenarios I had played out in my mind before our meeting, this was not one of them. In the end, it was me rather than Matt who was rendered speechless.

I had entered our meeting intent on demonstrating my focus on the business. I kept moving our discussion back to how we would plan my transition around our project milestones. I had developed a detailed work plan that would enable me to take my leave and still finish the project on time and under budget. Matt finally cut me off. "Tom, I am more interested in how we plan this around you. If we have to, we will bring someone in to support you. Let's focus on you right now. I will take care of the company."

I understood now why Matt had recently been recognized as a *Manager of the Year*. It is these moments of truth in life that define our character.

My HR representative was supportive, too. I think that she was a little surprised, though, by some of my comments in our first meeting. After I summarized my situation and my plans, she asked me what my greatest concerns were. I think that she expected me to bring up issues like bathroom access and pronouns.

"My greatest concern," I said, "is establishing my reputation as a successful career woman. I'm worried that I am going to face some new challenges in the way I communicate with people. I'm going to have to learn fast."

The die was cast. I had finally arrived at the moment I had been dreading. How was Pfizer going to respond? Was it up to its CEI rating? My future, I felt, was entirely in my company's hands.

THE NEXT SIX WEEKS were a whirlwind of activity. I met repeatedly with my manager and my HR representative. Both made it clear that Pfizer stood behind my transition one hundred percent. I would control the timing, but Pfizer insisted on controlling the communication process.

I was not to discuss my transition with anyone until I was given the green light to do so. We agreed that we would begin the communication cascade on May 6. I would not be present for the initial communications. I was not to use company email to communicate about my transformation. However, I was invited to provide input regarding what would be said about me at the meetings.

I decided that, following the announcement, I would remain on the job for two weeks as Tom before taking a medical leave. Many of my colleagues had known me for twelve years. I had added the two-week buffer because I wanted to give any who felt the need a chance to talk with Tom, the person they had known. In July, I would return to work as Tina.

The company assigned a small team to oversee my transition. They scripted a communications cascade and scheduled a series of meetings with leaders of the organizations that I worked with. They arranged for two outsiders from the Human Rights Campaign (HRC) to deliver a Trans 101 seminar to interested colleagues. Matt began to meet in confidence with senior leaders and peers to let them know what would be coming. He later teased me that, for three weeks, this was almost his full-time job.

The gist of the communications was this: Pfizer was firmly committed to diversity in the workplace. It would not look lightly on anyone who did not share this commitment. I was a valued employee and the company stood behind me, just as it stood behind all of its colleagues. As far as Pfizer was concerned, when I returned to work as Tina, I would return as a woman. They included a brief personal statement from me that explained my decision.

I had heard mixed points of view from other trans men and women about whether I should push to be included in the announcement meetings. I worried that my not being there might depersonalize the discussion. People liked me at work. Wouldn't it help to include me? On the other hand, this wasn't about me. It was about Pfizer taking a stand on its own values. What is more, without me in the room, discussion could be more honest. Maybe people had some questions that they would be uncomfortable raising in front of me. This meeting was for their benefit, too.

A WEEK BEFORE the big announcement, I was talking to a few of our administrative assistants about an upcoming meeting that they were helping to coordinate. One of them, Sue, had always admired my computer skills. She had also seen a picture of me a few months before, dressed for Halloween in a women's tennis dress. She turned to me and quipped, "You know, you'd make a great administrative assistant. In fact, you'd make a great woman. You have nice legs!"

My "nice legs" practically fell out from under me. Sue was teasing, of course, but on the way home that night I wondered what she would say when the announcement came out the following week. I was sorry that I would not be present.

FINALLY, THE BIG DAY ARRIVED. Early in the morning, Matt sent an email to our team announcing a mandatory meeting near the end of the day. I wasn't going to attend, but he included me in the invitation in order to avoid raising questions. I sent him an urgent note: a mandatory meeting was widely regarded by colleagues as code for layoffs. He had probably just pressed everyone's panic button. Did he really want to leave them distracted by worry for a whole day?

At four, I sat in my office, waiting to learn how the meeting would turn out. I stared at the phone, willing it to ring. At 4:30, it started to rattle. It was Matt. Would I please join my colleagues in the conference room?

I entered the room not certain what to expect. I was met with handshakes, hugs, and smiles. One after another, my colleagues extended their good wishes to me. I never felt so loved and validated in a workplace as I did that afternoon.

As I had predicted, everyone had initially assumed that the meeting had been called to announce a restructuring. Would their jobs be eliminated? Were we being reorganized? When my boss explained the purpose of the meeting, they heaved a collective sigh of relief. One of them teased me afterwards, "Oh, thank heavens! Tom's just becoming Tina. I thought something bad was going to happen."

IN THE TWO WEEKS that followed, hundreds of colleagues at work shared their happiness for me. They were particularly delighted to know that they worked for a company that stood so firmly behind its colleagues.

I was overwhelmed by the outpouring of support: "I admire your courage." "I am extraordinarily impressed with your bravery and strength of character." "I'm humbled by your honesty." "Your note is such a declaration of living with purpose and authenticity."

I was grateful for these accolades. But, was I courageous? I didn't think so. I was just trying to stay alive. Yes, I was trying to be my authentic self. But I was at the very start of my journey. I wasn't sure that it was fair to call the new me authentic until I had proven myself. After all, what had I really accomplished so far?

Publicly, I accepted everyone's compliments. Privately, I resolved that I would try to live up to them. I *would* be authentic. I *would* be open and honest. I *would* live my life with a sense of purpose.

TWO WEEKS AFTER THE ANNOUNCEMENT, I took my medical leave and headed to Boston for the first of my surgeries. While recuperating, I started the process for legally changing my name and gender. Over the ensuing months, I engaged with a hoard of bureaucrats and call center operators. I assembled a list of the records I would have to change. It included: a court-ordered name change, my driver's license, my passport, social security card, and voter registration; my bank accounts, credit cards, property deeds, vehicle titles, vehicle registrations, loan documents, investment accounts, 401Ks and checks; my will, my parents' will, my life insurance policies, my wife's life insurance policies; my medical records, dental records and prescriptions.

I would have to contact my universities, my high school, and my previous employers. If I ever hunted for a new job, I had to make sure that my transcripts, diplomas and employment records matched my new legal identity. At work, I had to update my employee ID, email address, Form I-9, my directory listing, pictures, office nameplate, travel records, and payroll data. If I didn't complete some of these steps in the right sequence, I could be flagged as an illegal alien.

I also had to update my credit history, my electric bill, gas bill, phone bill, sewer bill, frequent flyer accounts, loyalty club accounts, and subscriptions. I had to create new profiles for Facebook, Google+, LinkedIn, Amazon, and all my online accounts and iPhone apps. I had to update my records with professional organizations and the local police.

It wasn't as simple as changing a few fields in an online profile. In many cases, I had to submit a notarized copy of the court order and a copy of my new passport. I had to post an advertisement to potential creditors, pay processing fees, and hire lawyers. In the end, all of these changes cost Mary and me a little over two-thousand dollars.

THE MOST AGGRAVATING aspect of all these tasks was dealing with call center operators. Try as I might, my voice still had a masculine timbre. The operators almost always identified me as Sir.

Me: Hi, my name is Tina White, T-I-N-A. I am one of your account holders. I recently had a legal name and gender change. I am calling to ask you to update my account with my new name and to change my gender marker to female.

Operator: Yes, Sir. We can help you with that, Sir.

Me: Uh ... No, it's Ma'am. Your records list me as William Thomas White, but my legal name is now Tina Madison White. I need you to change my records to reflect my legal name and my female gender.

Operator: I'm sorry, Sir. Of course. ...

Conversations with my insurance provider and pharmacists could be even more exasperating. I was more fortunate than were many transsexuals in that I enjoyed certain insurance benefits. The problem was that few of the people I spoke to understood what was covered. It was so rare for them to field questions from a transsexual. When something was covered, it was often difficult to get it covered correctly.

My hormone regimen is a good example. As a transsexual woman, my prescribed dosage of estrogen is fifty percent higher than is typical for a post-menopausal woman on hormone replacement therapy. At first, the computer system flagged and refused my refills, forcing me to intercede. The call went something like this:

Me: ... Yes, I know that my dosage of estrogen doesn't match your standards. But your standards were written for women on hormone replacement therapy. These aren't the standards of care for trans-women. My doctor prescribed me twelve doses a month, not eight. My pharmacist says that you won't approve the twelve even though my policy says that hormones are included as part of my transgender coverage.

Call Center: I'm sorry, Sir, these are the approved dosages for women.

Me: It's Ma'am, not Sir. Look, I can understand the confusion. I'm seeking coverage under the transgender clause of my policy. This isn't for standard gynecological care.

Call Center: I see, Mr. White.

Me: Please, it's Ms. White, not Mr. White.

Call Center: [A pause. Then, in a tone of wounded aggravation] Yes. Well, OK, Ms. White. I'm afraid I am going to have get back to you.

At first, the constant use of "Sir" caused me great pain. Why couldn't they get it straight? But I gradually learned not to take it so personally. I was a rarity in their day. They were trying to provide good service. From their perspective, I was a source of stress, not because they objected to my being transgender, but because they had to think extra hard about our conversation. My voice, after all, was their chief cue.

I FACED THIS ISSUE MYSELF when I attended the birthday party of a transgender friend a few months later. Many of the celebrants were fellow gender outlaws. I loved them all and enjoyed the colorful atmosphere. But two of the partiers perplexed me: even after an hour of conversation, I couldn't read them. Were they men? Women? Were they women transitioning to men? Men transitioning to women? I couldn't tell for the life of me.

I didn't give a fig what the answer was. Either way, they seemed like cool people. But I started to feel a little sweat gathering on the back of my neck as I pondered how to reference them. If I got it wrong, would they feel hurt or annoyed? Would they label me ignorant or transphobic? Yes, I could ask them. But that might cause them embarrassment. It would certainly expose my ignorance.

This is when I developed my golden rule for dealing with people who are more conventionally gendered than I am. "I will treat your confusion with respect if you will treat my ambiguity with respect."

Most of the time, the cab driver who "Sirs" me isn't trying to hurt my feelings. He has his eyes on the road and his mind on the traffic— as he should. Even though a woman entered the cab, the voice he hears directing him to 27th and Broadway evokes an un-considered response, "Yes, Sir."

I have learned to treat such situations with humor. "Sir? ... You must have me confused with your last passenger. Was he as cute as I am?"

More often than not, the driver responds with a glance in the mirror and a quick apology. To get past the moment, we start a conversation. By the end of the cab ride, I have a new friend and fan. As I hand him my fare, he responds, "Have a good day, Ma'am."

SLOWLY, BUT SURELY, the wheels of bureaucracy began to turn in my favor. In June, I sent an update to friends and colleagues.

> *... The New Jersey courts made it official. In the future, they will send all of my parking tickets to Tina Madison White.*
>
> *I am still recuperating from my surgery. Mary and my doctors are excited by the results. ... At the moment, I confess that I look something more like FrankensTina: black-and-blue eye sockets, a scalp that is stitched together with a bushel of staples - and lips that look like Pirelli racing tires. Mothers, keep your children from the moors tonight! I hear there's to be a full moon.*
>
> *But seriously, all is healing well. I took myself off of pain meds this morning and have been walking the New England shoreline. I have never been happier.*

IN JULY, I returned to work two weeks ahead of schedule.

On my very first day back at the office, my ID card still had "William Thomas White" on it. It included a picture of the old me sporting my goatee. He's pretty cute, I thought. I wonder if I can meet him. My first order of business was to secure a new identification card and picture. But this, I learned, would take a couple of days.

Meanwhile, each time I went through our security turnstiles, my old picture flashed on a monitor at the security desk. I expected to be pulled aside by one of the guards, but they merely smiled and waved me through. Evidently, they had been advised about their "new" employee.

During my first few days back, I spent most of my time reintroducing myself to people and getting debriefed by my team on our software project. I was surprised at how easily my reintegration progressed. All of my meetings followed a similar pattern: five minutes of small talk followed by business as usual. Yes, everyone was happy to see me. But they also wanted to talk about my project. How was it going?

About half of the people recognized me as I entered their office. "Wow! You look REALLY good, Tina. How are you?" Their eyes clearly registered surprise. I suspect that they were relieved that they wouldn't have to look away whenever we spoke.

The other half of the people I met with didn't realize at first who I was. I had fun with this. I stood three feet away from them and stared expectantly. They stared back. "Yes, can I help you?"

"I should hope so, John, I'm here for our meeting."

"Oh my God! … You're back! … Holy cow. … That's amazing."

In either event, I was pleased to see how naturally the conversation moved back to company business. "I think our team may have an issue with the way you plan to track downloads. Can we talk about it?" They clearly considered my gender irrelevant to our work together.

For my part, I was surprised by my relative sense of ease. I had assumed that I would be a nervous wreck on my first day. But I wasn't nervous at all. Whether discussing personal or business matters, thoughts and words flowed effortlessly.

This surprised me. Shouldn't I be in a panic? Shouldn't I be worried about what everyone was thinking? What about my voice? What about my face? What about this business of coming to work in a dress?

But I was as calm as I had ever been—more so, in fact. It gradually dawned on me: for the first time in my life, I wasn't having to screen my thoughts or to carefully select my words. I just had to be me. The concept was laughably simple. This, I thought, is why I went through all of this. I finally get to be me.

The difficulty of communicating from the "wrong" gender can be difficult for others to comprehend. The best analogy I can think of is to imagine a conversation about the weather. Someone tells you that it is twenty degrees in the sun. If the two of you are American, you instantly register dismay. That's cold!

But if you are from a country that measures temperature in centigrade, you have to make a calculation. It takes time and effort. By the time you work it out, the emotional impact of the statement has dulled.

That was what communication had been like been like for me before. I had to continually translate back and forth between feminine sentiments and masculine expressions.

MY TROUBLES began at 4:30 on the afternoon of my first day back at work. I noticed with dismay that my nylons had developed a run. I had yet to master the art of carrying my briefcase away from my legs, so the latch had snagged on my hose.

"Damn!" I groaned. I was not going to commute home on my first day doing dishonor to the uniform. I crossed the street to a CVS store and purchased a new pair of hose. Rather than go all the way back upstairs to my office, I went into a women's room on the first floor of our building to change. But, though I had mishandled my briefcase, there was one thing I had not forgotten: Don't wear your engagement ring while you put pantyhose on—you will just get another run. (Mary had given me a beautiful engagement ring to match the one I had bought her years before.)

I took off my rings and laid them on top of the toilet paper dispenser with a mental note to be sure to put them back on. I changed my hose, then bolted for the train. Halfway to Chatham, it hit me: I had forgot the rings! It was a very red-faced Tina who had to call

Security that night. As I dialed the phone, I considered the fact that they still only knew me in the security system by my old name.

"Hi," I said. "This is William Thomas White. I left my wedding and engagement rings in the women's room on the first floor of the 219 building. Could you have someone check to see if they are still there?"

It took another minute to explain my predicament, but, yes, the rings were found. I could pick them up the following morning. The next day, I shared my story with some of the women on my team. They couldn't stop laughing. It was just the first of what they came to call my "rookie mistakes". In the months that followed, I would make many more.

IT PROVED TO BE the little things that tripped me up—like everyday office etiquette. As Tom, I had been expected to open doors. As Tina, I was expected to allow others to open them for me.

This wasn't a question of my preferences. It was what others expected. On occasion, I forgot myself and grabbed a door for the gentleman behind me. It was the result of years of conditioning. Previously, the man behind me would have gestured a thank you and walked through the door. Now, he looked at me in puzzled surprise and gestured for me to go ahead of him, "No, after you!"

Elevators posed a similar challenge. At the office, I often found myself on an elevator filled with men. When we arrived at the lobby, I stood there, wondering why no one else was moving. Eventually, it dawned on me: they were waiting for me, the lady, to go ahead of them. And they were getting a little annoyed. To their minds, I was holding them up.

A friend finally explained the error of my ways. "You are just outing yourself when you do that. Is that what you want? If you want to pass, you've got to adopt to the prevailing customs. Let women-born-women fight to change them. Your priority is to fit in."

Over time, I improved. At Home Depot, for example, I finally got used to the fact that men now regularly approached me in the parking lot. They pointed at my cart, filled with top soil and lumber: "Can I help you with that, ma'am?" I quashed my impulse to say no and gave them my best smile, "Oh, how sweet! Thank you."

Having lost several inches of muscle in my upper body, I confess that I was more than a little grateful for their assistance.

THE ONLY TIME I felt self-conscious at work was when I was in the company of strangers, people who had never known me before or after my transition. Would they find me an uncomfortable distraction? Would they take me seriously?

There were only a couple of instances where I felt taken less seriously than before. Typically, it was when I was the only woman in a room full of men. As they waited for the meeting to start, the men would lock eyes and fall into a discussion of the week's sports headlines. When the meeting began, they transitioned almost seamlessly from sports talk to the agenda. They barely looked my way.

THIS IS WHERE I learned to appreciate the importance of allies at work. Many companies, mine included, had recently begun to provide training to colleagues on how to be a good ally to people who are LGBT. Before coming out, I had always assumed that being an ally meant being an activist: standing up for someone faced with abuse or discrimination.

As I went about my daily routine, I realized that such notions paint an incomplete picture of allies. During my first year at work as Tina, what mattered most to me was the little things that colleagues did to make me feel welcome and valued. When I entered a room full of strangers, did everyone sit away from me? Was I greeted with as much enthusiasm as everyone else? All I needed was for one person to grab me by the hand, look me in the eye and say, "Welcome, Tina! I'm glad you could make it today."

It was little gestures like this that made the greatest difference to me. Though I was now comfortable being who I was, I was also aware that I was a visible outlier and a minority of one. I didn't want to admit it, but what I contributed to a meeting depended to a great extent on how welcome I felt.

This, I began to appreciate, is how many minority colleagues are likely to feel. Like me, they are probably brimming with ideas and energy. Whenever they join a new group, they have two choices: excitedly contribute all that they have to offer or sit on their hands and play it safe. Do they say what they think or what they think the group wants to hear?

All I needed was for one person in a room to pay a complement, lend an attentive ear, or offer encouragement. It restored my confidence. It muted my fears and put me back on my A-game. The greatest benefit of allies, I realized, wasn't what they did to change the organization; it was what they did to change me. Ally programs weren't just a feel-good intervention; they were good for the bottom line.

These experiences forced me to reexamine myself: was I a good ally? If someone was different from me, did I listen to them as attentively? Did I go out of my way to make them feel welcome? Did I show interest in what they shared? The men who had fashioned their meeting around sports trivia probably weren't trying to exclude me. They were just sticking to what felt comfortable and familiar. Was I guilty of the same behavior?

SO IT WAS, in the months that followed, that I gradually resettled into my life at work. In August, I delivered my first presentation to a large audience. I started to use the company fitness center and, with it, the women's locker room. I joined new initiatives and project teams.

But these milestones were marked by their singular lack of drama. My work life had returned to normal. Most of the time, I just did my job. I continued my efforts to reshape my voice, but my colleagues were more interested in the substance of my comments. I asked several of them if they found my voice a distraction. They invariably responded, "What voice? What are you talking about?"

ào

LIFE 2.0

When I heard the learn'd astronomer;

When the proofs, the figures, were ranged in columns before me;

When I was shown the charts and the diagrams, to add, divide, and measure them;

When I, sitting, heard the astronomer, where he lectured with much applause in the lecture-room,

How soon, unaccountable, I became tired and sick;

Till rising and gliding out, I wander'd off by myself,

In the mystical moist night-air, and from time to time,

Look'd up in perfect silence at the stars.

—*Walt Whitman*

ALL THIS TIME, my family had been holding its collective breath. Would Tina's career implode? Would she really be happier when she faced the realities at work? Would people accept her?

With Siblings, Christmas 2014

Now that I had passed my hurdles at the office, the reality of my transition began to sink in. However tentatively, my family had always supported my transition. But I think that it was Tom that they were supporting. Now it was official: they had a new family member in their midst. We had a lot to work out. Our family system had developed over fifty years. How would Tina fit in?

FOR MY PARENTS AND SIBLINGS, the most sensitive issue was how to handle our history together. When we gathered for family vacations, weddings and holidays, it was natural to reminisce about old times. Now that I was Tina, were they allowed to talk about their little brother, Tommy? Did they have to clear the walls of family photographs featuring the old me?

Many transgender people don't like to talk about their childhood. They announce to family members that "Joe (or Jane) is dead." They hide or destroy old pictures. They box up diplomas and trophies. They coach their family not to bring up their past at weddings.

I resolved early on to pursue a different course. If I wanted my family to honor my future I reasoned, I needed to honor their past. I was asking them to accept a little discomfort and to invest a lot of effort in order to support me. Wasn't it fair that I accept a little discomfort too? I explained to my family that, as far as I was concerned, little Tommy remained an integral part of our folklore. He had gone through hell to get me this far in life. How could I do anything but love him?

My intent was to comfort my family. But this was possibly the most therapeutic gift I could have given myself. I had lived my entire life filled with self-loathing. I had felt empty, weak, and ugly. But today, when I look at pictures of Tom, I see them with new eyes: What an amazing man! What a handsome man! What a kind and generous spirit. No wonder my family mourned his passing.

I have come to love it when my family talks about my childhood. I don't mind it when they pronoun childhood me as "he". I know that they do it because they love our memories together. In return, I ask only that they celebrate the reborn me. As we accumulate new memories together, it gets easier for everyone. We have a growing portfolio of stories that feature Tina.

Little Tommy had always struggled inside. Much as he had wanted to feel a part of the family, he had isolated himself. Why would I want to take away our few shared memories?

In an earlier chapter, I described my prom night with my high school sweetheart, Angela. Much to my sorrow, Ange died recently of cancer. I was happy that, before she did, I was able to come out to her and her family. True to her character, when Ange saw her first picture of the new me, she shot back an email: "You look like a whore. We'll have to work on that!" She suggested that she and her sisters take me shopping when they were next in New York City.

When we did finally get together, we relived our old memories, including our prom night. We laughed at the vision of me in her prom dress. As Tom, I had felt so ashamed of that memory. But now, as I recalled it with Angela, I felt a sense of pride. As confused as I had been back then, I had still known how to be a gentleman.

I also got a chance to have dinner with Ange's dad, Tommy. Ange and her sisters were there, too. I reminded him of the day, forty years before, when he had invited me to go with him to the veterinarian to have his dog, Max, neutered. "I've got to go for a little surgery myself, Tommy. Do you want to come along?"

"Thanks, but I'll pass, Tina."

As she had done years before, Ange scowled at what she considered indelicate humor. This time, though, she directed her glare at me.

Another memory I sometimes call forth is Sally's pregnancies with Haley and Cam. When she had been expecting, I often dreamed that it was I who was pregnant. I was delighted by the prospect of having children, but I was sad that I wasn't the one bearing them into the world. I so wanted to be a mother.

I don't recall discussing those feelings with anyone, not even with Sally. In the 1980s, such thoughts were more than a little disquieting. I just assumed that it was another problem for me to solve in private. Today, I enjoy reclaiming that memory. My sorrow makes sense to me now. And I can think of nothing unseemly about wishing that I could have born children. It is a beautiful thought.

NAMING CONVENTIONS and pronouns presented another tough area to navigate. What did I want my children and grandchildren to call me? What should I do when family members accidentally mis-pronouned me?

With Parents

Early in my transition, my mother and I went to Home Depot together. I was lost in thought, trying to pick out some perennials to buy. In the background, I heard someone shouting. It took a minute for the voice to register. It was my mother. She continued to shout as she waved at me and approached. "Tommy! ... Tommy! Look here!"

I wanted to crawl into the bushes and hide. On the way home, we discussed the matter. "Why did you have to change your name to Tina? Why couldn't you have changed the spelling of your old name to *Tommi* with an *i*?" she asked. "That would have been so much easier for me. I don't think I can promise to get it right all the time."

I understood where my mother was coming from. It wasn't just a matter of habit or a memory lapse. It was also a question of her doing honor to her own life. At some level, I was still her baby.

I get it. For me, no matter what my children do or become, there will always be a part of them that is three years old. I can still picture Haley and her stuffed animal companion, Bun, as though it were yesterday. I wouldn't let anyone rob me of that memory, not even Haley. My mother, I realized, wasn't resisting the new me. She just wasn't prepared to throw her darling baby away. Occasionally, she confused the two. What loving parent wouldn't?

In the end, we agreed on a compromise: I wouldn't get upset when she got my name or gender wrong so long as she never assumed that it didn't matter to me.

MY CHILDREN presented a different situation. I felt that I needed to give them more latitude. They quickly took me up on it: each chose a different way to refer to me. Depending on who I was with, I was variously referred to as "my other Mom", "Dad", "Tina", "T" or—I am not sure about Nathan. He cleverly found ways to avoid names and pronouns altogether.

Whenever I wrote to my children, I had to bear in mind with whom I was corresponding. Writing to several of them at once was especially challenging. I typically signed such letters, "Love, Me."

I didn't mind making these accommodations. Yes, they made my life more complicated. But I reminded myself, wasn't that what I was doing to everyone else?"

So long as the intent was good, I felt that this was an area that called for allowances and a little bit of fun. For example, my religiously conservative daughter, Lindy, was still struggling with how she and her children should refer to me. She knew from my last visit how deeply it pained me to be called Grampa Tom. "Grandma Tina," on the other hand, would force them to acknowledge my womanhood, something that did not sit well with their religious convictions. But Lindy is as loving as she is devout. She was trying hard to navigate this. "Why not call me *TranMa T?*" I quipped.

I was kidding, of course. While I might not mind that name as an occasional pun delivered at home, I would hate to be called that in public. But I was trying to lighten the mood. The effort that she and her family were making mattered a lot to me.

I wished that they had different beliefs on this topic. But I respected how seriously they took their faith. I was proud of their effort. Much to my relief, they generally settled on Grandma Tina, though Lindy quietly sticks with "T". Whenever she says it, I imagine the two of us on a basketball team, *Throw it here, T! Nice shot, T!*

Whatever works, L.

I WAS EQUALLY PROUD—if a little surprised—when Cam declared that he preferred to call me Dad. The occasion was his graduation from Princeton. He was an amazing student and was to be the recipient of many awards. That would mean special receptions with his professors and other parents. "How do you want to introduce me to everyone?" I asked. This was his day and I felt that it should be his choice. He thought for a minute. "As my Dad," he replied.

I never asked him to explain his reason. I like to think that it was his way of retaining some intimacy between us. Maybe he wanted to honor the person who had supported him and helped to pay for his degree. But it is possible, too, that he was honoring his mother by avoiding any confusion.

Surprisingly, the name that I found most difficult to cope with from my children was Tina. When Haley started to use it, I worried: "Wow! She moved to that pretty quickly. Is that her way of creating distance?"

Such is the paranoia that can creep into your head. It may equally have been her way of giving me her blessing: "I don't understand what you are doing or why, but I am going to call you Tina because I want to support you."

Only my children know the thinking behind their decisions. I find all of them acceptable because I know that each of my children has chosen the name that enables them to be as loving and authentic as they can.

WHERE MARY WAS CONCERNED, names were not an issue. She had nipped that in the bud a couple of years before. At one point, I had considered changing my legal name to something other than Tina. I was worried that Tina might be too girly. I approached Mary with several options. "What about Madison, Avery, Taylor, Morgan, or Brooke?"

"Oh, no you don't!" she retorted. "You got me used to Tina. Tina it stays!" Given all that she had been through, it seemed wise to

At AIDS Walk NYC

let the matter drop. With Mary's approval, I adopted Madison as my middle name.

THE MOST PRESSING ISSUE for Mary and me was how to describe our marriage. This was of particular concern to Mary. A lot of her social identity had been wrapped up in her wedded bliss with her Princeton man. All our lives together, our friends had commented on our storybook marriage. Mary loved hearing their purrs of admiration. She especially enjoyed retelling the story of our courtship and betrothal. What was she supposed to say now?

Whenever we met a new couple, I could see the frustration mount on her face. Inevitably, one of our new friends would ask, "so, how did you two meet?"

Mary explained to me, "I am not a lesbian. If I refer to you as *she* when I talk about our past, I am implying something about me that isn't true. But if I refer to you as *he*, I will be outing you. Either way, we risk inviting more questions than I care to answer. I don't know what to do."

In the end, we opted for simple transparency. What did we have to hide? If someone found our history together uncomfortable, we probably didn't want them in our circle of friends anyway. We were proud of our story.

As it turned out, our new relationship wasn't the issue we thought it might be. Our friends still told us that we had a storybook marriage. They just felt that it now had a more interesting plot twist.

OUR SECOND BIG ISSUE was how to express our love and intimacy with each other. Mary was clear: "I am not a lesbian, Tina. ... But what about you? Are you a lesbian? Do you still want to do that ... stuff?"

"No, not really. I still find women attractive, but I don't imagine becoming physical with them."

"Well, what about men? Are you attracted to men now? Are you ever going to want to go home with one?"

"It's interesting. ... I have to admit ... I find men attractive in a way that I never did before. Some of them are really cute. I notice their eyes and their muscles in ways that are new to me. But if I think anything more than that, I get grossed out. I can't imagine becoming physical with a man. After fifty years in the men's locker room, I think I just know too much."

"Well, is that something you are going to want to find out about?"

"No, I don't think so. Look … maybe if we were twenty years younger I'd think differently. But physical relationships just aren't a priority for me right now. I'm a lot more interested in getting to know the one person who's been a stranger all my life—me. And besides, I'm married to my best friend. At our age, I think that a loving companion is a lot more important than a roll in the hay."

"Yeah, but what if you change your mind?"

"Well, let me turn it around. You've been married to me for sixteen years. In all that time, did you ever find other men attractive?"

"Of course!"

"Well, did you want to go to bed with them? —I mean, really go to bed?"

"No! Of course not. … I'm married."

"Exactly. And I'm married, too. As long as I'm allowed to do a little window-shopping, I'm happy."

"Well, OK. So … how's it gonna work?"

SEX WAS AN EASY TOPIC TO RESOLVE. It was off the table. But even if we agreed that we had no interest in sex, did we now need to sleep in separate beds or bedrooms? What about hugging, kissing, and holding hands? Was it still appropriate for her to call me "Dear"? Could I still refer to her as "Sweetheart"?

And how should we behave when we were in public? We had never had to think about this before. All our lives together, society had applauded our sweet intimacy. Now we felt pressured to hide it. I finally understood the sorrow that gay and lesbian couples must experience when they have to conceal their feelings of love in public.

In the end, we let time work these issues out for us. We had such a huge bed and so enjoyed each other's company that we quickly agreed that our sleeping arrangements needn't change. Gradually, we returned to hugging and holding hands in private. We have always felt a close bond and like to feel connected. We just needed to reprogram the meaning behind our gestures as something not sexual. It came fairly easily.

Now, two years later, we give each other the occasional peck on the lips. We probably do it as an innocent form of mischief. We enjoy sitting close to each other when we watch TV. We are more like sisters now than husband and wife.

And we have found many new ways to express our love for one another. We express it in the way we hold hands and in the way we listen to one another so attentively. We declare it when we make each other coffee each morning. Mary expresses it when she laughingly points out the lipstick on my teeth. I let her know how much I love her when I help her to pick out new shoes. I still make her laugh every day; she still makes me feel important.

THE YEAR FOLLOWING my transition brought with it some wonderful opportunities to test-drive our new family model.

In May, I finally got to meet the only two family members who had yet to know me as Tina, my two granddaughters in California. Their parents, Nathan and Beth, had worried about how best to introduce them to the new me. I researched the issue and reported my findings: apparently, trans-gender people were a non-event to young

With Granddaughter Aliya

children. They only became concerned if they sensed that mom and dad were affected. If their parents looked worried, they knew that there was danger lurking. But if mom and dad seemed unconcerned, they shrugged their shoulders, let out a giggle (*that's silly!*), and returned to their play.

The night before Mary and I were to arrive, Nathan and Beth sat seven-year-old Aliya down for a talk. "Sweetheart, do you remember Grampa Tom?"

"Yes, he and Grandma Mary are coming tomorrow, right?"

"Well, yes. But Grampa Tom is going to look a little bit different than before."

They proceeded to explain that Grandpa Tom had always felt like a woman on the inside and that, from now on, he would be living as a woman on the outside, too. He now preferred to be called Grandma Tina.

"How do you feel about that, honey? You don't have to call him Grandma Tina unless you want to."

Aliya looked thoughtful. "Well, until I meet him tomorrow, let's stay with Grampa Tom. After that, I'll decide."

When Mary and I arrived, Aliya was waiting in the back of the car. I sat in the front while Mary joined Aliya. For the first five minutes, Aliya stared at me and listened silently as Mary and I engaged in small talk with Beth. Then, out of nowhere, she blurted out, "Grandma Tina … Grandma Tina … I can do cartwheels now!"

With that, the floodgates opened. Aliya chattered all the way home. That weekend, the two of us were inseparable. She even insisted that I sleep in her bedroom. "Grandma Tina and I are going to have a slumber party, Mom!"

We dressed as princesses—she as Snow White and I as Sleeping Beauty. Fortunately, I had packed a yellow nightgown and a royal blue bathrobe. We read together, swam together, and played in the park. Her baby sister, Avry, watched us from her blanket and burbled.

I introduced the only note of caution into our weekend. As we set up my special bed for our slumber party, Aliya began to giggle, "Grandma Tina, Grandma Tina … now that we're both girls, we don't have to worry if we dress in the same room anymore."

"Well, let's not do that just yet, OK?"

In June, Mary and I attended two graduations. First, we attended Cam's graduation from Princeton. This was his moment in the sun. He was graduating *summa cum laude* and *Phi Beta Kappa.* I tried to do what any parent is supposed to do in such situations: keep a low profile, admire your children, and take lots of pictures.

With Cam at Princeton

But I took secret delight when Cam introduced me to his friends' parents, "This is my mother, Sally, my stepmother, Mary—and this is my dad, Tina." I always greeted the other father with a firm, if womanly, handshake and looked him in the eye, "pleased to meet you." The startled looks on a few of the faces were priceless.

A week after Princeton, Mary and I traveled to Michigan to attend the high school graduation for Lindy and Jeff's three children, CJ, Michael, and Rosie. All of them had schooled at home. Although they were a couple of years apart, Lindy had managed things so that they graduated at the same time. She and Jeff planned to celebrate the milestone with about 150 people—most of them friends from church.

Things had improved a lot since my last visit to Michigan. Everyone now referred to me as Grandma Tina or T. Still, they generally avoided pronouns. I asked Mary to inquire discretely: did they really want me to attend? This was their celebration. I did not want to create an uncomfortable distraction. Mary returned to me with their reply: they not only welcomed me, they would feel hurt if I didn't come.

Nonetheless, I worried: I would be at close quarters with about 150 people, most of whom (I was pretty sure) did not approve of my declaration of gender. What is more, there would be a lot of young children present. I had learned from experience that kids often bring out the worst behavior in their parents.

Even adults who consider themselves open-minded are known to freak out when they see their children exposed to something unfamiliar. The mother bear instinct kicks in. Would I find myself surrounded by a pack of bat-wielding fathers and Bible-thumping mothers? I was certain that Lindy and Jeff would never allow this to happen. But I would be lying if I didn't admit to a little nervousness as I helped to decorate their home on the morning of the party.

As I had learned to do at previous events, I kept a low profile as the party began. I focused on serving and cleaning, and anchored myself to the kitchen. Every once in a while, I ventured into the front and back yards, watching closely for signs of discomfort. Everyone was friendly. In fact, everyone seemed perfectly at ease. From what I could tell, I was the only one thinking about my gender.

As the party moved into full swing, some of the children organized a game of volleyball. "Come on, Tina! We need you on our team!"

With Granddaughter Rosie

I looked around. Did any of the parents seem alarmed? They weren't even looking at us. That was all the encouragement I needed. I spent the rest of the day worrying about little more than my return of serve and ice cream refills.

As had happened so many times during my transition, I had gone from thinking myself the teacher to finding myself the student. I did not fool myself: I had not taught anyone anything that day. I was pretty sure that most of these people left the party with their beliefs intact. But those beliefs included a command to love and not to judge.

In a world as diverse as ours, I cannot hope that everyone will agree with and support me. But this Christian community had modeled a society that was guided by love and tolerance. They treated me as a human being and made me feel welcome. We found many things to celebrate and enjoy together that day—most importantly CJ, Michael, and Rosie. And we left it at that.

BACK HOME, Mary and I attempted to reconnect with friends and neighbors with mixed success. One of the things I discovered was that my closest friendships were the most difficult to keep.

Upon learning of my transition, our more casual friends were bemused and inquisitive. They hadn't been drawn into our drama. Nor had they felt betrayed. Most of them expressed surprise, wished us well, and went on with their lives as before.

For my close friends, the change in dynamics introduced too much complexity. They weren't opposed to my being transgender. They were opposed to having so much disorder introduced into their homes. I think, too, that they weren't sure how to reintegrate me.

Previously, I had generally hung around with the guys in front of the television. There was a well-established rhythm and banter. But I was a woman now. What did that mean to me? Did I still want to watch football? Could they still tell the same jokes?

Meanwhile, the wives in our circle of friends had a long-established rhythm of their own. Their primary relationship was with Mary. Did they now have to invite me when they had a girls' night out? Given my history, did we really have much in common? My presence complicated things.

As time passed, Mary and I found ourselves invited to fewer and smaller functions. We decided that it was time to make a fresh start in a new neighborhood. In the fall of 2014, we moved to Hoboken, New Jersey. It was a nine-minute bus ride from Times Square. We were city girls now.

IN CHATHAM, social life had revolved around the cocktail party and barbecue. In Hoboken, it centered on restaurants and bars. In fact, Mary informed me, Hoboken had the highest concentration of bars in the state. Like many of our new neighbors, we converted one of these,

Carpe Diem, into our patio and living room. It lay fifty feet from our front door. It was nice to be greeted once more with excitement, "Mary and Tina are here!"

Most of the time, we just sat with our new friends discussing work, family, and weekend plans. But occasionally, we would run into unfamiliar men whom Mary referred to as players. They were a new experience for me.

I had never had a man talk to my chest before. Nor had I ever had to deflect aggressive pick-up attempts. I gained new respect for the narrow lines that women must walk and the risks they face. How, I wondered, could I blunt a man's advances without sounding like a bitch? What was I agreeing to when I allowed him to buy me a glass of wine?

The experience was new for Mary, too. She generally recognized, long before I did, when men were making advances on me. She quickly set them straight, "Hey, that's my wife you're talking to!"

Personal Journal   September 2014

I think that I am still repressing my feminine identity to some extent. I have so worried about managing everyone's expectations. It is as though I want people to know that Tom is still in the room. But I love who I am. It is why I did this! I think that I have been affected, too, by worries that I might struggle to succeed as Tina. And so I have borrowed heavily from Tom's grab bag of successful practices. I need to allow Tina to be herself. I need to allow her to show the world what she is capable of.

LATE IN 2014, my company approved my participation in a weeklong leadership development program at the Center for Creative Leadership in North Carolina. The program, *Leading for Organizational Impact* was intended to help divisional leaders to work more effectively across boundaries and to think more strategically about their influence on their organization.

We weren't allowed to know exactly what would happen that week. We were told only that it would involve an intense business simulation and a lot of personal feedback. "Be prepared to come home feeling naked," was all a previous participant would tell me.

IN THE WEEKS leading up to the program, I grew increasingly apprehensive. It hadn't occurred to me when I signed up, but this was going to be my first professional foray into an environment where nobody knew me from my past.

I worried: did I owe all of my success to Tom? Was I merely trading on the equity and reputation that he had built up over several decades? Did people listen to Tina chiefly because they had listened to Tom?

The twenty participants who would be joining me in the leadership program knew nothing about Tom. My week was going to rest entirely on Tina.

AT THE TIME I transitioned, I was working in New York City. Both the city and the pharmaceutical industry were known for being LGBT-friendly. In contrast, most of the people in this leadership development program would be coming from places like Texas, Georgia, South Carolina, Virginia, North Carolina, and Tennessee. They worked in industries like construction, trucking, avionics, building maintenance, the military, and home goods.

How were they going to respond to a transsexual woman in their midst? Would they feel uncomfortable? Would they snicker? Would they take me seriously as a leader and colleague?

I decided to follow Sheryl Sandberg's lean-in strategy: If I came across anything that week that I was afraid to do, I would commit myself wholly to doing it. Whatever happened, I was going to go home knowing what I was capable of and what I faced in the business world outside Pfizer. If people were going to laugh at me, I had better know now.

All week long, I stepped up to every opportunity given and made myself as visible and vocal as I could. I ran meetings. I settled arguments. I directed, coached, facilitated, and presented. I did some things well and made some missteps.

As I had been led to expect, it was a demanding and intense exercise. We were leaders, charged with running a sprawling organization through challenging times. Everyone else took the simulation just as seriously as I did. At the end of the week, we readied ourselves for some revealing feedback.

The Center gave each of us a voice recorder on which to capture comments from our peers. When my turn came, I turned on my recorder and listened as the twenty participants and three program leads critiqued my performance. One-by-one, I learned how the others had experienced me, what they thought I had done well, and what they thought I had done poorly. I learned how each of my actions and decisions had impacted our company's performance and my teammates' morale.

HALFWAY THROUGH one of the feedback sessions, I noticed that some of my colleagues had begun to choose their words more carefully. They could see tears starting to form in my eyes. "No, don't worry," I said. "I'm loving every minute of this. Please don't hold back, I really appreciate your feedback. This is wonderful."

What they didn't understand was that I was crying tears of joy. Not once that week had my gender been mentioned. There wasn't a hint of discomfort in anyone's choice of words or body language. And the feedback was as honest as I could hope for. I was being treated no differently than anyone else. And while I had not been perfect, my peers found a lot to admire in my performance.

I had been just as successful and persuasive that week as Tina as I had ever been as Tom, possibly more so. I had put myself out there in a way that Tom had never been able to do. He couldn't. He was too busy struggling to manage his dualistic nature. As Tina, I had only to be myself. My peers were enjoying so much more of my potential.

I WENT BACK to my room that night stuffed my face into a pillow, and sobbed. I was releasing fifty years of pain. I loved Tom; I loved him deeply. But I had lived in his shadow all my life. For all of his limitations, he was a tough act to follow. Until now, I had worried whether a middle-aged trans woman could ever hope to compete with him, both at work and at home.

For me, February 12, 2015 ranked in significance with every other event in my life. This was the day that Tina was fully born into the world, her umbilical cord to Tom finally severed. I was my own woman now.

On the final evening of our program, I stood up to address my peers. "You have no idea what a gift you have given me this week. I came to this program uncertain whether I could survive let alone lead in a corporate world. But you made me feel valued for who I am and what I have to offer. Because of you, I feel that I can be me and look forward to a wonderful future. Because of you, I leave with the courage to be me. Thank you."

I HAD BEGUN my transition for the most basic of reasons: to stay alive. I had assumed that transitioning would keep me alive, but wretched. I would, like so many other transgender people, be shunned and ridiculed.

Now, a few years later, I finally understood what it felt like to live free and unafraid. I felt loved as never before. I thought about my life with a changed mentality: I was now its owner, not just a renter. I was no longer trying to survive; I was invested in building my future. I was excited.

For so many decades, I had been consumed by self-loathing and self-doubt. I had lost a part of each day battling my gender. Somehow, I had still managed to accomplish a lot—probably in order to escape my misery.

Now that I had stripped away all of those fears and doubts, I looked forward to seeing what I could do. I thought to myself: I might not be half the man I used to be, but I'm twice the person.

I felt, too, that I finally had a relationship with God again. I understood now that he had never left our conversation—I had. I had found him again, not by obeying a particular church or creed, but by listening to the voice inside me.

I had, in fact, wasted a lifetime trying to listen to everyone but myself—to the church; to family systems theorists; to philosophers of manliness, feminists, and social commentators. Institutions, I realized, have an important role in our society, but not if they shackle the soul, as I had allowed them to do. There must be partnership. I had been so phobic about my gender, that I had cut myself out of the conversation that is life.

A FEW MONTHS AGO, Pfizer eliminated my job—part of yet another restructuring. I had survived several such eliminations before; my colleagues encouraged me to post for other positions. I did so for a short time. But a voice inside me kept telling me that this wasn't what I was meant to do next. I decided to listen to it and to let go. To stay, I thought, would have been to remain in Tom's shadow.

I have been doing a lot more of that lately: listening and letting go. My father says that he can see the difference. He says that I am far more compassionate today than I ever was.

His observation surprised and hurt me at first. I thought that I had grown up with a strong social conscience. But he is right. I had always felt strongly about social issues and morality. But today, I am more likely to act on my convictions.

Since transitioning, I have become involved in a Habitat for Humanity project, the AIDS Walk of New York, and the Human Rights Campaign. Mary and I fund a variety of small-scale social entrepreneurship projects. Shortly before leaving Pfizer, I played a key role in getting an LGBT art exhibition installed in the main lobby of our headquarters. It wasn't that I had suddenly found causes worthy of my support. It was that I finally felt worthy to support them.

IN THE FINAL ANALYSIS, my reasons for transitioning had nothing to do with gender or sex. Yes, these were part of my story. But they weren't the *why*. They were the *how* and the *what*. The reasons I transitioned were anchored in a few basic needs that I share with everyone else.

The first was a need to be known. I had lived my entire life hidden from humanity. My mother and father didn't know who I was. Nor did my children. They only knew the person I had presented to them. It wasn't that I was trying to be false. When I had been younger, I had assumed that my struggles were part of growing up: I was a man and would learn to be a better one by acting the part. I presented my best understanding of manliness even as I worked feverishly and in secret to fix myself.

But once I understood the truth—that I wasn't a man and never would be—it was game over. I realized that I would prefer that my family know me as something shameful than that they never know me at all.

I WAS ALSO MOTIVATED by the need to know what it feels likes to be loved. When you present a false self to the world—even unconsciously—you cannot take pleasure in someone else's expression of love. Their very declaration feels like a betrayal. It is a reminder to the person within you that someone else is stealing the applause. Others aren't loving you; they are loving the shell that they see.

You learn to walk through life, sealed off from human contact as though behind a wall of Plexiglas. I transitioned to know what it feels like to feel loved for who I am.

I WAS DRIVEN, too, by the need to express my love. I had always considered myself a loving father and husband. I went to great pains to declare my feelings to Mary and my children. All of my friends described me as a loving person.

But there was a quiet desperation behind these declarations. It was as though I were shouting from the bottom of a well. I was rarely able to take pleasure in my expressions of feeling. I was too busy trying to convince myself that my feelings were real.

I used to feel guilty, for example, when I looked ahead to my parents' eventual mortality. What would I feel when one of them died? I worried that I might feel nothing. "But I love them!" I remonstrated. "How could I be so ungrateful?"

The issue, as it turned out, had nothing to do with my feelings for my parents. When I tried to bury the person inside me, I walled myself off from my own emotions. I thought more than I felt. I transitioned so that I could finally wear my emotions on my sleeve. I have shared more love with my parents during the past two years than I did during the first fifty years of my life. Though they continue to struggle with pronouns, the relationship we enjoy today is incomparably better.

FINALLY, I transitioned in order to be present for everyone I love. My children were often perplexed by my seeming absence from conversations. I was sitting right in front of them, but my mind was in another world. When I did respond, it was often with an awkwardness they could not understand.

212

My youngest daughter, Haley, is a frightfully effective mind reader. She often broke my moments of silence asking, "Daddy, are you OK? What are you thinking about? What's the matter?"

These moments always pained me. Part of me wanted to scream, "I'm dying in here!" Instead, I retreated into another lie, "Nothing's the matter, Sweetie. I'm just thinking."

My daughter, Evelyne, was the first to note the difference. "It is so much more fun talking to you now. I feel like you are completely here for me."

MY ONLY REGRET is the pain I have inflicted on Mary and my children. When I began my transition, there were many times when I felt that what I was doing to my family bordered on the criminal. The only thing that stayed my judgment was the certainty that this was not a choice. I would not have survived much longer.

Still, there is nothing worse than the thought that you are causing those you love incalculable pain. The father and husband that they had counted on to be there for them—to orbit around their world—is gone. I don't want to minimize what I took away from them. But to focus only on the person they lost is to miss two important considerations.

The first is that I arguably did more harm to my children in the years before I transitioned than in the years since. Yes, I was an outwardly loving and successful father. But children can tell the difference between someone who is wholly authentic and someone who is living in fear. They can tell when a parent is emotionally distracted and when they are fully engaged. When I see my children feeling especially anxious, I worry that they learned that emotion from me. All of them are courageous. But they learned courage from their mothers, not from their father.

The second consideration is that it ignores the gift that—I hope— I eventually did give to my family. I love the way that Evelyne recently described it. In an interview on the *Dr. Oz Show*, she said that my transition had been terribly hard on her—she cried for two years. But today, she says, she couldn't be more proud to be my daughter. As she put it, "If Tina can do this, there isn't anything in the world that I can't accomplish."

What more could a parent hope to pass along?

EPILOGUE

IT IS MIDNIGHT. I am in bed reading another management book. Nearby, Mary is lost in slumber beneath the blankets. I lay my book down and reach for her hands. Seventeen years ago, these hands were joined with mine in holy matrimony. Promises were made. We would love, honor and obey. We would cherish and protect.

Today, we know with a certainty what it is to give and receive love unconditionally. Our bodies no longer know the tight embrace of physical intimacy, but our souls know a tender touch and a quiet understanding that too few couples enjoy. Mary's hands have aged a little since we made our vows. They are gently lined and mottled with freckles. They are frailer. But I still find them lovely to behold.

I shift my gaze to my own two hands. Next to hers, mine are large and muscular. Their masculine size is their chief feature. Oh how often I have hated them for outing me! But tonight, as I cradle her fingers in mine, I understand the beauty of my hands. Their strength is there to hold and to protect her. And I love them for that.

So here we are, two aging Cinderellas, sharing life's mysteries as we dance into our sunset. I hope that it will be a beautiful one.

ða ða

APPENDIX

- A Brief Primer on Transsexuality and Transsexuals
- Gender Dictionary
- Religion and Gender
- Resources for Those Seeking Help & Support
- Resources for Getting to Know Us As People
- A Sampling of Successful Trans Women in Business, Science, and the Professions

A BRIEF PRIMER ON TRANSSEXUALITY AND TRANSSEXUALS[14]

FOUR THINGS TO UNDERSTAND ABOUT TRANSSEXUALITY

1. Being a transsexual is not the same as being a crossdresser, drag queen, homosexual, Inter-sex, or gender queer.

MANY PEOPLE lump transsexuals under the umbrella term, *transgenderism*. But *transgenderism* is a political and social umbrella. It is not a scientific category. It was conjured up as a neutral label for almost any individual not conforming to social norms of gender expression.

Though the science of gender is still in its early stages of development, we have ample evidence that there are fundamental differences among transgender sub-categories. Transsexuals, transvestites, and drag queens have distinct personal histories and motivations. The main thing they seem to share is public contempt.

Transsexuals are also sometimes mistakenly lumped together with homosexuals. But being transsexual has nothing to do with sexual preference. The sexual preferences of transsexuals are as diverse as those of the rest of the world.

Author's Note: I had once assumed that my transsexuality would give me a special window into what it feels like to be homosexual. It doesn't. I have no more sense of what a gay man experiences inside than does any

---

[14] Most of the statistics in this appendix are sourced from: Grant, Jaime M., Lisa A. Mottet, Justin Tanis, Jack Harrison, Jody L. Herman, and Mara Keisling. "Injustice at Every Turn: A Report of the National Transgender Discrimination Survey." Washington: National Center for Transgender Equality and National Gay and Lesbian Task Force, 2011.

other heterosexual. I do, however, understand what it feels like to be hated for no other reason than being different.

2. Transsexuality appears to be biologically rooted.

DURING THE PAST TWENTY YEARS, psychoanalytic explanations of transsexualism have largely been discredited and replaced with biological explanations. The emerging consensus among medical providers specializing in transgender care is that most forms of transsexuality develop in the womb, shortly after conception.

All mammals start their fetal development from a female template. If, at a critical stage, the fetus is exposed to certain hormonal signals, it shifts development tracks and starts to develop a masculine anatomy. It is as though the body is traveling down a train track and a switch is thrown: once the body heads in that direction, it continues along that track—permanently. (This isn't true of all animals. Some species can change sex even as adults.)

Among some mammals, man among them, the brain develops several weeks after the reproductive organs do. If the developing brain is exposed to different hormone signals than  were the sex organs, it can head down the other track. Some brain scan studies and autopsies have revealed that transsexual men's and women's brains more closely resemble those of the opposite sex. Sample sizes are too small, results too variable, and measurement technologies too crude to be conclusive.

> *Author's Note: But it makes so much sense to me. It explains everything I have experienced. In spite of my trying for fifty years to live as a man, I know of no other way to experience the world than as a woman.*

For all our learning, so much mystery remains in the world. Three hundred years ago, before the invention of the microscope, not one human being had ever seen a germ. And yet germs have been with us since the beginning of civilization, killing people by the hundreds of millions. Thanks to the science of germ theory, we are now able to save people afflicted by such scourges as influenza, typhoid, and leprosy.

Historically, humankind has defined gender based on what we can see—the genitalia. But just because we cannot yet "see" gender in the brain, it doesn't mean that it doesn't exist as something distinct from the genitals. We didn't discover germs until Anton van Leeuwenhoek invented the microscope. Perhaps we have yet to develop the lens to see gender in its fullest light.

Author's Note: We used to hang people as witches who we now know suffered from physical illnesses. Must we always destroy things we don't understand?

3. Transsexuality is not a psychological disorder.

At LEAST NOT IN THE SENSE that most people use the term. Aside from their deep unhappiness, transsexuals tend to be high-functioning people. In the United States, 47 percent have completed college and/or graduate school versus 27 percent among the general population.

Transsexuals function effectively in high stress careers. They are twice as likely as the general population to enlist for military service. They have held leadership roles at many companies, including Microsoft, Xerox, CIGNA, Ratheon, and Prudential. In 2013, the highest paid female CEO in the United States was a transsexual woman. Transsexual men and women have led some critical breakthroughs in information technology and medical science.

In one sense, transsexuality *is* a disorder. Left untreated, transsexuals tend to suffer from severe depression. It hurts a lot when your mind and body don't match. A recent survey of 6,450 transgender Americans revealed that 41 percent have attempted suicide—25 times the national average. And these are the people who are alive to respond.

Author's Note: If 40 percent of our "normal" children suffered such levels of despair, I suspect that healing them would be a national priority. What is more, we would put the promotors of quack remedies in jail.

4. The only proven cure for gender dysphoria lies in accepting one's gender identity.

DURING THE PAST CENTURY, many "cures" to transsexuality have been attempted—electro-shock therapy, talk therapy, aversion therapy, religious counseling—to name a few. What all of these approaches share is that they attempt to alter the mind to match the body. Documented successes are few and far between. More often, these approaches have made matters worse. They have largely been discredited by the medical community.

The only effective measure found to date has been to change the body to match the mind, coupled with rigorous psychological screening and counseling. This approach has met with an extraordinary rate of success. One measure of success is the percentage of patients whose lives significantly improved as a result of medical interventions. One study[15] pooled 28 other studies that included 1,833 participants. The participants had all undergone some sex reassignment procedures that included hormonal therapy. Eighty percent of the participants reported significant improvement in their symptoms of gender dysphoria. Eighty percent also reported a significant improvement in their quality of life.

Another measure of success is the avoidance of failure. How many of those who pursue gender-confirming procedures find that they later regret their decision? Rates of reported regret are typically well under two percent. One German study of 1,422 transsexuals found that less than 0.1 percent felt regret. Few medical treatments can boast of such a success record.

Author's Note: I would argue that transsexuals remind the rest of us what is important in life. They struggle—more than most—with the spirit-body connection. Is their identity rooted in their visible anatomy, or in the voice

---

[15] "Hormonal Therapy and Sex Reassignment: A Systematic Review and Meta-Analysis of Quality of Life and Psychosocial Outcomes", Murad et al. *Clinical Endocrinology* (2010) 72, 214-231

that cries from within? Personally, I find comfort in their answer: it is our souls that define us.

I cannot overstate the importance of psychological counseling. Not everyone who questions their gender is a transsexual person. Even those who are will almost certainly find that the psychological aspects of transition are far more difficult than the physical ones. Therapy is important.

FOUR THINGS TO UNDERSTAND ABOUT TRANSSEXUALS

1. For transsexuals, it isn't a transition to someone new.

FOR THE TRANSSEXUAL, "transitioning" isn't about becoming something new. They aren't becoming a woman or a man. They are finally coming out as the person they have always considered themselves to be.

A common reaction people have when they learn that someone is "transitioning" is to ask, "Why would you do that? What does becoming a woman solve?"

But the transsexual isn't trying to become anything. What they are trying to do is to end a lifetime of self-repression and pretense. They have decided to finally stop pretending to be something they aren't. They are finally becoming their authentic self.

This is why many transsexuals generally dislike terms like "sex-reassignment surgery". "Gender confirmation surgery" more accurately reflects their experience.

2. Transsexuals generally don't care to be thought of as transsexuals.

TRANSSEXUAL WOMEN consider themselves women. Transsexual men consider themselves men. It isn't wishful thinking on their part. It is the only way they know to process their reality. It is how their brain has been wired all their life. Many spend a lifetime attempting to "rewire" their brain to conform to social prejudices—but without success.

The ultimate goal of most transsexuals is to be accepted as the person they are inside. Far from wanting to preoccupy themselves with gender, their main goal is to put gender behind them. They want to move on to leading a normal life where they can finally take their gender for granted—just as everyone else does.

Sadly, only 21 percent of transsexuals surveyed feel that they can consistently pass as their identified gender. The other 79 percent are forced to live with what they experience as a visible birth defect—like a sixth finger. The greatest kindness you can show such people is to focus on who they are as a person. You will likely be amazed to learn how gifted they are.

3. Transsexuals are as diverse as the rest of the world.

IT'S LIKE THE OLD SAYING GOES: "When you've met one transsexual ... you've met one transsexual."

Only a few decades ago, society was saddled with gross stereotypes about what it meant to be Black, Asian or female. The stereotypes persist, but growing numbers of people see past them today. They recognize that women are incredible in their variety. They understand that someone's race does not define how they think or what they are capable of.

Transsexuals are no different. One of the reasons that transsexual stereotypes persist is that there is a bias in the profile of transsexuals who expose themselves to the media. There is nothing wrong with what these people choose to do. But transsexuals should no more be defined by these celebrities than a woman should be defined by Lady Gaga, Hilary Clinton, Mother Theresa, or Sarah Palin. We are all unique individuals.

Author's Note: The majority of transsexuals that I have come to know lead fairly conventional lives—as bankers, software programmers, waiters, truck drivers, policemen, lawyers, and teachers. Like most people, they want to be known for what they contribute to the world, not for what they carry between their legs.

4. We aren't out to change the world. We just want to live in it.

SADLY, TRANSGENDER MEN AND WOMEN are the one remaining minority in America without legal protections against job and housing discrimination. In most states, gender variance has been explicitly written out of equal rights legislation. In the military, transgender personnel are the one group still covered by "don't ask, don't tell". Even though they are twice as likely to serve in the military and 25 percent more likely to register to vote, gender variant people enjoy fewer rights than other citizens[16].

Transgender men and women are almost twice as likely to have achieved a college or graduate degree compared to the general population (47 percent versus 27 percent). This is all the more remarkable when you consider that, in grades K through 12, 78 percent have been harassed by peers and 31 percent by teachers and staff. Over a third (35 percent) have been physically assaulted and 12 percent sexually assaulted. And yet they stick around to graduate.

These accomplishments notwithstanding, gender non-conforming men and women are twice as likely to be unemployed. Twenty percent have been denied housing owing to their gender variance. Nineteen percent report that they were denied medical care by health professionals owing to their gender non-conforming status.

All that most of these men and women want to do is to lead healthy lives, love their families, and contribute to society.

HOW TO TREAT A TRANSSEXUAL: FOUR SIMPLE RULES

1. Treat them as they present themselves. A transsexual woman is a woman. A transsexual man is a man. She is "she". He is "he". If you use the wrong pronoun, don't get stressed. It happens. But don't let it pass. Being referred to by the wrong pronoun is painful. A simple

---

[16] As this book goes to print, it appears that the U.S. military is preparing to reverse this policy.

acknowledgement can turn their day around. ("I'm sorry Ma'am. I was focusing on your food order. By the way, that's a pretty dress.")

Author's Note: Some transgender people want to do away with the concept of gender altogether. Their preferred pronoun is often something like 'ze'." While I want to support them, I find it hard to keep track. I have decided to leave this battle to the next generation. In the meantime, I try to get to know people for who they are as an individual, not for their gender. I suspect that this is what those who defy gendered pronouns are really after.

2. Don't stereotype. Treat them as individuals. Transsexuals are as diverse as any other demographic group. A group of transsexuals is as likely to differ on politics, lifestyle, and values as any other random selection of men or women.

3. Don't assume that they want to be open. While some transsexuals are quite willing to discuss their personal journey, others want nothing more than to put that aspect of their lives behind them. Find a discrete way to test their feelings before asking personal questions. If you do ask questions, try to do so in a way that affirms who they are (AVOID: *Do you miss being a man?* BETTER: *What do you enjoy most about being a woman?*) Balance your efforts to understand their gender with efforts to learn about the rest of their life.

4. Be an ally. If you see a transsexual being mistreated, stand up for them! If you see them standing off to the side, make them feel welcome. Help them to bring their A-game into the world. We are all better off when they do.

GENDER DICTIONARY

SOME GENDER TERMS are subject to intense debate. Words like *queer* are celebrated by some groups and considered defamatory by others. Words like *transvestite* and *homosexual* were in common use a generation ago but are now generally considered offensive. As I wrote this book, I struggled with such word choices. For example, should I use *transvestite* or *crossdresser?* In general, I went with the term that best captured general usage and my state of mind at the time.

The dictionary below is organized topically. It borrows heavily from the PFLAG National Glossary of Terms and from the GLAAD Media Reference Guides[17].

SEX

Sex: Refers to biological, genetic, or physical characteristics that define males and females. These can include genitalia, hormone levels, genes, or secondary sex characteristics.

Assigned Sex: The sex (male, female, intersex) that is assigned to an infant at birth.

Intersex: Individuals born with chromosomal anomalies or ambiguous genitalia. They have both male and female characteristics, making binary identification impossible.

---

[17] GLAAD: The Gay & Lesbian Alliance against Defamation. Founded in 1985, GLAAD fights for appropriate coverage of the LGBT community in the news and entertainment media. Their lgb and transgender guides to usage can be found at: http://www.glaad.org. PFLAG maintains a glossary of terms at: http://community.pflag.org/glossary.

GENDER

Gender: A set of social, psychological, or emotional traits, often influenced by societal expectations that classify an individual as either feminine or masculine.

Affirmed Gender: The gender to which someone has transitioned.

Assigned Gender: The gender label assigned to someone at birth.

Gender Binary: The concept that there are only two genders, male and female, and that everyone must be one or the other.

Gender Dysphoria: A persistent unease with having the physical characteristics of one gender, accompanied by strong identification with the opposite gender.

> *In 2013, the American Psychiatric Association replaced the earlier diagnosis code, Gender Identity Disorder (GID) with gender dysphoria. To call it an identity disorder is to impose a value judgment—much as when the medical establishment regarded being gay as a mental disorder. This disorder isn't a matter of gender identity. The disorder lies in the intense discomfort experienced by people who feel that their body and gender identity don't match.*

Gender Expression: The manner in which a person chooses to communicate their gender identity to others through external means such as clothing and/or mannerisms.

Gender Identity: One's deeply held personal, internal sense of being male, female, some of both, or neither.

> *A common shorthand used to distinguish gender identity from sex is to describe sex as what's between your legs and gender identity as what's between your ears (in your mind).*

COMMON GENDER IDENTITY AND GENDER EXPRESSION LABELS

Transgender: An umbrella term for people whose gender identity and/or gender expression differs from what is typically associated with the sex they were assigned at birth.

Can be applied to anyone who does not conform to the binary gender norms. Some people object to this term because it consolidates groups that have very different experiences of gender and gender expression.

Cisgender: The opposite of transgender. An individual whose gender identity aligns with their assigned sex at birth.

Cisgender has its origin in the Latin-derived prefix cis-, meaning "on this side of", which is an antonym for the Latin-derived prefix trans-, meaning "on the other side of". Cisgender people's minds and bodies are on the same side of the gender binary.

Agender: A person who does not conform to any gender.

Androgynous: A non-binary gender identity. Can also be used to describe people's appearances or clothing.

Crossdresser (generally preferred to **Transvestite**): Typically, a heterosexual man who periodically wears women's clothes, makeup, and accessories as a form of gender expression. Crossdressers do not wish to permanently change their sex or to live full-time as women.

Drag: Originally used in Shakespeare's Globe Theatre to mean *DRessed As Girl*, referring to male actors planning female roles. **Drag Queens** are men who dress like women for the purpose of entertainment. **Drag Kings** are their female counterparts.

Gender neutral: Not gendered. Can refer to language (including pronouns), spaces (like bathrooms), or identities (being gender queer, for example).

Gender nonconforming: A person who views their gender identity as one of many possible genders beyond strictly female or male.

Gender queer: A person who has a fluid gender identity.

Generally, refers to someone who takes a more defiant view against the gender binary than someone who is simply considers themselves androgynous. They often prefer to express themselves in ways that incorporate both sides of the binary in order to call the very concept into question.

Trans. Used as shorthand to mean either transgender or transsexual.

Transsexual: A person who emotionally and psychologically feels that they belong to the opposite sex or a person who has undergone treatment in order to acquire the physical characteristics of the opposite sex.

People who identify as transsexual do not necessarily identify as transgender and vice versa. There is some debate about whether it is appropriate to use transsexual by itself or whether it should always be used as an adjective in conjunction with man or woman.

Transsexual Man (Trans Man, FtM, Transgender Man): People assigned female at birth who identify and live as a man.

Some prefer transgender because it focuses attention on gender identity rather than sexual anatomy. Others consider transgender an overly broad term.

Transsexual Woman (Trans Woman, MtF, Transgender Woman): People assigned male at birth who identify and live as a woman *(see Transsexual Man, above).*

TRANSITION

Transition: The process one goes through to discover and/or affirm their gender identity.

Transition can include a variety of personal, medical, and legal steps: telling one's family, friends, and co-workers; using a different name and new pronouns; dressing differently; changing one's name and/or sex on legal documents; hormone therapy; one or more types of surgery. GLADD suggests that the phrase sex change be avoided.

Coming out: The process of disclosing one's sexual orientation and/or gender identity to a chosen circle of friends, communities, or networks.

GLAAD describes it as a lifelong process of self-acceptance in which an individual decides whom to disclose what to.

Not Out (preferred to **closeted**): A person who is not open about their sexual orientation and/or gender identity.

Out: Describes people who openly self-identify as LGBTQ in their public and/or professional lives.

Questioning: Someone who is in a process of discovery and exploration about their sexual orientation, gender identity and/or gender expression.

Stealth: A term used to describe transgender individuals who do not disclose their trans status in their public lives.

SURGERY

Gender-affirming (or confirming) surgery: Surgical procedures that help people adjust their bodies in a way that more closely matches their gender identity.

> *GLAAD also supports the use of* **sexual reassignment surgery (SRS)**, *but many transsexuals find this term uncomfortable.*

Pre-Op / Post-Op / Non-Op: Transsexual men and women face a variety of surgical decisions when they transition. Some elect to have no surgery (non-op). Those who decide to have surgeries are pre-op before their surgeries and post-op after their surgeries.

> *Most transsexual men and women prefer to keep their surgical status confidential. Their surgical decisions may be motivated by their own sense of identity, by financial constraints, by medical considerations and a host of other factors. It is generally considered rude to inquire.*

SEXUALITY

Sexual orientation: An individual's emotional, romantic, or sexual feelings toward other people.

> *GLAAD suggests that this be used instead of "sexual preference" as the latter implies that orientation is a matter of choice.*

Asexual: An individual who does not experience sexual attraction.

Bisexual: An individual who is emotionally, romantically, and/or physically attracted to both men and women.

Gay (preferred to **Homosexual**): Adjective used to describe people whose emotional, romantic, and/or physical attraction is to people of the same sex.

Heterosexual: A person whose emotional, romantic, and/or physical attraction is to people of the opposite sex.

Lesbian: A woman whose enduring emotional, romantic, and/or physical attraction is to other women.

Pansexual: A person whose emotional, romantic, and/or physical attraction is to people of all gender identities and biological sexes.

POLITICS

Ally: Someone who does not identify as LGBTQ but who is supportive of LGBTQ individuals and the community.

Homophobia: An aversion to lesbian or gay people that often manifests itself in the form of prejudice and bias.

LGBT: An acronym for lesbian, gay, bisexual, and transgender that refers to these individuals collectively. Some people append Q (**LGBTQ**) to be inclusive of people who self-identify as gender queer, I for those who are intersex (**LGBTQI**), and A for people who consider themselves allies (**LGBTQIA**).

> *I don't mind any of these acronyms. They serve a purpose. But, if my condition has taught me anything, it is that we should focus on people's humanity.*

Lifestyle: A negative term often incorrectly used to describe the lives of people who are LGBTQ. The term is disliked because it implies that being LGBTQ is a choice.

RELIGION AND GENDER

IS GENDER VARIANCE A SIN?

ONE OF THE MAIN REASONS my gender variance filled me with so much turmoil was the worry that I might be committing a sin against God. I do not pretend to offer an authoritative answer to this question. It is a matter that everyone must explore with their own conscience.

I found two sites particularly helpful as I grappled with this issue. ReligiousTolerance.org offers a comprehensive set of resources for those wanting to explore religious perspectives on gender. While liberal in its viewpoint, the site takes great pains to capture the perspectives of many religious conservatives in their own words. Another site, TransChristians.org, details conservative objections to transsexualism and then offers blow-by-blow rebuttals.

Personally, I do not interpret the Bible literally. I believe, for example, in evolution. But I wanted to understand the biblical basis for the arguments that some religious conservatives used to justify their discrimination against gender-variant people.

In Western religion, arguments against gender variance seem to rest on two notions: 1) God created a binary world; 2) God explicitly forbids us to cross-dress and to mutilate our genitals.

BINARY CREATION?

TWO PASSAGES are often cited as evidence that God created a binary world.

> So God created man in his [own] image, in the image of God created he him; male and female created he them. (Genesis 1:27)

> And he answered and said unto them, "Have ye not read, that he which made [them] at the beginning made them male and female?" (Matthew 19:4)

233

Religious conservatives claim that we violate God's act of creation when we alter our gender. Who are we to question his decisions? God does not make mistakes.

But other religious scholars point to an important detail in the wording of these two passages. According to the scripture, God created them "male *and* female", not "male *or* female". "Or" is explicit that something is binary. "And" leaves room for interpretation. Arguably, it is religious conservatives who impose a binary model, not God.

This strikes me as a very close reading of the word *and*. I am comfortable with the notion that God created a world modeled, for the most part, on two sexes. But nowhere does the Bible say that he perfected the world or that he created a world without variation. We find variation everywhere.

What is more, mankind corrects and extinguishes God's creations every day. We improve God's soil, breed his animals, and vanquish his diseases. That something exists does not automatically make it good or unalterable. God does not expect us to resign ourselves to everything just as we find it.

Ecclesiastes suggests that we approach God's creation with a little more humility:

> *As thou knowest not what is the way of the spirit, nor how the bones do grow in the womb of her that is with child: even so thou knowest not the works of God who maketh all. (Ecclesiastes 11:5)*

I found this passage particularly comforting. Each year, more and more evidence accumulates that, for many people, gender variance is introduced while they gestate in the womb. There is so much going on in there of which we remain ignorant.

CROSSDRESSING / GENITAL MUTILATION

BUT WHAT OF DEUTERONOMY? It seems to offer pretty explicit proscriptions against crossdressing and sexual reassignment.

The woman shall not wear that which pertaineth unto a man, neither shall a man put on a woman's garment: for all that do so [are] an abomination unto the LORD thy God. (Deuteronomy 22:5)

He that is wounded in the stones, or hath his privy member cut off, shall not enter into the congregation of the LORD. (Deuteronomy 23:1)

Like most Christians, I do not feel compelled to obey every law laid out in the five books of Moses. I eat pork. I wear clothing made from two cloths. When a woman wears pants, I don't question her faith. I don't believe that a man with a flattened nose or a broken foot cannot approach God's altar.

In any event, these two rulings are arguably contradicted or updated elsewhere in the Bible. Isaiah 56:4-5 removes the ban on the genetically mutilated. In Acts 8:26-39.1, an Ethiopian eunuch is baptized and accepted into the Kingdom of God. In the Book of Matthew, Jesus strongly implies acceptance of the genitally mutilated:

For some are eunuchs because they were born that way; others were made that way by men; and others have renounced marriage because of the kingdom of heaven. The one who can accept this should accept it. (Matthew 19:12)

Many Jewish scholars suggest that the intent of the proscriptions against crossdressing were motivated by a desire to prevent men and women from committing adultery. For example, one commentary states it this way:

The root of this mitzva (commandment) is to keep us from sexual sin … and there is no doubt that if men and women's clothing were the same, they would mix and the earth would be filled with impropriety. (Sefer HaHinukh 564).

THESE ANALYSES are based on interpretations that are subject to debate. Honest hearts can disagree. In the end, two things persuade me that being transsexual is not a sin against God's will.

First, there are the lives and testimonials of hundreds, if not thousands, of transgender Christians, Jews, and other religiously minded people. Many of them are ordained pastors. In the Presbyterian Church, there is Erin Swenson. Drew Phoenix serves his United Methodist congregation. The Anglican Church allowed Carol Stone to continue her ministry even after she had undergone gender confirmation surgery. In the US, the Episcopal Church ordained openly transgender pastor Cameron Partridge.

These are good people—devout in their faith and sincere in their gender. If they are brave enough to accept and proclaim their gender, what have I to fear?

BUT I FIND the most persuasive argument in the Bible itself. In Galatians, Paul proclaims,

> *For as many of you as have been baptized into Christ have put on Christ. There is neither Jew nor Greek, there is neither bond nor free, there is neither male nor female: for ye are all one in Christ Jesus. And if ye [be] Christ's, then are ye Abraham's seed, and heirs according to the promise. (Galatians 3:27-29).*

As I read it, Paul couldn't be much clearer: our gender is inconsequential to God. It is our faith that matters. Elsewhere in the New Testament, the Lord says to Samuel,

> *The LORD seeth not as man seeth; for man looketh on the outward appearance, but the LORD looketh on the heart. (I Samuel 16:7)*

When I look into my own heart, I can find no cause to feel guilty. In fact, my heart feels purer and God's voice sounds louder now that I have unmuffled the voice that cries from within me. That voice was God's greatest gift to me. To stifle it for the sake of social conformity strikes me as the far greater evil.

RESOURCES FOR THOSE SEEKING INFORMATION AND SUPPORT

Gender and Public Policy / Legal Services

Human Rights Campaign (HRC). Largest civil rights organization pursuing equality for LGBT Americans. Produces several useful indices comparing government, business and health care organizations' LGBT policies and practices.

http://www.hrc.org/issues/transgender

HRC produces several indices that track LGBT laws, policies and practices for different institutions: *Corporate Equality Index*; *Healthcare Equality Index*, *State Equality Index*, *Municipal Equality Index*. Their *Buyers Guide* is useful for consumers who want to purchase from LGBT-friendly organizations.

http://www.hrc.org/resources

Lamba Legal. Committed to the civil rights of LGBT people and those with HIV through impact litigation, education, and public policy work.

http://www.lambdalegal.org

National Center for Transgender Equality. Pursues equality for transgender people through advocacy, collaboration, and empowerment.

http://www.transequality.org

Injustice at Every Turn. Revealing report based on the 2011 National Transgender Discrimination Survey of 6,450 transgender people. Survey is being updated in 2015.

http://www.transequality.org/issues/resources/national-transgender-
discrimination-survey-executive-summary

Sylvia Rivera Law Project. Works to guarantee that all people are free to self-determine gender identity and expression. Especially active in legal support and prison reform.

http://www.srlp.org

Transgender Legal Defense & Education Fund. Committed to achieving equality for transgender people through public education, test-case litigation, direct legal services, community organizing, and public policy efforts.

http://www.transgenderlegal.org

Gender at Home and In School

Campus Pride. Dedicated to safer, more LGBTQ-friendly colleges and universities. Produces *Campus Pride Index,* a guide to universities' LGBT policies, services, and practices.

http://www.campuspride.org

Gender Spectrum. Provides consultation, training, and events to help families, educators, professionals, and organizations understand and address gender identity and expression.

http://www.genderspectrum.org.

GLSEN. Gay, Lesbian, and Straight Education Network. Teachers dedicated to improved LGBT climate in K-12 education.

http://www.glsen.org

PFLAG. Parents, Families, Friends, and Allies United with LGBT People to Move Equality Forward. Grassroots network committed to LGBTQ equality through support, education, and advocacy.

http://www.pflag.org

TransActive. Provides services and expertise to empower transgender and gender diverse youth and their families to live healthy lives, free of discrimination.

http://www.transactiveonline.org

TransYouth Family Allies. Empowers children and families by partnering with educators, service providers, and communities, to develop supportive environments in which gender may be expressed and respected.

http://www.imatyfa.org

Gender at Work

Out and Equal. World's largest nonprofit organization dedicated to creating safe and equitable workplaces for LGBT people.

http://www.outandequal.org

Transgender Veteran Americans Association. Advocate for open trans military service, secure benefits for trans families, trans well-being, and trans veteran employment.

http://www.tavausa.org

Sheridan, Vanessa. 2009. *The Complete Guide to Transgender in the Workplace*. Santa Barbara: ABC-CLIO.

Understanding Gender

Most of the major sites offer downloadable overviews for free. Here are two that I found helpful.

What Transsexuality Is—Definition, Cause and History. — Brief overview of the history, definition, statistics, and biology of transsexualism.

http://transsexual.org/What.html

A Primer on Transsexuality — A "grade school level explanation" of what transsexuality is all about. Oversimplifies the science a little, but gets at the essentials. Especially good at describing why it hurts so much to have the "wrong body."

http://transsexual.org/aprimer.html

The three books below discuss gender in simple, engaging language. Each will appeal to a slightly different reader.

Bennet, DeAnna. 2014. *Born This Way: Questions & Answers about Being Transgender.* — Bennet answers 111 frequently asked questions based largely on her personal reflections. Will appeal to those who like a Q&A format ("What's it like to …?").

Herman, Joanne. 2009. *Transgender Explained for Those Who Are Not.* — Short, easy read by a transgender woman. You feel as though you are an audience of one with someone who is telling it straight and simple.

Teich, Nicholas M. 2012. *Transgender 101: A Simple Guide to a Complex Issue.* New York: Columbia University Press. — Well-rounded overview by a social worker and transgender man. Slightly more emphasis on societal perspective (e.g., history, mental health controversy, discrimination).

Two other books cover the topic a bit more technically.

Vitale, Anna. 2010. *The Gendered Self: Further Commentary on the Transsexual Phenomenon.* Point Reyes Station: Flyfisher Press. — Based on the author's experience in treating over 500 gender dysphoric individuals. Candid insights from a seasoned professional.

Seton, Sarah. 2008. *Transsexualism: A Medical Retrospective.* Aetheom Press. — Though its statistics are a bit dated, the author offers insights and scientific details that are particularly helpful to transgender individuals struggling with guilt. My favorite quote: "Contrary to current belief, transsexuals are not tormented by their condition: it is their condition, which prompts society to torment them."

Support for Significant Others

Many of the general support sites have special sections and materials for significant others. Below is a list of private discussion groups and resources developed specifically for significant others.

Daily Strength—Spouses of Transgender. Private support group for spouses of transgender people (59 members).

http://www.dailystrength.org/groups/spouses-of-transgender

Engender Partners Forum. Established by Helen Boyd. A private, supportive forum for the partners of TG/CD people (323 members).

https://groups.yahoo.com/neo/groups/engender_partners/info

Partners of Transgender People. A Facebook support group for partners of Transgender individuals (883 likes).

https://www.facebook.com/pages/Partners-of-Transgender-People/273878936075362

Transgender Partners. A support group for Committed couples where one (or both) identify as transgender.

https://www.facebook.com/transpartners

Kinsey Institute Resources for Significant Others. Two pamphlets for significant others, partners, friends, families and allies (SOFFAs).

http://kinseyconfidential.org/resources-transgender-people-friends-families/

Transgender Spouse Blog. A Huffington Post blog series with several contributors.

http://www.huffingtonpost.com/news/transgender-spouse/

Support for Those Transitioning

Lynn Conway's Site. Informational and support site for transgender and transsexual people created by a trans woman. Reflects years of fieldwork and empirical research.

http://ai.eecs.umich.edu/people/conway/conway.html

Transsexual & Transgender Road Map. Includes over 1,600 pages of original content to support every aspect of transition. A great guide to many more communities and resources.

http://www.tsroadmap.com/index.html

World Professional Association for Transgender Health (WPATH). Professional organization devoted to the understanding and treatment of gender identity disorders. Produces *Standards of Care*, now in its seventh edition. Includes a new search tool for locating healthcare professionals.

http://www.wpath.org

Boedecker, Anne L. 2011. *The Transgender Guidebook: Keys to a Successful Transition.* — Step-by-step, self-help guide by a licensed psychotherapist who works with the transgender community.

Brill, Stephanie and Rachel Pepper. 2008. *The Transgender Child: A Handbook for Families and Professionals.* — Comprehensive guidebook summarizes latest psychological research and offers detailed, practical advice (e.g., what to expect, how to deal with grief, how to talk to doctors and lawyers).

Erickson-Schroth, Laura, Ed. 2014. *Trans Bodies, Trans Selves: A Resource for the Transgender Community.* — Modeled after Our Bodies, Ourselves. Its strength is that it is encyclopedic and kaleidoscopic in its coverage. You learn about everything trans from every part of the transgender community. With so many contributors, it can be a bit overwhelming.

Levi, Jennifer L. and Elizabeth E. Monnin-Browder, eds. 2012. *Transgender Family Law: A Guide to Effective Advocacy.* Bloomington: AuthorHouse. — A product of Gay & Lesbian Advocates & Defender's (GLAD) Transgender Rights Project. Covers full gamut of issues, e.g., changing legal documents, parental rights, divorce, partner violence, and estate planning. Targeted at attorneys but readable by lay readers.

Rose, Lannie. 2004. *How to Change Your Sex: A Lighthearted Look at the Hardest Thing You'll Ever Do.* — Perhaps not as detailed or up-to-date as some other guides, but this book did more than any other to center me on my own personal journey.

Online Communities

These community sites are great places to gain perspectives and advice from other transgender people. They are listed by level of traffic. There are also many communities on the major social media sites, such as Facebook, Google+, and Yahoo Groups.

Susan's Place. Very comprehensive community site: news headlines, chat room, online forums, resource links, articles. My only complaint: its erotic logo perpetuates a stereotype and belies its serious content. It may alienate some potential users. From what I can tell, it is by far the largest forum: over 1.5 million posts on over 145,000 topics by almost 20,000 members.

https://www.susans.org/

Laura's Playground. Like Susan's Place, its visuals do a poor job of conveying its serious content. Something for everyone, including significant others. Over 19,000 members and 600,000 posts.

http://www.lauras-playground.com/

The Transgender Boards. Classic discussion board with 8,000 members, over 250,000 posts and 15,000 topics.

http://www.tgboards.com/

The Gender Society. Forum includes 70,000 posts on 9,000 topics.

http://gendersociety.com/

TG Forum. Its strength seems to lie in its blogs. Appears to have a much smaller number of posts and topics than the others.

http://www.tgforum.com/wordpress/

Religion & Gender

Institute for Welcoming Resources. Provides resources and training to churches and other religious institutions interested in supporting transgender worshipers.

http://www.welcomingresources.org

Religious Tolerance. Comprehensive set of resources for those wanting to explore religious perspectives on gender. Liberal in viewpoint, but captures perspectives of many religious conservatives in their own words.

http://www.religioustolerance.org/transsexu.htm#menu

Trans Christians. Offers encyclopedic coverage of conservative objections to transsexualism—and then offers blow-by-blow rebuttals.

https://sites.google.com/site/transchristians/

Gender Newsfeeds

Transgender News. Compilation of transgender news from various sources. Requires Yahoo Groups membership.

https://groups.yahoo.com/neo/groups/transgendernews/info

Google News. Enter *transgender* as a search term.

https://news.google.com/

Transgender on Huffington Post. Compilation of their transgender news, features, and blogs.

http://www.huffingtonpost.com/news/transgender

GLAAD Transgender. Recent media coverage of transgender people.

http://www.glaad.org/taxonomy/term/34557/feed

RESOURCES FOR GETTING TO KNOW US AS PEOPLE

SCIENCE, RELIGION and social commentary offer useful lenses for understanding transsexuality. But they are no substitute for getting to know the people themselves. In fact, I think that they often get in the way. Fortunately, there are a lot of resources becoming available that vividly portray transgender lives. Here are a few that I have found particularly helpful.

PERSONAL ESSAYS

I FIND these collections to be especially useful and fascinating. You gain many perspectives in one book. Contributors share their greatest insights and most poignant moments in a few pages.

Hubbard, Eleanor A. and Cameron T. Whitley. 2012. *Trans-Kin: A Guide for Family & Friends of Transgender People.* Boulder: Bolder Press. — Although the title suggests that it is a guide, it is really a collection of vignettes built from about 50 interviews. Includes experiences of significant others, family, friends, allies and transgender people. Excellent directory of trans-kin organizations.

James, Andrea and Deanne Thornton. 2014. *Letters for My Sisters: Transitional Wisdom in Retrospect.* Oakland: Transgress Press. — Transgender women share their experiences and hard-earned wisdom in 33 brief essays.

Keig, Zander and Mitch Kellaway, eds. 2014. *Manning Up: Transsexual Men on Finding Brotherhood, Family & Themselves.* Oakland: Transgress Press. — Eye-opening for me. Moving accounts by trans men, many of them people of color, as they struggle to adapt to their new social identity. As men, are they now people of privilege or targets?

Rohrer, Megan M. and Zander Keig, eds. (2010) 2014. *Letters for My Brothers: Traditional Wisdom in Retrospect*, 4th Printing. United States: Wilgefortis. — Searingly honest advice from the battle-scarred. These people share how they coped with shame, alcohol, violence, privilege and many other unexpected elements of transition.

Johnson, Jordon and Becky Garrison, eds. 2015. *Love, Always: Partners of Trans People on Intimacy, Challenge & Resilience*. Oakland: Transgress Press. — A collection of moving essays by partners of trans people. One of them, a moving essay by Blair Braverman, inspired me to write *Between Shadow and Sun*.

MEMOIRS BY FAMILY MEMBERS

Boyd, Helen. 2003. *My Husband Betty: Love, Sex and Life with a Crossdresser*. Berkeley: Seal Press. A searching look at the gender spectrum and a brutally honest account of what it feels like to be married to (or to be) a crossdresser. Includes interviews with a variety of interesting personalities.

————. 2007. *She's Not the Man I Married: Life with a Transgendered Husband*. Berkeley: Seal Press. — As her husband, Betty, considers living as a woman full time, Boyd struggles. She shares her confusion and anger, providing a fascinating observation of the ways in which relationships are gendered. Many memorable observations and quotes.

Fabian, Leslie Hilburn. 2014. *My Husband's a Woman Now*. College Station: Virtualbookworm.com Publishing. — Story of a wife's efforts to support her husband's transition even as she grieved the loss of her male partner.

Haskell, Holly. 2013. *My Brother, My Sister*. — Haskell, a well-known feminist film critic follows her brother's/sister's transition. Offers thoughtful commentary on what both of them went through.

Howey, Noelle. 2003. *Dress Codes: Of Three Girlhoods--My Mother's, My Father's, and Mine*. New York: MacMillan. — A daughter recounts her father's transition in suburban Ohio. A loving portrait of her complicated relationship to her father's femininity and her own.

MEMOIRS BY ADULT TRANSITIONERS

Boylan, Jennifer Finney. 2003. *She's Not There: A Life in Two Genders.* — A sweetly sentimental and deeply reflective examination of her changing relationships and personal growth as she transitions.

————. 2013. *Stuck in the Middle with You: A Memoir of Parenting in Three Genders.* — Examines parenthood based on her experience parenting in both genders and on interviews with non-trans people. Raises interesting philosophical questions about parenting.

Mock, Janet. 2014. *Redefining Realness: My Path to Womanhood, Identity, Love & So Much More*. New York: Simon & Schuster. — I especially enjoyed Janet's story because—even though it is so different from my own—I could identify with her humanity. What a wonderful, thoughtful soul.

Salazar, Lisa. 2011. *Transparently: Behind the Scenes of a Good Life*. Lisa S. Salazar. — A devoutly Christian husband and father struggles for ten years with his diagnosis of gender dysphoria before deciding to transition to womanhood.

Stevens, Grace Anne. 2015. *No! Maybe? Yes! Living My Truth*. Graceful Change Press. — Stevens artfully captures her mental struggle through the book's gradual shift in pronouns. You can hear the debate as it evolves inside her head.

MEMOIRS BY CHILD / TEEN / YOUNG ADULT TRANSITIONERS

Andrews, Arin. 2104. *Some Assembly Required: The Not-So Secret Life of a Transgender Teen*. New York: Simon & Schuster. — Arin does an amazing job of describing what it feels like inside to be a teen in the wrong body.

Herthel, Jessica. 2014. *I am Jazz*. Dial Books. — Written for preschoolers. Jazz shares, in simple, engaging language, what it is like to feel like you are in the wrong body.

Sallans, Ryan K. 2013. *Second Son: Transitioning Toward My Destiny, Love and Life*. Omaha: Scout Publishing, LLC. — Ryan chronicles his struggles with his body, his family his partner, and a near-fatal case of anorexia.

CELEBRITY MEMOIRS

These can be insightful, and poignant as well as a good read. I have not included them in the lists above because they tend to focus lifestyles and careers that are exceptional. I include in this category, memoirs by Kate Borstein, Caroline Cossey (Tula), Renee Richards, Kristin Beck, and Chaz Bono. You can learn a lot from them. But I would be wary of generalizing from them.

TRANSGENDER PROFILES

A Gender Variance Who's Who. "The most comprehensive [site] on the web devoted to trans history and biography. Well over 1,100 persons worthy of note."

http://zagria.blogspot.ca/

Person Inside—Success Stories . Less extensive than the others and more focused on business, science and the professions. Select as category from Success Stories menu (left).

http://www.personinside.com

Successful Trans Women / Successful Trans Men. See Lynn Conway's site above. She has captured profiles of an extensive variety of successful transsexual men and women. These were the inspiration for my own, more modest effort.

http://ai.eecs.umich.edu/people/conway/TSsuccesses/TSsuccesses.html /
http://ai.eecs.umich.edu/people/conway/TSsuccesses/TransMen.html

ACADEMIC AND CULTURAL REVIEWS

Beemyn, Genny and Susan Rankin. 2011. *The Lives of Transgender People*.
New York: Columbia University Press. — Based on a survey of
almost 3,500 individuals and 400 follow-up interviews. Portrays the
breadth of the gender spectrum.

TRANSGENDER PEOPLE ON TELEVISION

I have mixed feelings about television's headlong rush to produce
transgender reality shows. The exposure is good, but I worry that they
invite caricature and stereotyping. We don't live in the fishbowl that
reality television portrays us in. Transgender people spend most of
their days dealing with the same mundane issues as everyone else.

Three series are worth a look: *Becoming Us*, *I am Jazz*, and *I am Cait*.
Yes, there is some obvious scripting and posturing. But I am impressed
by these series' candor and by their even-handed editing. Caitlin
Jenner, for example, allows herself to be captured making some very
embarrassing statements that could easily have been edited out.

Becoming Us is probably the most realistic of the three in terms of its
portrayal of day-to-day family life. We see a family struggle through
some very deep angst. It is the most emotionally revealing of the three.

I am Jazz is the most uplifting. What an incredible family—so
incredible that I sometimes found it hard to relate. It can be difficult
to follow in the footsteps of supermom, Jeanette. Jazz, too, is amazing.

I am Cait is especially poignant because it contrasts Caitlin's
privilege and naiveté with the experience of trans women who are less
fortunate and further along in their journey. I hope that they keep this
element of the show. My two frustrations are Caitlin's political views
and the fact that most scenes portray trans people talking to other trans
people. It would be more realistic to show trans people interacting with
the rest of the world. That's what we do most of the time.

Another television resource is the award-winning Amazon series, *TransParent*. Jill Soloway is a brilliant writer and director. She has assembled an incredible cast. Her portrayal of Mort's transition to Maura is, in many respects, more realistic than are the reality shows. I identified with Maura in so many of the scenes.

My only complaint is that the series is set in what has got to be the most dysfunctional family on the small screen. There is *sturm und drang* everywhere. Maura, in fact, may be the most stable and well-adjusted member of her family.

This is not a criticism. It makes for fascinating television. But I worry that some viewers will come away with the notion that transgender people live lives filled with angst and drama and that our families are unstable. I look forward to seeing us portrayed more subtly in some lighter comedies.

TRANSGENDER PEOPLE ON DVD

There are many good DVDs. Two, in my opinion, have a particularly broad appeal. They are realistic and revealing but not too disturbing.

Reed, Kimberly. 2010. *Prodigal Sons.* Cinedigm. — A fascinating story with or without the transgender element. Ms. Reed starts to create a video focused on her return to her hometown. But she wisely allows the plot to change direction as something equally fascinating crops up. While it isn't especially informative about transgender issues, I like that it presents Ms. Reed as an ordinary person engaged with her family.

Arnold, Chris. 2013. *Trans—The Movie*. RoseWorks and SexSmart Films. — Captures the diversity of the transgender community and their struggles. Nice mix of personal stories and community events.

TRANSGENDER PEOPLE ON THE INTERNET

There are many fascinating videos on the Internet. Try searching for a talk show you respect (e.g., *Frontline*, *Dr. Oz*, *Oprah Winfrey*), together with terms like *transgender, transsexual, transgender families*. Alternatively, enter topics of interest on YouTube. Many transgender men and women maintain video blogs there. It is difficult to catalog these because they tend to come and go as each person transitions.

It Gets Better Project. Great collection of videos with inspiring LGBT video posts.

> http://www.itgetsbetter.org/video/

To Survive On This Shore. Photographs and interviews with transgender and gender-variant older adults.

> http://www.tosurviveonthisshore.com/

We Happy Trans. A site for sharing positive trans experiences. It is brilliant in concept, but does not appear to be getting updated.

> http://wehappytrans.com/

What Trans Looks Like. A Twitter campaign organized by the Huffington Post. Invites transgender people to share photos of themselves.

> https://twitter.com/hashtag/WhatTransLooksLike

Jones, Zinnia. *Gender Analysis: In-depth coverage of transgender topics, from someone who's been there.* — In each clip, Zinnia researches and reports on a topic, such as sex change regret, bathroom bills, and electrolysis.

> https://www.patreon.com/zinniajones?ty=c

SUCCESSFUL TRANS WOMEN IN BUSINESS, SCIENCE, PROFESSIONS

Take a look at these women. Do you really care what their gender is? Wouldn't you want them on your team?

WHEN I WAS STRUGGLING with the decision to transition, one of my chief concerns was the expectation that I would be committing career suicide. I found many examples in the media of successful transgender celebrities, performers, models, writers, and activists. I also found many examples of transgender professionals who had carved out a life focused on care for others in our community. I am eternally grateful to these people. They deserve a lot of the credit for opening society's eyes, advancing our laws, and changing people's attitudes.

But what about people like me? Could I find examples of transsexual women who— in spite of their failure to conform to gender norms—had carved out successful careers in fields similar to mine?

I began to scour the Internet for examples of people who were open about their transgender background but who were successful for things unrelated to gender. Following is a list of people whose lives and accomplishments particularly inspired me. They gave me hope during some of my darkest hours.

Business Leaders

LYNN CONWAY — EXECUTIVE, COMPUTER CHIP PIONEER

Career: Designed advanced supercomputers for IBM (fired in 1968 upon revealing plans to transition). Returned to work as a woman for Memorex and then Xerox PARC, where she led the LSI Systems Group. Coauthored *Introduction to VLSI Systems*, the standard text in chip design at 100 universities. Joined DARPA as key architect on Defense Departments Strategic Computing Initiative. Finished her career as a professor at the University of Michigan. Invented several technologies that revolutionized chip design.

Education: BS, MSEE, Columbia University.

Awards: IEEE Fellow. Computer Pioneer Award, IEEE. Member National Academy of Engineering. National Achievement Award, Society of Women Engineers. Electronic Design Hall of Fame. Secretary of Defense Meritorious Civilian Service Award. Honorary Doctorate, Trinity College.

MARGARET STUMPP — CHIEF INVESTMENT OFFICER

Career: 20 years as Chief Investment Officer for Prudential Financial's $80 billion investment management subsidiary, Quantitative Investment Management Associates. Her research and opinions have been covered in the *New York Times*, *Wall Street Journal*, *Newsweek*, *Forbes* and on CNBC. She has published articles in: *The Financial Analyst's Journal*, *The Journal of Portfolio Management*, and the *Journal of Investment Management*. She also worked at AT&T and Price Waterhouse.

Education: BA, Economics, Boston University. MA and PhD in Economics, Brown University.

Affiliations: Q-Group in Finance, Journal of Investment Management, CFA Institute, CQA, NY Society of Security Analysts, Executive Women of NJ, Financial Women's Association of NY.

AMANDA SIMPSON — TEST PILOT, FLIGHT OPS DIRECTOR, PUBLIC SERVANT

Career: Special Assistant to the Assistant Secretary of the United States Army (Acquisition, Logistics, and Technology). Deputy Director, Advanced Missiles & Unmanned Systems, Raytheon. Director of Flight Operations / Test Pilot, Hughes Missile Systems.

Activism / Public Service: Board member to: Raytheon Global Women's Network, Raytheon GLBT & Allies Alliance, Raytheon

Diversity Council. Winner 2004 Democrat primary in Arizona District 26. Associate Fellow, American Institute of Aeronautics and Astronautics.

In the News: First openly transgender woman political appointee to any presidential administration.

MEGAN (MICHAEL) WALLENT — MICROSOFT EXECUTIVE, WINDOWS EXPLORER LEADER

Career: Currently Corporate VP, Microsoft Business Systems. Previously General Manager overseeing development of Windows Explorer versions 5.5 and 6, reporting directly to Bill Gates.

Education: BA, Computer Science.

Personal Life: Lives with wife Anh and three children. Private pilot. Diehard Boston sports fan.

Activism: Member, Board of Directors, Out and Equal. Maintained very transparent blog detailing her transition.

Medical Update: In 2013, Megan announced that she is transitioning back to Michael. It isn't because she regrets her transition. Rather, she has learned that she has a genetic predisposition to blood clots and is in a high-risk category for hormone therapy. She prefers to stay alive in order to be with her wife and children.

GINA DUNCAN — MORTGAGE BANKER, STAR LINEBACKER

Career: Regional Manager, Wells Fargo Home Mortgage. President, Metropolitan Business Association of Orlando. Small Business Owner (Art in Voyage travel consulting).

Public Service: Ran unsuccessfully for Orange County Commissioner.

Personal Life: Star linebacker for undefeated high school football team. Homecoming king. Married 25 years with two children. Now lives with dog, Boo, in College Park, Florida. Loves skiing, college football and long distance running.

Entrepreneurs

MARTINE ROTHBLATT — ENTREPRENEUR, LAWYER & AUTHOR

Career: Founder & CEO, United Therapeutics (highest paid female CEO in 2013); Founder, Sirius Radio and GeoStar. Published *The Apartheid of Sex*.

Social Activism: launched the Terasem Movement, a transhumanist school of thought focused on promoting joy, diversity, and the prospect of technological immortality.

Personal Life: Married for 34 years with four children and four grandchildren.

GINA KAMENTSKY — INVENTOR, ARTIST, MUSICIAN

Career: Toy inventor, sculptor, comic book artist, animator, and musician. Well known in the toy industry as the creator of the hit game *Chicken Limbo*. Worked at Fischer Price Toys before becoming an independent toy designer. Gina has collaborated on the design of a miniature golf course, invented interactive candy, dolls, card games and wacky kinetic sculpture. Her creations have been featured in the *New York Times*, *Metropolis*, *LA Style*, and *Home Magazine* and are housed throughout the United States.

Personal Life: When not inventing, Gina can be found playing bass fiddle in the hillbilly band The Fritters or zooming around Massachusetts with the East Coast Biker Chicks.

NICOLE ASHLEY HAMILTON — IT PIONEER, ENTREPRENEUR

Career: Developed Microsoft's first search engine. Named as inventor on seven U.S. patents. Founder / CEO of Hamilton Laboratories. Previously managed software development departments and projects at Prime Computer, IBM, Microsoft, and RealNetworks.

Education: MBA Valedictorian, Boston University; BS and MS, Electrical Engineering, Stanford University.

Personal Life: Two sons. Self-described tomboy. Loves fast motorcycles, hiking and bicycling. Wardrobe comes from REI. Firearms instructor and competitive shooter.

AUDREY TANG — ENTREPRENEUR, SOFTWARE PROGRAMMER

Career: Free software programmer, described as one of the "ten greats of Taiwanese computing". Best known for initiating and leading Pugs, a joint effort to implement the Perl 6 language. Has also contributed to SVK, Request Tracker, and Slash. Has led Chinese translation efforts for various Open Source books. A reputation for "penetrating insight into code and an uncanny knack for encouraging the people who write it."

Education: IQ reportedly 180. Unable to adapt to student life, dropped out of school at 14.

Personal Life: At 24, began to life as a woman, citing a need to "reconcile my outward appearances with my self-image."

KATE CRAIG-WOOD — TECHNOLOGY ENTREPRENEUR

Career: Focuses on Green IT, Cloud Computing. Selected at 20th most influential person in British ICT by Computer Weekly's UKTech50. Co-founded Memset Dedicated Server Hosting. Board member of Intellect UK. Fellow of British Computer Society. Steering Board Member of European Cloud Partnership.

Public Service: Chair of Intellect UK's Climate Change Group; Outspoken advocate for women in IT.

Personal Life: Loves motorcycling, surfing, SCUBA, Skiing. Licensed helicopter pilot.

MICHELA LEDWIDGE — WRITER, DIRECTOR, PRODUCER, SYSTEMS ARCHITECT

Career: Founder / Director of MOD Productions. Focused on Visual Storytelling. Won Sydney Film Festival's Peter Rasmussen Innovation Award for her cutting edge screen projects. Board Member, Australian

Directors Guild. Lecturer, University of Sydney. Set up the first web site in New South Wales (1993).

JANET FURMAN — ENTREPRENEUR, MUSICIAN

Career: Founder of Furman Sound, a professional audio and AC power products manufacturing company. Business development counselor at SCORE. Live Recording Technician for the Grateful Dead.

Personal Life: Amateur bass player. Avid runner, featured in Runner's World.

Education: BSEE, Columbia University.

Science, Academia

DEIRDRE MCCLOSKEY — NOTED ECONOMIST

Career: Distinguished Professor of Economics, History, English, and Communication, University of Illinois at Chicago. Previously on the faculties at the University of Iowa and University of Chicago. By reputation a conservative economist of the University of Chicago school, she describes herself as a Christian libertarian.

Publications: Author of sixteen books, most recently, *Bourgeois Dignity: Why Economics Can't Explain the Modern World*. Author of 400 scholarly pieces.

Honors: Honorary doctorates from universities in Sweden, Guatemala, Denmark, Ireland, and the USA. Phi Beta Kappa Lecturer, National Endowment for the Humanities Fellow, Guggenheim Fellow.

Education: BA and PhD in Economics, Harvard University.

RACHAEL PADMAN — CAMBRIDGE ASTROPHYSICIST

Career: University Lecturer, Cambridge (UK), Deputy Project Scientist, James Clerk Maxwell Telescope (Hawaii). Miller Research Fellow, Berkeley (California).

Education: Electrical Engineering, Monash University, PhD in Astronomy, Cavendish Laboratory.

Research Interests: Millimeter wave optics and receiver systems; Low-mass star formation; Spectral-line data reduction software.

JOAN ROUGHGARDEN — EVOLUTIONARY BIOLOGIST

Career: Taught at Stanford University from 1972 to 2011. Now semi-retired as a faculty member at Hawaii Institute of Marine Biology. Author of 8 books and 178 articles. Associate Editor or Co-Editor of *Philosophy and Theory in Biology, American Naturalist, Oecologia,* and *Theoretical Population Biology.*

Contributions: Proponent of social-selection theory of evolution as an alternative to Darwin's sexual selection model. Argues that the Bible does not conflict with evolutionary science.

Awards: Stonewall Book Award, American Academy of Arts & Sciences Fellow, Guggenheim Foundation Fellow, Dinkelspiel Award for Undergraduate Teaching.

Education: AB in Philosophy and BS in Biology, University of Rochester—Phi Beta Kappa. PhD in Biology, Harvard University.

LEANDRA VICCI — RESEARCH EXECUTIVE, ENGINEER

Career: Lecturer of Computer Science and Director of the Applied Engineering Laboratory Department of Computer Science University of North Carolina, Chapel Hill, NC.

Personal Life: A self-professed techno-geek, her high school activities bear this out: science club, radio club, math club, duodecimal club, chess club. She placed second in New Jersey's 1957 physics competition and had a ham radio license.

Passions & Perspectives: Science, technology, classical music, mountaineering, rock climbing. Lives on a farm with her long-time partner, Ina. "Since my transition ten years ago, the gender issues that used to dominate my life have evaporated entirely, while I'm still the techno-geek that I've always been."

Health Care, Pastoral Care

Dr. Rebecca Allison — Cardiologist

Career: Chief of Cardiology, CIGNA. Fellow, American College of Physicians. Fellow, American College of Cardiology. Repeatedly voted a "top doctor" in *Phoenix Magazine*'s annual poll.

Education: BS, University of Mississippi. MD, *magna cum laude*, University of Mississippi Medical Center.

Activism: Chair, American Medical Association Advisory Committee on LGBT Issues. President, Gay & Lesbian Medical Association. Recipient, Human Rights Campaign (HRC) Equality Award. Director, World Professional Association for Transgender Health (WPATH).

Reverend Erin K. Swenson, Th.M., PhD — Minister, Psychotherapist

Career: Presbyterian Minister practicing in Atlanta, Georgia. The first known mainstream Protestant minister to transition from male to female while remaining in ordained office. A practicing parish associate and pastoral psychotherapist.

Community Leadership: Board member, More Light Presbyterians. Chair, Health Ministries Committee of the Presbytery of Greater Atlanta. Co-founder, Southern Association for Gender Education. Travels nationally, presenting to conferences, churches, organizations, seminaries, and universities.

Personal Life: She continues to maintain warm, supportive relationships with her ex-spouse and their two grown daughters, as well as with the rest of her family.

Performing Arts, Creative Arts

Sara Davis Buechner — Concert Pianist, Educator

Career: Has served on faculty at University of British Columbia, Manhattan School of Music, and New York University. Performed with New York Philharmonic, Philadelphia, San Francisco, Buffalo and Cleveland orchestras. Maintains an active repertoire of almost 100 concertos. Has given master classes at the Royal Academy in London, the Juilliard School, Indiana University, and the Kobe-Yamate Gakuen in Osaka, Japan. Chief music consultant to Dover Publications.

Awards: Queen Elisabeth Music Competition. Gold Medal, Gina Bachauer International Piano Competition. Bronze Medal, Tchaikovsky International Piano Competition.

Discography: Has produced 16 albums featuring works of Mozart, Brahms, Bach, Dvorak, Busoni, Stravinsky, Tchaikovsky, Turina, Martin, Rozsa, Foster, Friml, Gershwin, Lamb, and Addinsell.

Education: BA, MA, Juilliard School of Music. PhD in Music, Manhattan School of Music.

In the Media: Featured in the *New York Times*, *Paris Match*, *Macleans*, and *Noticias de Argentina*. Has appeared on *Entertainment Tonight*, *Extra*, *In the Life*, *Studio Four*, and *National Public Radio*.

Personal Life: Lives in Vancouver Canada with her partner Kyoko.

LAURA JANE GRACE — PUNK ROCK MUSICIAN

Career: Founder, lead singer, songwriter, and guitarist of punk rock band, Against Me! Founder, Total Treble Recording Studio and record label, Total Treble Music. Album, *New Wave*, selected as Spin's Album of the Year.

Personal Life: Continues to live with her wife, Heather Hannoura, and their daughter, Evelyn, in St. Augustine, Florida.

JENNIFER LEITHAM — JAZZ BASSIST, COMPOSER, VOCALIST.

Career: Member of the Jennifer Leitham Trio. Has played for k.d. Lang, Doc Severinsen, Mel Tormé and Peggy Lee. Recorded on over 125 albums, including 10 of her own.

Personal Life: Transitioned while touring with Doc Severinsen. Subject of award-winning documentary, *I Stand Corrected*.

Media (Journalism, Film, Production)

LANA WACHOWSKI — DIRECTOR, SCREENWRITER, PRODUCER, COMIC BOOK PUBLISHER.

Career: With her brother, directed *The Matrix*. They wrote and directed the two Matrix sequels. Co-founder, EON Entertainment. Owner, Kinowerks, a green-friendly production and special effects studio. Founder, Burlyman Entertainment, a comic book publishing company. Previously, a comic book writer for Marvel Comics and Epic Comics.

JENNIFER BOYLAN — AUTHOR, ACTIVIST, PROFESSOR

Career: Faculty of Barnard College at Columbia University (New York); Professor of English, Colby College. Hoyer-Updike Distinguished Writer at Ursinus College. Member, Fulbright Scholarship Judging Committee, US Department of State.

Education: BA, Wesleyan University. PhD, Johns Hopkins University.

Publications: Author of 13 Fiction and Non-Fiction Books. Op-ed Contributor to New York Times. Two of her books detail her transition (*She's Not There*) and her life as a transgender parent (*Stuck in the Middle with You*).

Media: Guest on *Oprah Winfrey, Live with Larry King, 48 Hours, the Today Show, Barbara Walters*, and NPR.

ACKNOWLEDGEMENTS

I WISH, in particular, to thank Mary, Evelyne, and my parents. They suffered through every revision of this book. Continually reliving some of the most difficult moments in our family history wasn't easy for them. Each revision cost them a fistful of Kleenex.

Quince Mountain didn't teach me how to write; he reminded me how people read. Weening a corporate wonk from PowerPoint back to the beauty of the printed word is a worthy labor.

IN THIS BOOK, I mentioned that it can feel demeaning to subject your body, soul, and life to the discretion of a team of relative strangers. I feel blessed with the team of medical professionals who guided and cared for me along my journey. I feel a special closeness to Dr. Kathrine Rachlin, Dr. Christine McGinn, Christie Block and Dr. Jack Pula. They shepherded me through some trying times.

I am deeply indebted, too, to James Walker, Inna Katz, Dr. John Taylor, Dr. Jeffrey Spiegel, and Dr. Michael Beehner. And, of course, I am thankful to the teams that supported all of these professionals. I know who does most of the work!

Access to healthcare is critical to transgender men, women, and children. I am sorry that the majority of my brothers and sisters have not been as fortunate as I. I hope that we can remedy that. Aligning the body as closely as possible to the mind brings wonderful relief.

AT A RECENT Trans-Health conference in Philadelphia, a college student complained about the resistance that her team was facing from campus administrations. I asked her, "Have you thought about contacting HRC? They are really good at influencing institutions."

"Oh, we would never do that," she replied. "They are in bed with corporate America."

Well, I for one am grateful to HRC. They have admitted to a checkered past with the transgender community. But I am certain that my life is better because of them and that they have had a beneficial impact on institutional policies. I am confident, for example, that a lot of organizations have added transgender insurance coverage as a result of HRC's influence. I am thrilled with the direction that they are heading in. Their recent activism against so-called bathroom bills has been nothing short of phenomenal. I couldn't ask for a more zealous ally.

I am thankful, too, to all of other organizations that have emerged to fill this important area of need: the National Center for Transgender Equality, the Transgender Legal Defense & Education Fund, Out & Equal Workplace Advocates, Campus Pride, PFLAG, Lambda Legal, WPATH—and many others. They are all making extraordinary contributions. As they say, it takes a village.

FINALLY, I want to thank my friends who were there for me when I needed them most—Matt Hurlburt, Chris Altizer, Lori Fox, Alaina Kupec, Victoria Datta, Angela Orlando, Tammy Forlenza, Richard McIntyre, Pfizer's OPEN Community, Drew Whitler and my team at the Center for Creative Leadership, my friends at HRC, and my girls at the Gender Identity Project. I am a better woman because of you.

ABOUT TINA AND MARY WHITE

TINA WHITE works to transform businesses, communities, and people. She has worked as a commercial and investment banker, a management consultant, a business information manager, and an organization strategist. She holds an AB in Economics from Princeton University and an MBA in Marketing, Finance, and Organization Behavior from the University of Chicago Booth School of Business.

Since coming out, Tina has become more vocal in advocating for transgender people and their rights. Her chief contention is that, aside from their struggle with gender, transgender people are very normal human beings. They are capable of making great contributions to the world—if only we would let them. She looks forward to the day when gender variance is no more remarkable than variance in skin color and ethnicity—though we clearly have work to do combating prejudice and misinformation in these areas as well.

Tina has appeared on National Public Radio and the *Dr. Oz Show*. She has founded a website (www.personinside.com) devoted to helping the world to better understand and embrace transgender people.

MARY WHITE is Tina's wife of eighteen years and a key contributor to this book. She recently retired from a career as an information systems project manager. She networks actively with other transgender people's significant others in order to ensure that they find the support and community they need. Whether transitioning couples stay together or separate, Mary seeks to encourage loving and thoughtful dialogue. She has shared her experiences on the *Dr. Oz Show*.

CONNECTING WITH TINA WHITE

Web Site: www.personinside.com
Email: TinaMadisonWhite@gmail.com
Twitter: http://twitter.com/TinaMnWhite
LinkedIn: www.linkedin.com/in/TinaMadisonWhite
Facebook Author Page: www.facebook.com/PersonInsideUs